th first time

True Tales of Virginity Lost & Found

(including my own)

KATE MONRO

ICON BOOKS

Published in the UK in 2011 by
Icon Books Ltd, Omnibus Business Centre,
39–41 North Road, London N7 9DP
email: info@iconbooks.co.uk
www.iconbooks.co.uk

Sold in the UK, Europe, South Africa and Asia
by Faber & Faber Ltd, Bloomsbury House,
74–77 Great Russell Street,
London WC1B 3DA

Distributed in the UK, Europe, South Africa and Asia
by TBS Ltd, TBS Distribution Centre, Colchester Road,
Frating Green, Colchester CO7 7DW

Published in Australia in 2011 by
Allen & Unwin Pty Ltd, PO Box 8500,
83 Alexander Street, Crows Nest, NSW 2065

ISBN: 978-184831-240-1

Typeset in Minion by Marie Doherty

Printed and bound in the UK by
CPI Mackays, Chatham, Kent ME5 8TD

Contents

About the Author

Kate Monro's career has taken in spells with the rock band Blur, publishing mavericks *Dazed & Confused*, experiential marketing and PR agency Cunning, and most recently creative advertising agency RKCR Y&R.

www.virginityproject.typepad.com

Introduction

Writing this book has made for some interesting conversations. I can't tell you how many times I have perched, poised between two choices as someone has asked me what I do for a living at a party. Shall I opt for the more pedestrian answer, freelancing as a personal assistant in the creative advertising business? Or shall I tell them that in my spare time, I interview people about virginity loss? I think you can guess which one I go for.

Bam. In five seconds flat, I have bypassed the niceties and got straight down to brass tacks. You don't need to bother with small talk when you tell people that you investigate sexual experiences in your spare time. The conversation has just moved onto an entirely different level.

But I didn't plan this. Writing a book was never on my list of things to do, particularly not one about virginity loss. So how did it begin? What led me to a point where this sort of exchange was, and still is, a regular occurrence?

It all began on a beach. It was the end of the summer in 2005 and as we basked in the Californian sunshine, a dear friend and I had entertained each other by reminiscing about our misspent youth. We had known each other since we were teenagers but we had never had *that* conversation.

'How did you lose yours?' he asked, finally.

He didn't need to specify which 'yours' he was referring to. I knew exactly what he meant. From the practical details: the venue, the background music and the choice of attire (somebody's garden, Spanish euro-pop and a sun-bleached pink T-shirt, since you ask) to the emotional nuts and bolts, we soon began to relive this unique experience and to talk about how it had changed our lives.

What had been our expectations for this much-anticipated moment? Compared to the reality? And what did we see *now*, sitting on this beach so many years later, that our tender teenage minds couldn't comprehend at the time? As our respective tales came to life, I was struck by the contrasting dramatic elements of these stories. They contained humour, sadness and joy. In fact, they contained all the ingredients for a top-quality drama.

They would make a brilliant book.

There it was. I am not exaggerating when I say that I was captivated by this idea. I had a perfectly good job in a marketing agency but I was looking for something different to do with my life. I wanted to flex my creative muscles and I wanted to do it in a unique way. This idea couldn't fit the bill any more if it tried. In the days that followed, I kept trying to push the whole concept aside but it kept coming back at me. My friend and I were not the only two people with tales to tell. This was the *universal* experience that almost all of us will encounter, no matter who we are or where we come from. There must be millions of stories out there that were every bit as good as the two that had just been recounted.

I decided to run the idea past my friends. This was probably the best litmus test I could have taken. Asking people to think back to their first sexual experiences garnered an immediate response. People's faces changed the instant I asked the question. Good, bad or indifferent, every single person that I spoke to had something to say. My mind was made up. I bought a Dictaphone, I started making phone calls and I got cracking.

Looking back, I am amazed that people agreed to take part, given that virginity loss has the potential to be one of the most vulnerable moments of your entire life, but that didn't seem to put people off. Once again, I appealed to my friends for help and a little like the loss of virginity itself, my first fumbling efforts didn't look promising. Jamie, my 24-year-old colleague, agreed to be a guinea pig and patiently put up with my attempts to break new journalistic ground as I quizzed him intently at my kitchen table one Saturday afternoon. But it was a start and at least I remembered to switch the tape recorder on (something I would not always remember to do in the future).

I followed this up with a trip to Yorkshire. This time, the subject was a very game – and cherished – 91-year-old family friend. To my utter astonishment, my mother had asked Edna if she would like to take part in this project and she said yes. Over the following eighteen months, I found myself travelling, literally and metaphorically, to all sorts of unexpected places, with all sorts of unexpected people. The subject matter seemed to capture people's imagination. In the case of Edna, despite the fact that her generation were not given to such conversations, I sensed that she was seizing an opportunity, not just to give me the information that I wanted, but also to tell me a love story. She and her husband had been married for 50 years.

Slowly, as my interviewees referred me on to friends, family members, lovers and neighbours, a slow trickle became a steady stream. Without ever intending to, I morphed into a different person. A person who could walk into the home of a complete stranger, sit down with a cup of tea and proceed to quiz them on the finer details of their sex lives.

While it wasn't too hard to pin these people down, I came to see that they had different reasons for being there. Some of them did it just because I asked them to, but for others it was a rare opportunity to talk about their personal lives. How often do you get to do that in a non-judgmental environment? It is a well-known fact that much of the value of the therapeutic process lies in the sheer relief of having someone listen to *you* talk, with no interruptions. People grabbed the opportunity to sit with me for a moment, away from the maelstrom of their lives, and reflect on an experience that most had never shared with anyone before.

And boy, did they reflect.

I was astonished at what came out during these sessions. Virginity loss was the inspiration for some epic stories. As people spoke to me, they spun tales of shame and joy. Their stories contained breathtaking romance and mind-numbing mundanity, often in the same sentence. They talked about great expectations and equally grand disappointments. I watched as people revived ghosts from the past, and laid them back to rest. Sometimes it seemed as if these ghosts were right there in the room with us. I felt like I was mining a rich and untapped seam of personal history.

Men were the biggest surprise. We all know that men don't want to discuss their intimate lives with a friend, let alone a stranger, don't we? Men shocked me with their ability to speak openly and honestly about the critical moments of their sexual lives. It was almost as if no one had thought to ask them what they really thought before. I was only too happy to be the one who got to listen.

Frequently my interviewees looked lighter as they spoke. Occasionally, this translated into a physical process. I watched one man sweat from the start of his interview to the end, the drops springing from the indent above his cheekbones and rolling slowly down the sides of his face. His story was difficult to tell.

Unpacking the past is a powerful experience. Reliving a formative, and often teenage moment as an adult can be revelatory. But clearly my interviewees were not the only ones taking a trip back to the past. I was going somewhere too. I often asked myself why I was spending my weekends interviewing people I had never met before about their sex lives. Was I just nosy? Or was there a deeper need driving me?

On the surface, it was about social history. I got so much enjoyment from the fact that I was documenting the lives of my fellow human beings. I hoped that some day in the future, this unusual collection of stories might help people to understand something about the intimate nature of our lives as one millennium moved into the next. But I also knew that there was a *gut* motivation for my endeavours.

Perhaps it is easier to understand if you ask yourself the same question. What are you doing here, reading this book? What is it that you need to know? Are you just curious? Or do you need the reassurance of knowing that your experiences are the same as other people's? Because we all have the desire to fit in and I am no different. On a subconscious level, I needed to know that my hopes and fears were the same as everyone else's. Not just women's, but men's too.

Having got this information, something else propelled me forwards. On the days when I questioned the logic of asking strangers to tell me about their sex lives, an underlying momentum kept me going and it was this: the cast-iron belief that other people might benefit from what I now knew.

Every time an interviewee looked me in the eye and said, 'I don't suppose anyone has ever told you this before ...', just as I was thinking to myself, thank *God*, I'm not the only loser who has ever had that thought, I knew I had to share these stories.

Structuring these very human insights into a cogent stream of information has been an interesting process. I will start, in the first chapter, by asking a question to which I previously thought I knew the answer. How do we define the loss of our virginity? How do we know for sure when that moment has occurred? After all sorts of conversations with all sorts of people, let me tell you the answer is not as straightforward as you might think. Defining virginity loss is a highly personal matter.

The second chapter tracks the incredible changes in the lives of the women that I interviewed for this book. The oldest woman I spoke to lost her virginity in 1940 and the youngest in 2008, 68 years later. Comparing these stories proved an intriguing tool with which to understand these developments.

In response, chapter three will look at how men's lives have moved on. If women have become more independent in almost every department, have men returned the favour by adopting more feminine traits? Only time, and their tales, will tell. They certainly could not be accused of skimping on detail.

The fourth chapter will look at a modern phenomenon: the virgin. I call it a phenomenon because after a journey that has taken in some questionable adventures, it was always the story about the married virgin that messed with people's minds the most. Virginity, for many people in the modern world, is a taboo. Chapter four will explore the many different reasons why people retain their virginity, some of them due to personal choice and some of them not.

Finally, the last chapter will look at the present day. How far have we travelled? We have more information about sex than our parents ever did. Does that mean that we are we having better first-time experiences? And finally, while we can't change the raw facts about our stories, can we at least change how we feel about them? Chapter five examines the transformative power of a story that we will never forget.

This brings me back to the beginning, because if I take a long, last look back at the beach and the day on which an unplanned book was born, I see one other important detail. Many years had passed since my friend had lost his virginity, but he could still tell me *exactly* how he felt about it. The memory of that moment was easy to conjure up, even 30 years after the event. For that reason alone, this was not a difficult book to write. It didn't matter how much time had elapsed; this potentially life-changing event was the catalyst for some inspired storytelling.

In a world that celebrates sex on every street corner, every advertising hoarding and every television set, there is very little written – or said – about this very private sexual moment. I will be eternally grateful to a brave selection of individuals for taking the opportunity to help change this. As I found out, there is a first time for everything, including the telling of a very secret story.*

---

* All names – apart from the author's – have been changed.

1

Like a Virgin?

'Virginity can be lost by a thought.'
ST JEROME, 340–420 (FATHER OF THE CATHOLIC CHURCH)

Virginity loss has taken me on a fascinating quest. I thought I was just going to record an interesting bunch of stories and be done with it, but no. Along the way, it has come to my attention that there are very few subjects in life that raise as many questions – or eyebrows – as the subject of virginity and its loss. Maybe it is just because I was ever-so-slightly obsessed with my subject but as I looked around me, I realised that virginity is more or less everywhere you look.

One of the first stories that we are taught is about virginity loss. We all know the story of Adam and Eve. No sooner had these two hapless teenagers given in to the temptation of the 'fruit' than the course of their lives, and ours, was irrevocably changed. Once that bridge had been crossed, there was no turning back for Adam and Eve. This irrevocability has been a constant theme throughout the history of virginity loss. Mostly, it must be said, for women.

Christianity and its iconic female representative, the Virgin Mary, continue to play a role in the lives of millions of men and women every single day. Virginity, particularly outside of marriage, is revered, respected and on some occasions demanded, not just by the Christian faith but by many faiths. But if you think that virginity only has significance for religious people, you are wrong.

Virginity packs just as big a punch in the secular world. In 2008, 22-year-old Nathalie Dylan decided to auction her virginity on the internet to pay for her master's degree. Over 10,000 people were motivated enough to make a bid. The highest came from a 39-year-old businessman who was allegedly prepared to pay £2.6 million for this once-only offering. This probably isn't the first time you have heard a story like this and I doubt it will be the last, but it does tell us something about the value and the *power* of virginity, even to people who have no religious leanings whatsoever.

Some of us might find the idea repellent. After all, what kind of man would pay such a large sum of money to 'win' a woman's virginity? Is this the twisted modern-day equivalent of a hunting trophy, albeit a rather expensive one? And what motivates a woman from an affluent Western country to auction her virginity in so public a manner? Either way, here were two people who understood the power of virginity only too well; not only that, but both of them were prepared to leverage it to their own advantage.

We still use virginity as a metaphor for something precious and unique. Once it is 'broken', it can never be replaced. Or so you might think. I have found some fairly weird virginity-related news stories in my time but this one took the biscuit. In 2005, the *Wall Street Journal* ran a story about a 40-year-old medical assistant who couldn't think what to give her husband of seventeen years for their wedding anniversary. Here was a man who already had everything, so she went one step further. Yep, you guessed it; she gave him her virginity. Jeanette Yarborough paid a surgeon $5,000 to reattach her hymen, just so that she could lose her virginity all over again. 'What an awesome gift to give to the man in my life who deserves everything', she said. 'It was the most amazing thing I could give him as a woman.' This operation has grown in popularity in recent years, although, sadly for the women concerned, not usually for Jeanette's reason.

These are extreme examples. But for most of us, male or female, religious or not, whether we want to hold on to our virginity for as long as we can or shake free of it at the first opportunity, notions of virginity and its loss have concerned us since the beginning of time.

The Romans placed virginity on a pedestal, quite literally, by creating the concept of the vestal virgins. The vestal virgins were female priestesses. They entered into a 30-year contract of chastity and service to the state but in return, they were accorded phenomenal power and influence. A pardon from a passing vestal virgin could save a condemned man from the gallows. A vestal virgin could own property and write a will, rights unheard of for a woman in ancient Rome. But as you might expect, there was a price to pay for this freedom. A vestal virgin who dared to break her vow of celibacy came to a very sticky end, buried – alive – in a chamber beneath the streets of Rome.

By contrast, sometimes just when you think that virginity might have had some stature, it has been completely disregarded. In 1554 a German physician, Johannes Lang, described the ominously named 'green sickness' as 'peculiar to virgins'. His controversial solution? Sufferers should 'live with men and copulate. If they conceive, they will recover.' 'Green sickness' is in fact a form of anaemia. Iron is found in blood and when women menstruate, they have the potential to lose iron and can occasionally turn a rather ghostly shade of green. Even in an age when virginity was generally revered, not everybody thought that hanging on to the 'V' card was such a great idea.

I found these deviations into the world of virginity fascinating, but one question remained timeless and unanswered. If virginity is so important to us, then how do we define its loss? Do we have one blanket definition to cover all eventualities? Or a hundred? Because no matter where I went or to whom I talked, it never ceased to amaze me how many different and very creative ways people found to define one experience. We might think we are in agreement about this, but we are not.

People have often searched for physical proof of virginity, particularly a woman's. Medical literature begins to mention the hymen, the inconsequential piece of skin that *can* partially cover the entrance to a woman's vagina, in around the seventeenth century. The story goes that when a woman first has sexual intercourse, this piece of skin can break and cause the woman to bleed. This explains why even today, some cultures believe that the bloody bed sheet is proof enough of a woman's (freshly lost) virginity.

One of my female interviewees surprised me by telling me that she had lost her virginity on the back of a bike. She explained further:

OK, so people say they know when they lose their virginity. I didn't know. But I did know that I took the dog for a walk, I was feeling lazy so I thought I'll tie the dog to the bike and I'll ride down the road and the dog can run beside me. And that started really well until the dog saw another dog across the road and shot in front of the bike. Of course I went over and I hit myself on the crossbar and I started to bleed. So it wasn't really a big thing for me, losing my virginity. Although it did hurt.

This story makes my next point for me. Using the female hymen as a barometer with which to test a woman's virginity is clearly not a good idea. When it comes to the hymen, the only thing that can be proven is this: if it existed in the first place – because many women do not have hymens – it can be broken easily and in a variety of different ways, including sports (particularly horse riding), the use of tampons and of course the one to really watch out for, dog walking.

History relates a number of equally tenuous ways in which we have sought to define the existence of female virginity, whether by physical means or occasionally by slightly more ephemeral methods. I turned to Anke Bernau and her brilliant book, *Virgins: A Cultural History*, for some examples:

> The late-thirteenth-century *Women's Secrets*, popular and influential well beyond its own period, suggests that apart from downward-pointing breasts, other 'signs of chastity' are: Shame, modesty, fear, a faultless gait and speech, casting eyes down before men and the acts of men. Urine also features prominently in such discussions: 'The urine of virgins is clear and lucid, sometimes white, sometimes sparkling'. A virgin urinates from 'higher up than other women, because 'the vagina of a virgin is always closed, but a woman's is always open'. Certain plants, such as ground up lilies, or the 'fruit of a lettuce' will make a virgin 'urinate immediately'.

She makes similar discoveries about the *absence* of virginity:

A nineteenth-century expert takes a different approach in listing alleged signs of *lost* virginity: 'Swelling of the neck, rings around the eyes, the colour of the skin and urine.' He also mentions the popular story of a monk who claimed he could tell a virgin by her smell.

It's easy to laugh at such stories (and to wonder how a monk, of all people, managed to gain such finely honed olfactory skills), but not a lot has changed when it comes to the testing of virginity loss, whether for men or women. We are *still* evaluating its existence with methods not much more reliable than our sense of smell.

Perhaps it is precisely because virginity *is* such a nebulous, ever-changing proposition that we have often chosen to fall back on such unreliable and unproven tests of its existence. Men were just as confused. All sorts of people engaged me in conversation about this project, including my car mechanic, and I can still picture the look of utter confusion on his face as he asked me the question: 'But Kate, how does a man *know* when he has lost his virginity?' To which I can only say this. During the course of almost 50 interviews and many more conversations with people of all persuasions, around the beer-soaked bar tables of my local pub and the kitchens and living rooms of various friends, I discovered that the definition of virginity loss is a deeply personal issue. It can be defined in any number of ways, largely depending on how we *feel*.

But as a generalisation, it often comes down to technicalities. Even if we don't articulate it as such, the first incidence of penetrative sex is frequently the one that counts. For this reason, I was tempted to entitle this first story with a cheap quip like 'getting off on a technicality'. Because this story does involve the technical loss of virginity, but perhaps just not in the way that we were expecting.

Charlie Thomas. Born 1962. Lost virginity in 1978 aged sixteen

I always knew that I wanted to interview lots of different types of people for this book. In the 1990s, during my tenure at a magazine called *Dazed & Confused*, we collaborated with fashion visionary Lee Alexander McQueen to produce a special issue of the magazine. The theme? Fashion and disability. Lee put Olympic athlete and double amputee Aimee Mullins on the cover of the magazine wearing nothing but a sleek pair of Adidas track pants and her custom-made running 'legs'. It was challenging and it was brilliant. Sexuality and disability are not always seen as comfortable bedfellows. The experience made an impact on me. Over a decade later, I knew that I didn't want to present a homogenised, two-dimensional view of virginity loss. I wanted every section of society represented in all their shapes, sizes and permutations. I certainly didn't want to fall victim to the underlying assumption that just because a person might find it physically harder to have sex, that this might be analogous to their level of interest in the matter. What I didn't realise was that I already *had* made an assumption. A really big one. When I finally did find a disabled person who was prepared to share their story with me, I never expected it to be one of the best virginity loss stories that I had ever heard.

Born in 1962, Charlie Thomas was the unfortunate victim of thalidomide, a drug that was given to thousands of women in the 1950s and 1960s to relieve morning sickness. Tragically, and unbeknown to them, it also caused dramatic birth defects. Charlie Thomas is a tall, handsome man who just happens to have arms that finish at his elbows. A smart, popular boy, we join his story at the age of sixteen, just as the Sex Pistols were ransacking the late 1970s and just as Charlie's mother and stepfather had moved from very 'happening' London to the very non-happening Welsh countryside:

It was the late seventies and my school consisted of Welsh people who were into Elvis and absolutely everyone wore flares. But there were also the children of the hippies who had moved to the country and formed all these hippy communes. One of them was a lesbian commune. Can you imagine how popular they were with the local villagers? They were lesbian, dope-smoking, patchouli-smelling English people and they were all witches as far as the Welsh were concerned.

There I was, in the middle of all this and then she walked into the room. She was the daughter of one of these lesbian couplings and she was called Stella. Stella had huge bosoms, reeked of 'teenage' and sashayed down the hall in a way that stopped everybody in their tracks.

Our village was having a village hall disco one night. Imagine my surprise that day when Stella came up to me on the bus and said, 'Are you going to be at the disco tonight because I'd like to dance with you?' Pandemonium. You know, it was just a little bit too much for the other passengers. The weird English punk guy with the short arms getting propositioned by the witch girl with the big boobs.

The evening came and went and I walked her back to the end of the lane where her commune was and we had a bit of a kiss, but she had this really annoying all-in-one denim trouser suit on so any idea of getting hold of those breasts was just not happening because it was like a second skin.

Cut forward about a month and she invited me back to hers for tea. By this time we were almost officially girlfriend and boyfriend and it was the weirdest house you've ever been in. There was a woman called Gloria who looked like a man and had a moustache. An actual moustache. Now I look back on it and I just think, yes, they were a bunch of lesbians in a hippy commune. It was the late seventies in Wales, what do you expect? But at the time, for this little straight boy, it seemed really weird.

Anyway, the mother sent us off to Stella's room with our tea and Stella got her Jimi Hendrix record out. She was still in her school uniform and she lay down on her bed lolling her legs slightly open and I was sitting on the floor so you can imagine the view that I was experiencing. Then she just went, 'Touch me'. What she actually meant was, you have got carte blanche to go straight to base three.

It was basically being offered to me on a plate. The sexiest bitch in the school, with the biggest tits, was showing me her vagina and saying, 'Touch me'. I had never really got anywhere with anyone and there it was, all there, for me. I bottled it.

I wasn't ready for it. I needed the base one and base two, you know? I hadn't even touched her nipple. I wasn't ready to insert my fingers into places that they didn't know what to do with once they'd got there. So, in a rather desperate moment of attempted comedy, I put my finger on her knee, because techni-

cally that could be construed as 'touching' her, and thinking that I'd also answered with wit to mask my insufficiencies.

Cut forward again to a month later and there was a gang of about five or six of us that were the dope-smoking, punk-rock-liking, beer-drinking naughty people, who also had the parents who cared the least. We would hang around together, staying up till four and sleeping in the living room. On one of these nights, Stella and I were the only two left. It was three in the morning and there wasn't enough bedding for two so we slept together.

One thing led to another and she lay down and opened her legs and I sort of got on top of her, I had no notion of foreplay or anything like that and I managed to put it in her with a little bit of assistance, and then I started putting it in and out and in and out again. And I remember thinking, is that it? Is this what I've been waiting for? Because this is shit! This is nothing! I didn't come either, so I didn't really understand the feeling that can go with it. I'd done it. I'd done the act but I didn't have the feeling.

It wasn't long after that that we were doing it every night and I'd kept it from her that I couldn't come. We used to do it in the public toilets up the lane from the disco where everyone used to go. It was so popular that you could usually recognise the grunts of a familiar co-worker. Then one night she just sat back on the toilet bowl and went, 'Where's your fucking spunk?' Or something like that. She was a game girl, Stella; I was a very lucky boy.

That weekend, I saw a film called Candy *and I was wanking while I was watching it. Suddenly I felt this really weird sensation, kind of like buzzing. My ears went a bit weird and I stood up and ran into my room, still with a hard cock, and carried* on wanking, my legs felt wobbly for a second and I thought, oh my god, what's going on, and then suddenly, yes! Finally, I've orgasmed! I've come. Produced sperm. Da da, da da! I'm a man! And that was my virginity.

I was desperate to see Stella again after that, obviously. I think I got one more in, and that was the one where I finally managed to have sex with her and come. A week later, Stella's best friend Nancy asked her if she could borrow me because she wanted to lose her virginity. College was beckoning and she was buggered if she was going to go off to college still a virgin. Stella actually said to me, 'Would you mind sleeping with my best friend?' I was kind of like, 'Err, sure, yes, I'll do that.'

And I did. I actually enjoyed that a lot more because I almost thought I knew what I was doing by then. Happy days. Directly after that, when I went off to my A-level college, I was quite confident and buoyed with the success of my double whammy in the summer holidays.

I met an older woman next who introduced me to LSD and the clitoris. She was 30 and I was seventeen. I called someone a cunt in the pub and the next thing I knew I was being punched in the face and I was on the floor with a woman leering over me with pink hair, Dr Martens and a boiler suit. She was pointing at me shouting, 'Shut up! I like my cunt!' and it was literally, like, 'Wow!' at first sight.

She was a communist and she was very angry. She looked at me and saw a man who'd been disabled by the state because basically, that's what thalidomide had done. She wanted to unlock my anger by fucking my brains out and giving me acid. She was partially successful. Sexually speaking I had a lot more of an idea about what I was doing by the end of that summer.

I had a lot of partners over the years because I was in rock-and-roll bands and I was shagging everything I could get my hands on. Some moves were not an option to me, because of the disability stuff; there were some areas that I literally could not reach. So I became damn good at oral sex to make up for that. Making the leap and learning how to go down on women was a huge step forward for me because then I could absolutely guarantee their pleasure.

Many years later, this is pathetic of me I know, I tried to sleep with Stella again but it didn't work. Halfway through the date I realised that I didn't actually fancy her any more and I was just trying to get closure on something that ... didn't need closure, so that was as far as it went.

I have been married to my partner for fourteen years now and I'm an old hippy. I believe that the physical plane is not as important as the spiritual one, and I'm also a pagan insofar as I'm anti-Christian insofar as I believe we should have as much physical pleasure as is possible. And practise it as much as possible, because it will help us reach Nirvana. Rather than abstention from physical pleasure. No! I don't agree with that. Absolute rubbish! Wank, fuck, do all of that as much as possible, that's what I say. Because, come on, who of us here can quite honestly say that in times of stress, bringing yourself off in the bath or whatever doesn't relieve the damn stress, and make you feel better afterwards? How on earth can that be a bad thing?'

This is why talking to men was so interesting. I know how my own body works but it never occurred to me to think about how boys might feel about their own physical development. Erections, ejaculation, wet dreams; these are potentially exciting but highly alarming events in the life of a young man. Why wouldn't they be? You only need to ask a woman about her first period to answer that question. This was the first of many steps to understanding why virginity loss is every bit as dramatic for a man as it is for a woman, but perhaps just in a different way.

Having penetrative sex for the first time was of little consequence to Charlie. That's not to say that it wasn't exciting or even emotional, but contrary to the commonly held belief that we lose virginity when we reach this all-important milestone, it wasn't *Charlie's* defining moment. That came later, and at the same time that he did; the moment that he had intercourse and ejaculated. It was almost as if this visceral physical experience was evidence of something else that he mentions. Something of great importance to almost every man I ever interviewed for this project: the concept of 'becoming a man'.

What an impactful phrase that is. Charlie followed this up later by saying to me that 'you can't come until your voice has broken; the two things tend to happen at the same time. You're not a woman until you have periods, right? So you're not a man until you can come.'

The loss of virginity can be a physical process with physical consequences, ejaculation being just one. But this is tangible evidence for what can also be seen as an *emotional* change. It became clear as I went along that while we frequently do mark the loss of virginity by observing significant physical milestones, the process of virginity loss can have almost nothing to do with the corporeal world.

I was hardly the first person to realise this. St Augustine was born over 1,600 years ago. I loved him for his well-known aphorism, 'Lord, give me chastity, but not yet', but he also had something interesting to say about virginity loss. A philosopher and theologian, his words rang true as I sought to understand why virginity loss often has nothing to do with physical practicalities.

'*[Neque] enim eo corpus sanctum est, quod eius membra sunt integra*', said St Augustine. Or, 'the holiness of the body does not lie in the integrity of its parts'.*

Augustine was ahead of the curve. He believed that virginity could reside in the mind and that, as such, it could never be forcibly taken because it did not physically exist. If the mind had not consented, then neither had the body. This was a radical piece of thinking for the time; particularly given that people's attitudes towards female virginity were a lot less evolved than they are now. Even if a woman had lost her virginity against her will, it is quite likely that the finger of blame would have been pointed at her anyway.

Jump forward 1,500 years and I discovered that Augustine's words had the potential to resonate just as much now as they did then. When I came up against my first really difficult interview, with a woman who most definitely *had* lost her virginity against her will, I had an unplanned opportunity to test the power of Augustine's words. Martha was a friend of a friend and she agreed to talk to me for very personal reasons. She was a religious woman. She had also been date raped by her first boyfriend in Paris in the 1960s. This was to be the first time that she had ever told her story to anyone.

I hadn't had any training for scenarios such as these. I had rushed into this project without thinking that far ahead and I certainly hadn't considered how I might deal with potentially

---

* St Augustine, *De Civitate Dei* ('City of God'), Book I.

traumatic storytelling situations. I quickly learned, though, that coupled with basic human kindness, listening really was the best policy. People wanted their stories to be heard. I just needed to sit and witness them.

As we sat alone together, the tape recorder nestled between us; it was difficult for her to recall such painful memories. When she had finished telling me her story, I felt compelled to read her another Augustine quote: 'No matter what anyone else does with the body or in the body that a person has no power to avoid without sin on his own part, no blame attaches to the one who suffers it.' I wondered if it might make her feel slightly better about what she had just told me. I felt terrible when she burst into tears, but she quickly followed this up by telling me that she had never heard these words before and that they had helped. I was glad and amazed. Amazed that the words of a man whose robes had swept the streets of ancient Rome could still have such an uplifting effect on the life of a woman telling a story in a Soho members' bar so many centuries later.

If nothing else, I had also discovered the sheer *power* of definitions. For the duration of her life thus far, Martha had allowed herself to be defined by her so-called lack of purity. As you can imagine, this wasn't a happy situation for her. As if dealing with the trauma of rape were not enough, she also had to deal with her conscience because, technically speaking, as far as some people were concerned, she was now sullied. In the eyes of her ancient fellow Christians, Augustine's contemporaries, she would have been defined as morally lacking and therefore damaged goods. But by looking at virginity loss from a new perspective, and ironically a saint's at that, she had eased the grip of *some* of the guilt that had dogged her for over 30 years.

Hannah St John. Born 1964. Lost virginity in 1982 aged eighteen

For a lady of Martha's age, virginity loss might also have been considered a loss of innocence. Because once we have been inducted into 'the ways of the world', as my grandparents might have called it, we cannot go back. We cannot '*un*-know' what we now know. Our childhood is effectively at an end. We have lost our innocence. My next interviewee, like many before her, blurred the line between virginity and innocence. She also demonstrated that you could lose your innocence lock, stock and barrel. But does that mean that you have lost your virginity?

This is probably the right point at which to tell you about my blog, The Virginity Project. Several years into researching this book, I realised that I needed an outlet, a place to let off steam about my adventures. I realised that there were too many unexpected and extraordinary stories to ever be able to fit in one book. I also figured there probably weren't too many other people in the world doing what I was, so I decided to start a blog. Ultimately, I ended up starting a conversation, with people from all over the world.

At first, I just posted my own thoughts and experiences but over time people began to engage with the material and, much to my delight, they began to tell me their own stories. People from different countries, with different perspectives and opinions about virginity loss, felt compelled to email their stories to a stranger and allow her to share them with other readers. I got stories from women and stories from men. I got stories from religious people, gay people, from incredibly old people and in some cases I got stories from people who had lost their virginity in the previous ten minutes. Really.

I loved every single one of them but what astonished me was the variety of opinion. The stories and emails I got sent only backed up what I already thought: that our perceptions of what constitutes 'loss', 'innocence' and 'virginity' are nebulous, ever-changing and almost impossible to pin down. I will get to Edna's story later on, but for now, here is the potted version. My 'aunty' Edna lost her virginity in 1940. She was 25 years old and despite the fact that she had grown up in a house with two brothers, she had absolutely *no* idea what a naked man looked like until her wedding night, let alone what the sexual act consisted of. She was innocent.

These days, unless you live in a sealed box, it would be almost impossible to recreate this scenario because sex is everywhere you look. Innocence is a much harder concept to protect. Perhaps, in this respect, virginity and innocence really did go hand in hand in Edna's day.

By the time I went to school in the 1980s, innocence and its rather unlovable sister, virginity, were desperately uncool, something to be rid of at the first opportunity. Or, as an interviewee of a similar age to me once said, 'the word virgin was bandied about a lot at school, almost as an insult, "Oh, so and so is a virgin", especially if they were not very good-looking'. Ouch. Not only was it an indication of how lame you were but it might be a judgement on your appearance as well. No one wanted to be thought of as innocent or virginal and if we were, we made sure we guarded this incriminating information closely.

Not a lot has changed since then. Films like *The 40-Year-Old Virgin* and *American Pie* continue to be box-office hits because they depict the teenage-tinged dilemmas that we all relate to. For this reason, Hannah's story really stood out. She genuinely couldn't have cared less what anybody thought about her well-documented virginity, despite constant pestering from her classmates about the precise status of her relationship with her boyfriend.

More to the point, if it were still 1940, Hannah could have married with a clear conscience because, technically speaking, she was still 'pure'. But she was most definitely not innocent. 'We were having so much fun having lots and lots of orgasms together that it never seemed necessary to go all the way', she said, showing that there are many different ways to experience pleasure that do not involve the loss of virginity.

Hannah is an artist and as I climbed the stairs to a studio stacked full of her creations, I had little idea of what to expect. As it happened, she poured not just a glass of red wine for me but, very generously, her entire life story into my tape recorder. She also asked an interesting question. Is virginity always something that we lose? Or could it be something that we find – or 'gain', as she preferred to call it? Hannah began by explaining exactly where the gaining of her own virginity began.

My friend Fanny Martin came to school one day, it was so funny. I was probably about eleven, and we were all in the changing room after games. We were at that age where we were still very innocent so we weren't that embarrassed about talking about masturbation because we didn't really know what it was.

So Fanny Martin said, 'Oh god, I was in the garden messing about with my neighbour in his sleeping bag, and he's rubbing me down there and I got really hot all over, and then I got this amazing feeling'.

So we were all looking at her like, well, what do you mean? How do we get the feeling as well? 'Well, you just kind of rub', she said, and I remember we were all crowded round as if we were talking about making a cake. And then she was saying, 'You know, that little bit in there, you just keep rubbing that and it feels really nice' and everyone was like, 'Shall we?' It was a bit like homework. Like, 'OK, we'll all go home and try it then.'

So of course it's game on. I'm lying on my bunk-bed, the dog's on the bottom bunk and I'm thinking about the 'homework' and I remember just rubbing away thinking, well, Fanny Martin doesn't know what she's talking about, and I am literally thinking, I wonder what's for tea, when … OH MY GOD.

That was it.

I almost fell off my bunk and I remember thinking, did my brain just do that? I was stunned and amazed. I remember feeling like I was on a rollercoaster and the night sky was full of stars. I was overwhelmed that your body could do that and I think I was completely unstoppable from that point on. When we went back to school the next day, no one ever mentioned it. Everyone had probably gone home, had massive orgasms and then never discussed it again.

When I was fourteen I went away to school. I was lucky because my time at boarding school turned out to be some of the happiest years of my life. It was also where I met my first love who I lost my virginity to and I took his as well. It was the most beautiful time to be in love because you don't have any other pressures. It's like a little golden rosy nugget because what are you going to have any worries about apart from your next exam?

Even though Matt and I got together when I was fifteen, we didn't have sex until I was nearly eighteen. A lot of people were surprised that we waited but despite the fact that we were not having actual sex, we were doing absolutely everything else. We were having so much fun having lots and lots of orgasms together that it just never seemed necessary to go all the way.

But after two years of snogging and loads of oral sex, I think we just got to a point where we had been doing everything else for long enough and it was almost like, 'Well, shall we?' So we talked about it and we just decided we were going to do it that weekend. I remember going to get the condoms and dropping my money all over the counter in Boots and all these old ladies helping me to pick the coins up.

I really remember that first time because we put a little towel in the bed just in case I bled. When we actually had sex I remember thinking, oh, OK, so that's what it feels like. I mean, it was fine but I have to say that the earth did not move.

I did sort of wonder if my body had been wired up to have orgasms just through foreplay. Perhaps if I had never had an orgasm and then had penetrative sex maybe my body would have reacted differently. In fact I still find it easier to have an orgasm without having penetrative sex. For me, an orgasm is a much more powerful feeling than having an actual penis in my vagina.

But the experience was actually fine and it was nice. It wasn't like I thought, oh, I won't do that again, because the earth had moved for me so many times with him already anyway.

I was very lucky to lose my virginity that way because I don't think most people do. It was almost like an old-school marriage type scenario where you've been courting for long enough and building up to the main event and it felt like a safe situation. It certainly didn't feel like I had 'lost' anything. I had lost my innocence long ago; I'd had so much cunnilingus. I think it should be called 'gaining' your virginity not 'losing' because it's the most gorgeous thing to do. How can that be a loss? That's just patriarchal fifteenth-century crap.

Matt is someone who you think, in dreamland, I could have actually just married and never had another lover. In fact, subsequent lovers were disappointing after that experience, because I think that I had had the cherry on the cake the first time and my expectations were set quite high.

It was actually really sad because I ended our relationship to go out with this really glamorous, sexy guy that I met at art school who was rich. The only guy I've ever been out with that was rich and he was fucking crap in bed. And he had a minute willy as well. Not that size matters but I just remember sleeping with him and thinking, Christ, this is shit.

Matt and I are in and out of touch. I hadn't spoken to him for a couple of years until recently when he phoned me up out of the blue at my old studio and just said 'Can I come around?' I remember saying to my assistant, 'Go. I don't know what it is but I know it's something really bad.' And then he came round and he said, 'My dad died.' It was twenty years after our relationship had ended but he obviously needed to see me, I suppose because I am an integral part of his history and he is an integral part of mine.

Now I have an eight-year-old daughter who watches Beyoncé on the TV and gyrates around the room in quite a sexual manner. My stepmother was around recently and she turned around to me and said, 'Do you let her watch this?' Because you know what it's like with Beyoncé. She's basically shagging with clothes on, and I hadn't even thought about it. I immediately felt really guilty and thought, am I a terrible mother?

I hope that I am informative to her as she grows up. I hope that I'll be able to be a guide for her. Because at the end of the day it won't be me, bloody snogging, finger fucking and shagging. Of course I didn't do the shagging until I was eighteen but I did all the rest of it and actually it was bloody nice so I don't want her not to do that.

But I do really want her to feel that her virginity is precious. I don't want her to get shagged by some nasty bloke in the back of a cinema against a bloody wall, I would love her to love somebody and have her virginity taken in a loving situation, even if it doesn't last, because that's what I had and it really was lovely.

Andy Mackenzie. Born 1963. Lost virginity aged thirteen, seventeen and 28

The dictionary defines a virgin as 'a person, esp. a woman, who has never had sexual intercourse'. If we set aside the rather retro gender bias of this definition and find out how 'sexual intercourse' is defined, then perhaps we might be able to agree on how we go about losing it:

Sexual intercourse: the insertion of a man's penis into a woman's vagina, usually with the release of semen into the vagina. (*Chambers Compact Dictionary*, 2005)

Isn't it interesting to note that even today, our benchmark for definitions struggles to move with the times and establish a more all-encompassing view of intercourse and, ultimately, of virginity loss? Because according to this 2005 edition of the English dictionary, no gay person has ever lost their virginity. The act of making love, technically speaking, has to involve the insertion of a penis into a vagina.

The truth is that the way we define 'sex' is every bit as personal as the relationship that we have with virginity loss. What constitutes 'sex' for one person might mean something very different for someone else. Bill Clinton unwittingly brought this to our attention during his infamous liaison with Monica Lewinsky. Now, I happen to be a fan of Bill Clinton. In fact, I ran into him while writing this book. I was hard at work in the London Library in St James's Square one day when I noticed a sign saying that he was doing a book signing session at the local bookstore. I hung around while I ate my lunchtime sandwich and, eventually, out he came. The effect that he had on the waiting crowds, the journalists, the builders from the site next door and the passing tourists was mesmerising. He made a point of shaking every single person's hand, including mine. I was absolutely thrilled, but really Bill, can you honestly say that oral sex should not be considered 'sexual relations'?

Apparently you can, because when Bill Clinton was finally asked to tell the truth about the nature of his relationship with Ms Lewinsky, he famously stated that he had 'not had sexual relations with that woman'. In a final stroke of comedy, a judge was asked to approve a three-page definition of what constituted 'sexual relations'. As a result, such is the power of words (and the law) that Bill and Monica's special time together was deemed not to be of a sexual nature.

Clearly, this is a tale about politics, morals and the many reasons why people in power, particularly married people, should not engage in sexual relations with a third party – but at the time, it also started a ferocious media conversation about how we define 'sex'. Back in the real world, the people that I have spoken to differ every bit as much as presidents do.

I once worked with a gay man who told me that he had never had penetrative sex with another man in his entire life. But he certainly considered himself to be in possession of an active 'sex life'. Conversely, I have a straight female friend who once said that 'kissing is just the same as shaking hands'. And while kissing can hardly be construed as sexual intercourse, she leads us to an interesting observation. A kiss was of little consequence to my friend, but it could mean everything to someone else. Virginity loss is the same. The levels of importance that we attach to our sexual interactions frequently do define the way in which we view them. This is certainly true of my next interviewee. Andy, a gay man who was 42 when I interviewed him, had had many different experiences, any of which could be called virginity loss, until he had an experience that actually meant something to him.

In doing so, he also illustrated another, more universal idea. We needn't define the departure of virginity with a single moment. Virginity loss can be a process or a continuum; a series of events, if you like, that over time produce a result. This isn't a 'gay' thing. Eighteen-year-old Cheryl, a heterosexual woman who wrote to me via my blog, felt it too:

I can't help but think that 'losing your virginity' is something you should grow into; not something which is over in a split second amidst pain or embarrassment. I was seventeen when I had my first sexually active relationship. I had never orgasmed before other than on my own. After a few months of sleeping with my boyfriend, I started to feel the twinges of a possible orgasm. And then he made me come. That's when I really started to lose my virginity.

Andy, my next interviewee, took an entire afternoon to explain his own 'process' to me and I think you will understand why when you read his story. Listening to him made me realise exactly what I was asking people to commit to when they sat down and told me their stories. It wasn't just that I was asking them to reveal their intimate moments, I was also asking them to reveal something else: their lives, in all their glories, failures and ups and downs. You cannot have one without the other. They are inextricably linked and lives are messy, complicated and dramatic, just like the people who live them.

I had known Andy for almost five years when he generously decided to tell me his story. We had shared all sorts of adventures and fun times together but I had never known much about his background. I had heard whispers of it; that he had lost a brother, or was it a mother? Either way, I never felt it appropriate to ask until Andy offered his story to me of his own volition. He obviously understood exactly what this would involve, but I did not:

There was a social difference between my parents because my mother was a wealthy woman in her own right and my father was a working-class Catholic guy. They were both quite old when they got married so it was a 'last resort' sort of arrangement. They didn't actually get on. They weren't hostile; it just felt more like having a father who was a lodger in the house. There was no growing up knowing that your parents were having sex, because they weren't. It was a complete blank as far as that was concerned.

My mum stayed at home being a housewife and that was the way that we grew up. As time went on, she began steering us against our father, I think, because she was stuck in this gormless marriage with no romance and very little warmth. It was the seventies and there were a lot of women constantly down their GPs' with stress and depression and I remember that there were always jars of pills in the cupboards. She also dabbled with psychics and mediums, which was not a good mix. It was quite a burden for us because she would come home from her trips to the psychic and tell us that our father didn't have very long to live.

I remember having a friend at primary school who would come over on Friday nights and have a sleepover. It was only a small bed and I don't remember us fooling around or fiddling with each other's bits, but there was a closeness and there was something about the intimacy that I thrived on. There may have been a frisson of sexual excitement, but there was no way I could have articulated any realisation that I might have been gay at that stage.

I began to get a better idea at around eleven years old. That was when it all kicked off. I remember several instances when you think, oh right. Hang on, something's up here. The first of these was in the first year at secondary school when we performed 'Snow White and the Seven Dwarves'. We were in the green room and the head boy was getting changed next to me. He was the epitome of what a head boy should be, you know, stunning, clever and a great body.

So there I am, getting changed into my dwarf outfit and he was getting changed into his Prince Charming outfit. I had my back to him and when I turned around he was wearing a pair of black underpants, which I had never seen in my life. I remember my heart stopping as I turned round to look at this vision and even though I was only eleven, I knew in my heart that I fancied him.

Of course this was the seventies, so being gay was still pretty much not said and if it was, it was only in the 'Danny la Rue', 'Larry Grayson' sort of way.

At this point, I still didn't understand what sex involved, because no one had actually told me. I remember walking home one day with one of the girls from the choir. We were walking past Sketchley's and she was talking about sex and I was nodding along, you know, pretending to know what she was talking about and all of a sudden she said, 'Right,' she said, 'Come on then. Tell me what sex is.' And I said, 'Right, well, sex is when a man and woman get in the bath, they fill it up and then they get in the bath together. And then,' I said, 'the sperm comes out of the man's penis and it swims through the water and into the woman's vagina!'

So I think biologically from what I'd read in books about sex, that was a pretty good guess. I was halfway there. Clearly I didn't know that you had to actually put the penis in the vagina. But she certainly did and I remember she was killing herself laughing because it was so naïve.

I have to say that this new-found knowledge was quite abhorrent to me. I found it pretty appalling because I knew that my parents didn't get on and it was even worse to think that they had actually had to do that together.

I went to the local church and it was this that connected me to my first sexual experience. I was thirteen and we sang in the church choir together. He was in his twenties. Nowadays there's all this stuff in the media about paedophilia and being led astray, but it didn't feel like that to me. I wasn't dragged, I wasn't coerced. I was very much a willing participant and I suppose by thirteen, I mean, God, in some cultures, you're married at thirteen.

It wasn't immediate, it was just, you know, bonding first of all. He was very well educated and he was funny and nice-looking. We used to listen to a lot of music, because obviously he was older than me so it was like learning about Pink Floyd and Fleetwood Mac and Santana. I used to go back to his for tea. All the clichés were there, scones and tea, a pot of Earl Grey, which was all very impressive to me. And then it just became very natural and it happened very slowly. I think you go through life and it does click with certain people.

For me to have a mentor at the age of thirteen was a godsend because I had such a weird home life and a really shoddy life at school as well. I mean, my attitude has always been to just get on with things but it was really difficult psychologically. So it was great for me to have this mentor, who obviously loved me in that old-fashioned way, almost like a centurion taking a young boy under their wing and educating them, which he did. We used to listen to Frank Zappa and the Rolling Stones, but classical music as well because he had been a choral scholar. So it was Debussy, Mozart and Beethoven too.

We only did blowjobs. It wasn't an anal sort of thing. I know everyone thinks of losing your virginity as actual intercourse, *but actually a blowjob can be just as intimate as something going into a hole and at the time I certainly considered it to be losing my virginity. At that stage, anal intercourse was just a bit too frightening and he didn't ever try it. That stage of losing my virginity didn't happen until quite a few years afterwards.*

I suppose people would say that he took advantage of me but he made me feel confident, and as soon as I realised that something could happen with him sexually – Whoopee do! You know, all my sexual instincts went full steam ahead.

Once I had got going, that was it. There was a cruising ground near where I lived and I often used to go down there on my way home from school. This was in the days before the internet and 'Gaydar', so cruising grounds were really active and popular. It wasn't always about quick anonymous blow-jobs in the bushes either. It was around this time that I began to grow up even more and realise what nice people gay guys are and that everyone just inherently needs to be held. You need the intimacy and the snogging and the kissing, and it doesn't have to be anything else. That can really lift you up and carry you through anything.

Around this time I met a British Airways steward out cruising one night and that was the first time I ever went back to anybody's flat. I was quite old-fashioned in my upbringing and I was never going to be rushed into anything. It was all done at my pace, but I liked him so I stayed the night.

I suppose losing your virginity, for a girl, must always be painful but anyone who's ever put their finger up their bum knows that it's probably going to be a bit uncomfortable for a guy as well. But this felt like the right time so I went for it. The funny thing is that I don't actually remember anything about the experience. What I do remember is the music that was playing in the bedroom. It was Judie Tzuke, 'Stay With Me Till Dawn', and that seemed very prophetic to me.

My mother was suffering really badly with depression by this point and had dug herself into a total rut. It's obviously much more complicated than that, but she hung herself when I was nineteen. I had left home and my brother found her hanging outside the back of the house. Things had gone on for such a long time and some people feel that there's no way out, so it wasn't a surprise.

But then nine months later my brother took an overdose and my father found him one morning, dead in bed. That really did shake me. Because my mother killing herself wasn't a surprise, it was an awful sort of conclusion; but with my brother it wasn't. I hadn't seen that coming at all. My biggest, hugest regret, and always will be, was that I was having fun down in Brighton whilst my brother was obviously not coping and I had no idea.

I went to Italy for a year after my brother died. I needed to get away from everything that was familiar. When I came back, I started working but I took bits of time off where I would literally lock myself in and draw all the curtains for months at a time. I had money, so I could do that, but it took about ten years to recover from my mother and my brother's deaths, especially my brother's.

I was still also trying to cope with my sexuality. I had realised that this was going to be more difficult than I thought because the gay crowd seemed to be quite hedonistic and self-absorbed and I had led quite a straight life with a real mix of people. My mother had been a gregarious woman and had brought us up to talk to a 'duke and a dustman' in the same way and always to be interested in people. I liked watching football and going to the pub so I was never going to fit into the gay clique.

It wasn't until I was almost 30 that I had the experience that you could genuinely call 'losing your virginity' and my God, he had a dick like a Coke can. It's only clicked a few times in my life with a few people and he was one of them.

Gay guys are quite funny because if you are a 'big bear' type of gay man then you tend to go for other bear types and if you've got a moustache, you tend to look for another guy with a moustache and it's all very much to do with the body beautiful, but this guy was enormous and I was skinny.

He picked me out in the sauna through a crowd of other guys who were trying to get it on with me and I wasn't having any of it. There was so much steam that I could actually sense this huge guy before I could see him. I could hardly see his face but I could see this enormous chest and I was turned on straight away. He sat down next to me, pushed the other guys out of the way and took over. Then he literally picked me up and took me back to his place. Of course, when I saw the size of him that was a bit of a worry but I just knew that I trusted him, I liked him and I knew what I wanted to do.

It took a while. We had to take our time. In fact, we tried for a bit and then we watched Coronation Street *and then we tried again for half an hour and it got a bit easier because by then I had started to relax a bit more. And then finally after another hour we got there. That was an amazing moment. I remember hanging on to the bedstead, he had one of these wrought-iron beds and I was holding on with both my hands and I was just tingling all over. I had never experienced anything like that in my life. My whole body was quivering. I was just so fucking pleased. It was the biggest turn-on ever. It was just, like, 'Yes!'*

For a definition of losing my virginity, fully, properly, that would have been it, with him. Because it had been an effort on my part, obviously, but also because there was that amazing spark that I felt as soon as we encountered each other. I just knew that he was 'the one' because I had had the courage to actually go back with him, which was pretty unusual for me.

Afterwards he took me out for dinner and then we came back and I spent the night with him. But I didn't pursue it. I wish I had done, because I now know that going through life, it doesn't click very often for me and when it does, it's worth pursuing. I should have stayed to see what happened next but I didn't.

I woke up on my 30th birthday and I clearly remember getting up and thinking, fuck it. I'm not going to care what people think about me anymore. People are always going to think something about me because I lost half my family or that I'm gay or effeminate or that I'm skinny, and I had to get to 30 to think, fuck it, I've just got to get on and not worry what people think about me. That was a turning point.

All through my twenties and thirties, I could satiate my sexual appetite by just cruising and getting it on with someone in a bush for five minutes or maybe an afternoon. Sometimes you stay and chat, but mostly it was nothing and I was too scared to get really intimate with someone. But now it gets to the stage that I am 42 and it would be nice to have that closeness. I now want to be the sort of guy that I would want to go out with. I've got over the hang-ups about my sexuality and even though I've still only had 'proper' sex a couple of times, it's a good time for me to, you know, start the next chapter of my life.

Andy could have defined his virginity loss in any number of ways, any of which depended on where he was standing in his life. This was a constant theme. The passage of time changed the way that people perceived their virginity loss. Definitions were not carved into stone. On the contrary, definitions grew and changed in the same way that *people* grew and changed.

Crucially, for Andy, his picture appeared to complete itself when he threw in a 'connection' or an emotional feeling for another man. This is important because it also connects him to a word upon which his entire story appears to hinge. Trust. He meets this huge bear of a man, a man who, given that he virtually picks Andy up and carries him home tucked under one arm, could presumably crush him with the other one if he chose to. But he doesn't.

Andy senses this and in return, 'gifts' this man with what he considers to be the ultimate prize: his virginity. He lets someone into his life, physically as well as metaphorically, further than he has ever allowed another person to go. It sets the scene for one of the most meaningful sexual encounters in his life and one which, even now, he is able to recount in such explicit detail. During an experience which involved a significant amount of physical effort, Andy learnt to trust not just another person but, perhaps more critically, himself. Something that he hadn't always felt he had done before.

We have consistently used the word 'loss' to describe the passing of our virginity and yet this experience appeared to be a personal victory of sorts for Andy.

Diane Hill. Born 1946. Lost virginity in 1963 aged seventeen

Pursuing stories for this book provided me with all sorts of distractions from everyday life, and at no point was this more aptly demonstrated than during my encounters with Diane Hill. My 'beach' friend that I mentioned in the Introduction to this book put me in touch with her. 'You should interview Diane,' he said. 'She is bound to have an opinion on virginity loss.' He was not wrong. Diane is a teacher of Tantric sex.

It took me the best part of two days' driving to get to the other end of Britain in order to do this interview, but it was worth the effort. Diane had invited me to stay in her house. The landscape was wild and beautiful and as I lay in bed that night, the elements lashed so violently against the walls of her old stone house that I was convinced that very little would be left standing by morning. All in a day's work for Diane, but completely new meteorological territory for a city dweller like me.

The next day, we sat in Diane's living room and talked about the equally dramatic journey on which her life had taken her. We discussed her early experiences as a sex worker and how that work informed the life that she had now. We talked about the workshops that she conducts for men and women, sometimes in single-sex groups and sometimes mixed. She also told me about the powerful transformative effect that this work has on people's lives. I had a chance to see this work in action a lot more quickly than I anticipated. A couple of weeks after our interview, she phoned me up. 'We usually give away a place on each of our courses for free. This time that place is for you. Are you up for it?'

I was horrified. How I wished I hadn't been so effusive in my praise for her good work. But I also knew that I was being offered an opportunity on a plate. I told her I would ring her back. I needed time to think about this unexpected offer. My book was primarily about other people's stories but along the way, I realised that I was discovering rather more about myself than I had bargained for. I was pleased with my progress. So much of this experience seemed to be about pushing boundaries and trying new, unexpected things. My mind was made up. I phoned her back. It was a women-only group. How much trouble could I get into? In the interests of my highly unscientific explorations, I decided to get over myself and find out.

As it turned out, the weekend was a carefully orchestrated mix of chaos and structure, with a large dose of therapy thrown in. It was nerve-racking, and I was constantly pushed out of my comfort zone, but it was also one of the most profoundly satisfying weekends of my life. It felt like passing my driving test ten times over, but occasionally without the addition of clothing.

The most challenging part of the weekend, at least for me, came on the last day. Diane had asked us all to bring a piece of music with us. Her only stipulation? This piece of music had to mean something to us. She didn't tell us what it was for. In retrospect this was a good idea because had I known, I might not have turned up.

It all became clear when, on the last afternoon, Diane teetered into the room wearing secretary-style spectacles, killer heels and a short, tight pencil skirt. She whipped out a copy of Tom Jones's 'Sex Bomb', flicked 'play' and proceeded to entertain us with the raunchiest strip tease that I have ever witnessed. Truth be told, it was the *only* strip tease that I have ever witnessed. When she had finished, she made her announcement. 'Ladies, this is what we are going to do for the last "structure" of the course.' I wasn't sure what I was more disturbed about. The fact that I was about to strip naked and dance in front of a roomful of people or the realisation that I was about to do it to a Bob Dylan song.

Needless to say, Bob and I are pretty well acquainted these days. On the final day of that course, reader, I let go of my fears, I stripped down to my birthday suit and I danced to Bob Dylan for my fellow womenfolk. It was undoubtedly one of the most challenging moments of my life; strangely, the naked thing didn't bother me but having the entire room's attention to myself did. Most significantly, I knew that I had crossed an important divide, one that I would never come back from. Even if my secret had only been shared with a select few, *I* would always know that I was the person who had the balls to do a freestyle dance, naked in front of a room full of strangers. Public speaking never felt quite so challenging after that.

Except of course my witnesses were not strangers by this point, and that was the other fascinating aspect of this weekend. Watching the ways in which this work affected other people was breathtaking.

On the first night, a nervous, chattering woman arrived for the course. She was delightful, but there was something missing and I couldn't put my finger on what that might be. The next morning, as we sat in a circle and told the group a bit about ourselves, it became clearer. Rachel was a virgin. She was in her early forties and she had never had sexual intercourse. While I do not believe that virginity loss is a prerequisite for happiness, I do think that most people require the love and the physical affection that you can only get from being in close, intimate proximity to another human being.

Rachel had never known that. She was an academic success but her personal life had paid the price. When she told us about her sense of loss at never having had a physical relationship, it was one of the saddest stories I have ever heard. This made what followed all the lovelier.

It had been difficult for her to sit and reveal the truth about her life, but it was worth it because it was clear to every single person present that something had changed inside Rachel by the end of the course. A weekend of boundary-pushing, of sharing and exploration with her fellow human beings had a palpable effect on her. We watched a different woman dance around the room on Sunday afternoon. She looked light and peaceful, blissful even, as if a lifetime's weight had been lifted off her shoulders.

Two years later, I ran into Rachel again. I was happy to see her for many reasons but mainly because I could tell that somewhere along the line, she had found the missing part of her personal jigsaw puzzle. Maybe she was still technically a virgin and maybe she wasn't, but as Diane Hill's story shows, the technical loss of virginity is not always the one that counts:

I didn't know anything about sex. When we did get television, which was probably about 1953, anything on TV that even faintly hinted at anything sexual, I knew that I had to be sent out of the room. You know that it's something that's not right.

There's a lot of stuff been written about this. About what you know, and what you are told. Because as a child, you have a very deep, inner knowing. And what happens to us is that our intuition is denied and that's why we get so fucked up, because we don't trust ourselves. Because the authority, parents, teachers, whatever, tell us that what we're feeling is wrong. And that's the journey really, to get back.

I've come full circle. I do a job that feeds me, nurtures me. I teach women and I teach men how to have pleasure. That's my group work; my private work is giving people pleasure from a Tantric perspective. I'm very generous with my body. Because I think that sexual energy is the best thing there is for health. I teach them how to relax into pleasure. We're not taught that in this society. We're taught to go for more and more materialistic stuff, which doesn't satisfy, because it's an endless journey. You can never have enough.

When I was about fourteen, some boy kissed me and got spit on me and I was terrified I was going to get pregnant because I knew nothing. And neither did my friend Carol. We were both anxious about this, and I think she started to get into self-pleasuring, as we call it in Tantra. Exploring herself. I think I probably started to do a little bit too, but felt really guilty about that.

Later, I joined some sort of Christian youth club and the boys at the cathedral school came over and put on a kung fu exhibition. This boy chopped a block of wood in half, like they do, and I was incredibly impressed. Incredibly impressed at this and it was love, obviously. That was a lovely intimate time, just exploring the body. But we didn't make love. Because it wasn't a big thing, like it's a big thing now, to have penetrative sex. It wasn't. And that's the whole perspective of Tantra. People think you've got to have penetrative sex to have had sex and it's not about that, it's about the whole body. I think that's probably what we were doing, actually. There was no goal. Which was nice.

I was lucky to have that experience because the next thing that happened was that I was pregnant at seventeen. The guy next door in the electrical shop was the father of my first two children. I used to go out with him delivering televisions and he fucked me, basically, and I got pregnant immediately. Immediately.

It happened in the back of the van, it was really quick and I remember it not being very nice. It was not pleasure. Just sort of when you don't connect with that part of your body. Because you get into a situation, well, I got into a situation, women get into a situation, when you feel obliged. You don't want to say no. Because it felt like ... I didn't want to upset him.

Then of course all hell broke loose because you didn't have unmarried mothers in those days. Got to marry him. You can always divorce him later. What will your father say? All that money spent on your education and now look at what you've done. So I was married within two weeks. Top hat, tails, Rolls Royce, the whole bloody thing.

I was with him for two and a half years and it was never like making love, and that's how we continued until I left him really. After I turned my husband out, I had lots of different experiences with different people, some beautiful, some not, and I found myself living in the red light district in Liverpool. I used to watch the girls take the guys behind the lorries from my window. It was fascinating and I became friendly with the women, I thought they were great, so open, great women, you know. So one day, I went down the road and I thought, oh well, let's give it a go, let's give it a bash and at the same time I had a guru, so I had the spiritual stuff, but my day job was as a sex worker.

On some levels, it was no different to working in Tesco's. I mean, I would have hated working at Tesco's, and on another level, if you're in your authority, in the place of the goddess, if you like, it can be a beautiful experience. It's the oldest profession. The sacred prostitute. When the men came back from war the prostitutes would be in the temples, and their job would be to bathe, massage and make love to the men so that they could go home refreshed and all the stress of the war would be gone. And that was a very respected job.

The biggest thing I learnt is that it's not about sexuality. Men are looking to get back to mother. They all come from woman, and they're looking to get back there. And they think that sexuality is going to do it. And for at least a few seconds, minutes, it does.

For me, it was research, but it was unconscious research. I guess that's how it is in life. You do this, you do that, and then you look back and piece it all together. For me it's been a journey from ignorance to completely understanding. And then of course, you teach what you've learnt.

I had been invited to a Tantra workshop, which I didn't want to go to. I'd heard about Tantra in the sixties and I didn't like the sound of it, obviously because I had big problems around sexuality. But I went because it kept coming up and I thought, well, maybe there's something here for me.

The first night was horrendous and on the second day I had a couple of very strong experiences. We were doing a meditation and I saw this tiny little woman dancing in front of a bunch of women and she was free and I thought, I want that freedom. And then she came really close and it was myself, I was looking in the face of myself. So I thought, okay, this is my journey. I knew it was going to be hard because I knew where I was and how far I had to go, but I just did it and I know now that what I do is good. I know that I'm doing my bit for humanity, because I'm giving back what I've learnt and understood.

Tantra is a way of using your sexual energy to move into a higher state of consciousness because, I think, how you are sexually is how you live your life. I work with people in groups, teaching them how to self-pleasure. Some people are really quick, can't be bothered, some people are too finicky, it's too cold in here, the music is too loud, it's too this, it's too that. That's where they are in life. Some people go on for hours, you know, and really take their time, so you can actually go right down into sexuality, and see what sort of person you are.

To get to that stage, we have to become vulnerable. And everything that's in the way of that vulnerability has to be looked at, and sorted out. I mean, sexual energy is our life energy; it's our creative energy. It's the energy of joy. It's who we are. But it's almost like: on top of that very beautiful energy are all sorts of guards and restrictions that hold it down. And the first bit has to be sexual healing.

Ultimately, I think that losing your virginity should be that gateway into pleasure, a gateway into something very innocent and beautiful. It should be about moving from ignorance to awareness, to becoming totally sexually self-contained, to being a person who makes love or becomes intimate because they choose to, and not because they have to. Of course that could come years after you technically lost virginity. And for some people, maybe never.

Diane's story wraps this chapter up beautifully by taking two diametrically opposed definitions of virginity loss and knitting them together in one story. Despite the contrasting viewpoints that we have heard, most people in the street, and in fact most people in this book, will tell you that they lost their virginity when they first had penetrative sex. In the 'traditional' sense, virginity loss is a physical experience and most of us know exactly when it has happened.

The first part of Diane's story is testament to this fact. Her virginity loss is a raw, physical act that results in the birth of her first child and it has far-reaching consequences for the remainder of her life. Perhaps for this reason, she ends up going on a path of discovery towards a very different, and one might say ephemeral, definition of virginity loss.

St Augustine identified this idea over 1,500 years ago. Andy, our gay interviewee from earlier in this chapter, articulated it when he described his own virginity loss not as a one-off act but as a process, or a series of incidents, each one moving him nearer to a sense of completion. For many of the people I spoke to, virginity loss could be seen as a mental as much as a physical process, a journey of discovery, of fulfilling potential – sexual or otherwise – and of becoming the person that they wanted to be. Virginity loss, in all its different forms, had become the metaphor for that change.

Or as Diane Hill put it, 'it should be about moving from ignorance to awareness, to becoming totally sexually self-contained'. Diane teaches people how to become 'sexually self-contained', and in that sense she teaches people how to lose their virginity. 'You can actually go right down into sexuality,' she said, 'and see what sort of person you are.' She encourages people to examine their sexual identities, to challenge them and, in the process, to effect great change. It's a simple idea and despite my initial trepidation, I watched it transform people's lives.

She also used an interesting phrase when she described her own life as 'a journey from ignorance to completely understanding'. In many ways this is not just Diane's but society's journey over the last 50 years. After many thousands of years of living in a patriarchal society, the leap that not just women, but men as well, have taken in the last half-century is nothing short of monumental. Some of the stories in this book will demonstrate this leap to you. Some of the voices that you hear might argue that we have gone too far in the opposite direction, but no one will disagree with the following: we have more freedom in our lives than we have ever had before.

We can be gay. We can be straight. We can be married, single or all of the above at different times in our lives. The dictionary struggles to come up with a decent definition of virginity loss because our lives can no longer be encapsulated into neat two-line descriptions. Modern Western life has eradicated the need to define ourselves in this way. The life stories of Diane and many others like her are symptomatic of these changes.

But as we will see, it has not always been this way. The journey to get here has been a long and interesting one. Perhaps it is more pertinent to conclude this chapter by asking the following question: does it actually *matter* how we define virginity loss?

It has mattered. It has mattered a lot.

2

The History Girls

Virgin noun 1 *a person, esp. a woman, who has never had sexual intercourse.*
CHAMBERS COMPACT DICTIONARY

People often looked at me in surprise when I told them that I was interviewing men as well as women because, they said, 'it's only really women that lose their virginity, isn't it?'

This baffled me, partly because I know what's going on in *my* head. Why would I only want to interview people who are the same as me? I wanted to know what was going on in *everyone's* heads, particularly the heads of men. But at the same time, you can't push history aside. In many ways, they are quite correct. Historically speaking, a woman's virginity has been of far more interest to most people than a man's. After all, literature would never have invented a metaphor like 'the plucking of the rose' to be used in conjunction with male virginity. We simply wouldn't deem it important enough. The dictionary definition of the verb 'to deflower' compounds the point further: 'To deprive (a woman) of virginity. 2. To despoil of beauty, freshness, sanctity, etc. 3. To deprive or strip of flowers.' (dictionary.com)

Good lord. Such was the extent of a woman's potential 'loss' that it could deprive her of not only beauty and fresh-ness, but sanctity as well. This was serious stuff. A woman's virginity has always been venerated to an unrealistic level, but why? Could it be the Virgin Mary's fault? Could she be the one responsible for the modern-day dilemma that dogs almost every woman – how to be all things to all people? After all, who else could have achieved such an improbable combination of roles: wife, mother, daughter and … a virgin?

The truth is much simpler. The question of women and their virginity is largely down to ownership. From the moment that man first felt a sense of value about what he owned, whether it was his home, his animals or the land they grazed on, the fate of womankind was sealed. A man needed to know that in the event of his death, his possessions would be transferred to the correct heir. He needed to be 100 per cent sure about the paternity of his children. The best way to do this? Marry a woman who has never had sex before.

This was true not just of kings and queens or rich land-owners, but of everyone. A virgin daughter had as much value to the middle classes as to the nobility, but for slightly different reasons. For a family with aspirations of moving up the social ladder, a virginal daughter, particularly a beauti-ful one, had value well beyond her worthiness as a decent human being. Can you see virginity's stock rising? This is how the female of the species became a commodity, because a woman who could make a good marriage brought all sorts of opportunities to the table for her family. A woman's vir-ginity, therefore, had a tangible value.

That value reflected upon everyone. If you wondered when morals would get involved, here they come. A father who could not keep control over his daughters was not seen to be cutting the social mustard because a woman's virgin-ity was inextricably tied not just to her marriageable value, but to the *reputation* of her family as well. Ultimately, it was incumbent upon a woman to protect not just her own reputation but that of those around her as well.

Tragically, as we all know, a woman's virginity has always been harder to protect than a man's. There are countless sad stories of women who, through no fault of their own, had their virginity, and therefore their 'value', obliterated. As if the psychological fallout of sexual assault were not enough to deal with, women were also ostracised from their communities because their stock had fallen. Who wants to be associated with something tarnished, spoilt and ultimately, valueless? Thankfully, while our anatomy is not set to change shape anytime soon, our ability to live independently is. In an age when more women have the financial clout to support themselves, they are not burdened with the weight of other people's expectations in quite the same way that they used to be, at least in much of the Western world.

But it was clear to me that the shockwaves were still felt by many of the women I interviewed for this book. The oldest woman I interviewed was 101 years old, and while she could be forgiven for not being able to recall the precise details of her virginity loss, she was quite sure of one thing. It was gone by the time she had married. She knew this because, had such an error become common knowledge, the consequences would have been drastic, not just for her, but for her family as well.

Researching this book was a sobering journey at times. My mother took an active interest in the work, mainly because she loves social history but also because, at 77 years old, she is acutely aware of the differences between her own life and mine; between the opportunities that we have or haven't had in our respective lives. As she herself says, 'my generation got married so that we could have sex'. You might think that she's joking, but she is not. While sexual intercourse before marriage was frowned upon for both sexes, deeply entrenched ideas about women meant that for at least one half of the Western world's population, the stigma attached to the loss of virginity was always going to be tougher territory to negotiate.

So how did we get to the present day? How did we journey from the stories of the very grand old ladies who allowed me to ask them impertinent questions – the same women who were bred to guard their modesty with their lives – to the young women of today who can choose to do as they please? What happened along the way? How did we change? And most importantly, what happened to our virginity? Through a series of interviews with women of different ages, I will show you exactly what happened.

Edna. Born 1915. Lost virginity in 1940 aged 25

My mother came with me on this first part of my journey as we drove north towards Yorkshire to interview our dear family friend, Edna. Finding older people to interview was a challenge. The social conventions of Edna's generation decreed that subjects of a sexual nature were strictly off limits. A 'lady' would never talk about such matters! Talking to Edna confirmed that all the old clichés were true. According to her, one would *never* say that one was 'going to the toilet'. One would only ever refer to 'brushing one's hair' or 'powdering one's nose'.

But as with my mother I often detected, if not anger, then certainly regret at the constraints placed upon these women and their natural inclination to really live life. 'You'll have these once a month and don't let your brothers know,' said Edna's mother to her when she began her periods. She was not expected to share the news of this startling development with a single living soul.

But it was all change now, and women of 'a certain age' almost universally leapt at the opportunity not only to set the record straight, but to break free from the past. 'You must interview me as well,' said a woman in her seventies when I called to arrange an interview with her husband. 'My generation weren't brought up to talk openly about virginity and sex.'

Speaking to me appeared to be a small act of rebellion for this generation of women. If nothing else, I got the impression that they wanted to help women of my age – and those younger than me – to understand why our lives are so much richer now. We didn't get all this freedom overnight. Someone had done the groundwork.

I hadn't seen Edna for a long time and I had no idea how lucid she was going to be, or indeed, how candid. At 91 years of age, she was to be one of the oldest people to be interviewed for this book. She might even change her mind about the interview before I got there. It was a chance I had to take, but I needn't have worried.

'How are you?' we asked as we arrived at her bungalow.

'I've got one foot in the grave and the other on a banana skin,' she quipped as she teetered across the room to say hello. Ninety-one she may have been but she was as sharp as a tack.

The two world wars provided significant bookmarks in Edna's life. She was born a year after the beginning of the First World War and she married her husband, Henry, 25 years later, a year into the beginning of the second. The two world wars changed the fabric of everyday life in all sorts of ways. Edna's life was no exception. As a child, when a strange man appeared around the side of her house she had no idea who he was. That man was her father but he had been away for such a long time that she didn't recognise him. Families like Edna's were separated, relocated and if they were lucky reunited, often after spending years apart.

Dry, factual information had meant nothing to me when I was studying history at school 30 years ago. I hadn't been the slightest bit interested in learning about things that seemed to bear so little relation to my life as a teenage girl in the early 1980s. But I was now. I wanted to be able to put the stories of my older interviewees into context and to understand what had made these people the way they were. If people could be bothered to take the time to tell me intimate details about their lives, then the least I could do was to understand where they were coming from.

Ironically, for many women, war bought them their first taste of freedom. Four years into the Second World War, a stunning 57 per cent of Britain's labour force was made up of women. This was anathema to many people at the time but most of the male population were busy fighting to protect their country and a workforce had to be mobilised. That workforce included women.

We are not just talking about knitting woolly hats for soldiers either. In every area of industry, from engineering and aircraft production to shipbuilding and railways, women got their hands dirty. Grandparents looked after small children as their fitter and more able daughters went to work. Quite apart from challenging the popular misconception that women had neither the capability nor the physical strength to do such work, the psyche of the average British woman changed during this process. For the first time, women earned their own money and they decided how they would spend it. Via the most testing of circumstances, women gained independence. Life had irrevocably changed and it was going to be difficult to go back to the kitchen once the war was over.

Alongside these fundamental changes ran a 'live now and pay later' attitude. Young people literally did not know if they would survive to the end of the week. I know what I would do if I thought my days were numbered. In a memorable television interview, the 85-year-old actress and writer Joan Wyndham came straight to the point: 'One night there was a really bad raid and the whole shelter was shaking and I thought: "Ah well! The opposite of death is life so I might as well go and get myself de-virginised!"'

With the help of an obliging neighbour, she did just that. She wasn't particularly impressed with the result. 'I'd rather have a jolly good smoke and go to the pictures any day,' she said afterwards. A read of her wartime memoir *Love Lessons: A Wartime Diary* reveals that she revised that opinion later on. But she illustrates the stark reality of people's lives. People had more sex because they didn't know if or when they would see their loved ones again. In an era without contraception, this meant taking risks. Many got pregnant, some out of wedlock. People got married, often hastily, and for those who decided to go it alone, a tough path lay ahead.

But while the war changed the landscape every day, much else remained the same. Though she was every bit as outspoken as Ms Wyndham, Edna did not come from the same bohemian background and even if she had, the value of her virginity had been firmly instilled in her mind. Her stock would be higher if she remained a virgin. At least until she was safely married to her husband Henry.

I mentioned the many reasons that people had for talking to me, and Edna was not backward in coming forward. She was naturally outspoken; however, there was more to it than that. She was eager to tell me about the sexual mores of the day but she also had a personal message to impart about love, and ultimately, about friendship. The latter was particularly important to her because she and Henry were married for over 50 years. This would be her last chance to share this information because she passed away within six weeks of telling me this story.

The First World War was already a year old when I was born in 1915. Both of my parents were involved in it so I stayed with my grandmother in the countryside. She had big boobs and feather beds and I loved it. I used to get into bed with her in the morning in this feather bed, and the boobs, and that was my first few years of life.

Eventually my mother gave up war work and we went back to live in Manchester where I had been born. One day I was playing and a man passed around the house and I didn't know who he was. My mother was sitting on the table and she had had her hair cut. She used to have beautiful hair and she had an Eton crop and she was smoking a cigarette, and he came back and found this woman who he had left with lovely long hair and didn't know what a cigarette was, sitting on the table, smoking and reading a newspaper. That was my father. My little brother was born nine months later.

Though I had two brothers, I never knew what a man looked like until I got married. Now, how my mother kept the two brothers from me, with one bathroom, has always been an enigma. You'd have thought I would have had an idea, but I didn't. Sex was a forboden [sic] subject. And going to the lavatory was a very private matter and that's how it was. My mother never gave me any advice. When I started periods, she just said, 'You'll have these once a month and don't let your brothers know'.

Eventually, as I grew up, I left school and got a job as a receptionist in a hotel in Mayfair. I used to meet lots of chaps and I hung on to my virginity. It was taken for granted that I would. Some of these chaps would grope around but I had had this austere sort of childhood and no one was going to get too near me. Men fumbled and tried to find their way through like the prince did in 'Sleeping Beauty' and he had to get through all those brambles and everything. Well, they never got that far with me.

I was in love several times, deeply in love. I was going to commit suicide when it ended but I decided not to in the end. Also my father was ill. We thought he had cancer but he actually had TB. He contracted it in the trenches during the war. It lay dormant and took a hold of him when he got older. I used to visit him in the hospital and he would write me these wonderful little poems. I was in love with a man from Peru at the time so there would be a little poem entitled 'My friend from Peru' and another time it would be something else. Anyway, he died, just before the Second World War.

Although I was engaged to the chap from Peru, there was no familiarity at all in those days, a kiss goodnight and that was it. Eventually, he went back to Peru and I was to go out to Havana and get married to him. In the meantime, I met Henry and fell in love with him and we decided to get married. Unfortunately, how it worked out with dates, our wedding day, 12 January 1940, was also the anniversary of my engagement to the chap from Peru and all these roses arrived and my mother was absolutely furious. She said, 'What are you going to do with them then?' and I said, 'You put them on Dad's grave'. So that was that and Henry and I got married.

Before our wedding, I would go up to London at the weekends when Henry was free but we always had separate rooms. One night he did come into my room and got into the bed and things could have gone on from there, but with my austere upbringing I knew that this wasn't right so off he went. I had half lost my virginity; when I say that, I'd been fooled around with and manhandled by previous boyfriends but when I got married, that was when I really lost my virginity.

I was frightened on my wedding night and when I saw how he looked, I laughed. I'd never seen anything so funny. In spite of having two brothers I didn't know what a man looked like. My mother had never told me anything. She never said anything about what would happen when I got married, I had to find out by myself. On the first night, I might tell you, I thought 'this is much ado about nothing', but then I got to quite like it.

In days gone by virginity was a commodity that was sold. Today virginity is a very cheap thing. On the one hand, I don't think the ideal thing is to keep yourself pure and meet the right man and save yourself for marriage, I don't believe in that at all. But I feel sorry for young people now because they're taking their young days and making the most of them but I think there is going to be a regret later on. I don't think poor girls setting out for an evening's boozing and then all finding a one-night stand is a good way to start.

I think it is very likely that if you're in love with someone and you're not married, that it can happen in a natural sort of way; that happens. But to go out with the intent, that you've got condoms in your bag, I don't like it. The whole point about marriage is that you grow into a deep friendship. You grow older together and you become deeper friends. Henry and I were very deep. We were very good friends.

Edna's story was interesting and significant for many reasons but most pertinently, she tells us a shocking amount about how much people did not know. Sex and virginity were not openly discussed between parent and child. Despite this, the idea was still communicated to Edna that her virginity was something she had to hold on to. Even though she had no genuine understanding of what 'losing it' meant in the first place.

But many would find out. The war produced concrete evidence of people's so-called misconduct. It was unavoidable. Out-of-wedlock babies conceived in a moment of passion were hard to conceal. Sexually transmitted diseases contracted by lonely soldiers were hard to get rid of but easy to bring home. In a worst-case scenario, a happily married man might return home from the war to find a 'cuckoo' in the family nest that hadn't been there when he left. As a result, a dialogue of sorts began; or, at least, the acknowledgement of people's 'misdemeanours'. The war caused loneliness and it caused heartache but ultimately, it started a chain of events that led to social change.

It didn't happen instantly.

Sandra Jones. Born 1943. Lost virginity in 1963 aged twenty

A number of key characters moved heaven and earth to help me find the right people to interview for this book. Quite often, they came from the most unexpected sources. Andrea was a 'soul girl' when we went to school together in the 1980s. She wore a box pleat skirt and a Pringle sweater. I was a punk. We came from different tribes and as such we had very little to say to each other. Twenty years later, I bumped into her at a party and we couldn't stop talking. When I told her about my project, her response was immediate.

'I love it', she said. 'Why don't you come to Liverpool and I'll see if I can get you some interviews.' She was as good as her word and it wasn't long before I was on a train to stay with Andrea and her husband. She had corralled her eclectic circle of friends into talking and the weekend yielded some absolute gems. Sandra Jones was the first of these.

Sandra insisted on telling her story not just to me, but to her partner and to Andrea as well. 'I have nothing to hide,' she said, 'and I come from an era where everything was hidden.' She didn't want that tradition to continue. Instead, she leapfrogged us from Edna's era straight through the 1950s, and landed us squarely in 1963.

Although the war had a far-reaching social impact, daily life continued much as it had previously done for many people, particularly for women. 'Women are born to love,' Monica Dickens wrote in *Woman's Own* in the 1950s. 'They are born to be partners to the opposite sex, and that is the most important thing they can do in life ... to be wives and mothers, to fix their hearts to one man and to love and care for him with all the bounteous unselfishness that love can inspire.'*

No one wanted women to change. Why would they? Women ran homes and raised children. But seismic shifts were under way for everyone. Religion was beginning to lose its popularity and people were moving, albeit subconsciously, towards a more self-evaluated sense of morality instead of looking to the Church for guidance. The civil rights movement was gathering pace. All over the Western world, men and women from different cultures and backgrounds were finding their voices and beginning to protest against the conservative status quo. On 1 December 1955 Rosa Parks, a 42-year-old black woman, famously defied segregation laws by refusing to give up her bus seat to a white person. Rosa was emblematic of a sea-change not just for racially segregated America, but for millions of people worldwide regardless of age, colour or gender.

Teenagers were becoming a force to contend with. The concept of adolescence genuinely did not exist before the 1950s. People did not go on gap years when they finished school. They grew up, got married and started to give birth to children of their own. But in the 1950s, the vague rumblings of discontent, coupled with a feeling that ordinary people had the power, created the perfect climatic conditions for something radical to happen. Sandra Jones described the moment when she heard 'Great Balls of Fire' by Little Richard for the first time: 'I was passing a house and I heard it coming out of the window. I froze, like a physical reaction.

* From Cate Haste's brilliant book *Rules of Desire: Sex in Britain, World War 1 To The Present* (Vintage, 2002)

It was the most exciting thing I had ever heard. I just stood there and thought, what on earth was that?'

I have always loved the irony of the first paragraphs of Sandra's story. Smoking was actively encouraged 50 years ago because people didn't know any better. Sex, on the other hand, was seen as the devil incarnate. This was about to change.

Growing up in rural Wales in the fifties was interesting because I grew up in what was a Methodist environment, where anybody could drink or smoke. It was considered to be backward not to. My parents smoked, my grandparents smoked, we all smoked. I started when I was sixteen or seventeen and it was taken as read that I would.

Although I grew up in a Methodist area, we were Church of England and we went to church. My father was a highly respected person within the community but he was also a compulsive gambler which nobody knew about, so there was that dual life, if you like. I grew up loathing hypocrisy with a vengeance as a result of that.

In those days we used to spend a lot of time out on the hills playing with other children. We really had that freedom that children don't get anymore. There was a boy that used to knock around with our little gang called Johnnie Reeves and it was around about that time, the twelve or thirteen stage, that my sister Rose and I realised that we had no idea what Johnnie Reeves looked like without his clothes on.

One day we jumped him and removed everything. We took all his clothes off and Juliet Denton, who was with us, had got a little brother so she knew a little bit about the way little boys were made. Once we'd got Johnnie Reeves down on the ground, we were inspecting him very closely and we were literally sitting on him to stop him running away and Juliet Denton piped up, 'Johnnie Reeves, get it up.' I shall remember this until my dying day, because Rose and I both said at the same time, 'Get it up? Get what up?' I can remember Johnnie Reeves replying, 'I can't. Honestly, I can't get it up.' We were completely ignorant.

There was no sex education at school and no one told us anything at home. We found out a lot when we went to stay with my grandmother. She used to buy Woman's Own *and we got a lot of information from reading the problem pages despite the fact that the problems were never spelt out. We had to do an awful lot of reading between the lines to guess what they were talking about.*

As I developed into a teenager, I became a terrible flirt because up until I was thirteen years old, I was a tomboy. I was always up trees and jumping rivers in the woods and I really wasn't aware of my sexuality. Then when I was about fourteen, I started to grow my hair because I was becoming aware of music and I was going for the ponytail look, which you had to have, and all of a sudden boys started taking an interest in me in a different way and I liked that.

For a few years, I dated just about every boy possible and I did an awful lot of snogging. But no sex and I never let them touch me. I was very well conditioned that if they tried to touch you anywhere, you didn't let them. It was a strange time to grow up because nice girls simply did not do it. If you did, you were nasty.

We were also living in this community where the Methodist preachers were very powerful. The chapel was the life and soul of the community and 'rock and roll' was considered to be the work of the devil. Of course I got into rock and roll as soon as I heard it. I was eighteen years old and I was a beatnik.

Around that time, I got together with Ian. I had been on a canal boat for the holidays, we were hitching back home and Ian had picked us up and given us a ride. That was really the first time that I thought to myself, I have got to be noticed by him. He was part of the desirable set in North Wales, they had cars and they did things. So I started going out with him and I fell in love with him.

He was inexperienced and I was inexperienced so we started with snogging at first and then heavy snogging. And then we started to pet: kissing, tits, feeling each other, the usual routine. We tried not to fuck. We really tried not to go all the way so we spent a lot of time petting. When I say a lot of time petting, I mean about eighteen months' worth of petting and all the while it was getting hotter and hotter and we were wanting to do it more and more. And then we did.

It was a pretty disappointing experience but we did manage to get it in and then afterwards we had a total faff about what to do if I got pregnant, which we hadn't thought of before because we hadn't planned on doing it.

He was a medical student and that becomes relevant here because he knew that a solution of vinegar and water would kill the sperm and wash it out. So I turned myself upside down and he poured vinegar and water solution into me and that was our answer to the birth control problem.

But of course now that we had done it once, we couldn't stop doing it and the combination of not being able to stop having sex and the constant vinegar and water gave me what we later learnt was 'honeymoon cystitis'. I related this cystitis to going 'all the way', so I didn't go straight to the doctor because I wasn't married, and in Ian's studies he hadn't got to the stage where he'd learnt about cystitis so he was as baffled as I was.

In the end I actually became quite ill and I developed a kidney infection so I had to give in and go to the doctor and get antibiotics. The doctor must have known that I had had sex but he never said a word.

Once I'd finally done it, although it wasn't particularly good, I knew that I liked it. It was to be explored. Ian and I were so immature and unknowing as to do with sex. It was only because we had both studied some psychology and we were both interested to know more that we did get better. We got the Kama Sutra and we read it and we experimented. If Ian or I heard something interesting from any of our friends, we shared it and we'd have a go. We played.

The pill was only just becoming available but you had to be married to get it. We had discussed Ian getting rubbers, as we called them in those days, but he was too shy to ask for them. For a Methodist, as he was, you had to admit you were having sex to ask for them. Apart from the vinegar and water, we hadn't taken any precautions. It worked for a while and then just after I finished university, I got pregnant.

I could have had an abortion. As soon as the doctor realised Ian was a medical student I was offered an illegal one straight away, which other girls would not have been offered in 1964. I didn't consider it at all, I knew I wanted to keep it even though that was really very difficult timing. We had to get married, of course. There was no question. Ian's mother and father were big names in their Methodist parish.

You could have said that a new dawn came with me getting pregnant because it was the sixties and within two or three years of us getting married, everybody was bonking, but more *significantly, they were saying that they were bonking. That was when times really began to change. My sister actually lived with her boyfriend before she was married. Now she was only eighteen months younger than me. But that's how quickly times were changing, because there was no way Ian and I would have got away with living together just a couple of years previously.*

Do not ever suggest that we should go back to how things used to be. Younger generations have got access to information and it is a very good thing. It was really hard for us to get information because nobody told us anything. When I was reading those Woman's Own *magazines at my grandmother's house, it was like a little mystery tour. You were having to pick up the clues in the stories because nothing was ever directly named or said. Hypocrisy just ruled when I was young. I could have quietly had that abortion, even though it was illegal. No one would have known and I would not have been expected to talk about it.*

We made sure that your generation were never brought up as ignorant as us. I never saw my parents without any clothes on. I had no idea what a naked person looked like.

Sandra's story identifies the pivot on which the 1960s really swung and it appears to be 1963, the year she lost her virginity. Philip Larkin was inspired enough to write a poem about it:

Sexual intercourse began
In nineteen sixty-three
(Which was rather late for me) –
Between the end of the *Chatterley* ban
And the Beatles' first LP.

Larkin references *Lady Chatterley's Lover*, the infamous novel by D.H. Lawrence, because its publication brought the UK to a standstill. Its sexually explicit content was apparently so shocking that its publishers were taken to court under the Obscene Publications Act of 1959. When the twelve jurors passed a verdict of 'not guilty', it signalled the beginning of a new, more permissive era.

It wasn't quite permissive enough for Sandra Jones. When her predicament became clear, there was little doubt about what would happen next. Marriage was the only option. Which made it all the more galling when, only a short time later, her younger sister was living 'in sin' with her boyfriend. Sandra had fallen pregnant on the wrong side of the moral tipping point. People's perceptions of what constituted acceptable behaviour were changing on a daily basis in the early 1960s. There was another reason for this: science had just invented the contraceptive pill.

Never underestimate the importance of allowing a woman to control her own fertility. Little else altered the balance between the sexes in quite the same way as the contraceptive pill. The pill gave birth to something radical: a generation of people who could have sex for no other reason than to please themselves. The umbilical cord between sex and reproduction had been cut. This must have seemed shocking, groundbreaking and brilliant all at the same time.

Sherrie Smith. Born 1956. Lost virginity in 1971 aged fifteen

People often refer to the sexual 'revolution' of the 1960s but I think that 'evolution' might be a more appropriate term. People do not change hundreds of years' worth of history and habits overnight. The women I spoke to certainly didn't think so. A genuine, dyed-in-the-wool change of consciousness takes time. The 1960s may have given women the permission to do things differently, but I got the impression that it was the 1970s that really sealed the deal.

Sex books might be ten a penny now but the 1972 publication of *The Joy of Sex* broke the mould. Here was the cast-iron proof not only that people had sex for pleasure, but that there was a whole variety of different ways in which one could 'do it' too.

The Joy of Sex was swiftly followed by another groundbreaking tome, Nancy Friday's *The Secret Garden*. *The Secret Garden* took *The Joy of Sex* and wiped the floor with it because here was a book about women's sexual *fantasies*. This might not sound like a big deal now but in the foreword to her book, Nancy Friday revealed the following gem. When the idea was first pitched to publishers, one of them famously said: 'I don't know why you are bothering to write this book because women do not have sexual fantasies.' Someone somewhere is eating those words very slowly and painfully. *The Secret Garden* was a publishing phenomenon.

Interviewing the women for this book frequently felt like watching history change in front of my eyes. Each of the women I talked to took me nearer to understanding how my own life had come to be what it is. My next interviewee was fourteen years old when the 1970s began, and standing behind her was a rather horrified set of parents. Try as they might, there was nothing they could do to stop Sherrie becoming the woman she wanted to be. Sherrie had been educated, but that was not the most potent indicator of the direction her life would take. The most powerful piece of information Sherrie possessed was the knowledge that she did not need anyone else in order to survive. When push came to shove, and it did, she knew that she was capable of supporting herself. This was the point in our history when virginity really got handed back to the person who had owned it in the first place: the individual.

Sherrie is a woman who has embraced many different roles in her life. Playgirl – quite literally, Sherrie was one of the country's first Page Three girls – feminist, artist, wife and mother. As ever, I knew none of this as I stepped over the threshold of her home. 'You must interview my friend Sherrie,' Hannah St John had said to me a few weeks previously. 'She'll give you a great interview.'

After a frantic journey through rush-hour traffic, I arrived in a panting heap at Sherrie's north London home. She took one look at me and led me towards the kitchen through a hallway festooned with fairy lights, candles, children and pets. Within seconds I was seated at a table. A steaming bowl of pasta was placed in front of me, and a glass of wine to my side. We chatted about London transport and wintry weather. Once I had caught my breath, she shooed the husband, children and pets out of the room and told me this story.

The gap between my parents' generation and my own was a chasm. It was huge. We had nothing in common and nothing to talk about. We had come out of the dark ages but my parents still wouldn't allow me to see the sex education film at school. Did that inhibit my desire to have sex when I wanted to have sex? No! It just made me more curious. I was living a very closed life and I wasn't by nature a very closed person. I desperately wanted my own life and I knew the only way I could have that was by leaving home.

I'd had all sorts of snogging things with boys by this point. I had nearly lost my virginity with this gorgeous dark-haired gypsy boy from the local fair. I wanted to but I just thought, no. Lying in a field behind a fairground really isn't where I want to do this, to go that far with someone. So I stopped him and every time I saw him in the street after that he just used to smile at me.

When my father fell ill, I was packaged off to an aunt's house and that's where I met the man I lost my virginity to. He was an artist and it was lust. Pure, driven, hormonal lust. I was fifteen years old, he was 23 and my aunt never spoke to me again after that because she thought that I had led him on, which is probably true. I was very much the driving force. But I was also sensible. I was mad in many ways, but I was sensible. There was no way I was going to end up pregnant and begging my mother for help so I went to the doctor and got the pill. I asked him very nicely not to tell my mother and he said, 'Yes, that's fine but you'll have to give me £20.' That was a week's wages to me at the time. Bastard. But I got the pill and I was prepared.

Looking back, I never really thought about it in terms of losing my virginity. I know that's odd because I've talked to girlfriends about it and it was a big thing, but I didn't really think about it, perhaps because it was a very gradual process. I had actually had my first orgasm before we had sex properly and it was a complete surprise to me. We were just playing around and I remember suddenly feeling as if I was going to wet myself and I thought, my god, what's this? No one had ever mentioned orgasms to me before so I really wasn't clued into what the sensation was. I wasn't really looking for it but it just happened and it was like, OK, I'll have some more of this, thank you very much. This is really nice!

I was completely fascinated by the whole process of sex and once this guy had made me come, that was it. It was like a door opening to another world that I wanted more of. Losing my virginity wasn't a fumbling, horrible thing like it is for so many. He knew what he was doing, it just kind of happened and it was brilliant.

It was manna from heaven for me on so many levels because sex also equalled freedom, absolutely. And strength. Finding out that you can actually reduce most men to a pulp when you are young and beautiful was incredibly empowering. If I could exert that kind of power over an older man at that age, then I really could do whatever I wanted. I was totally delighted and happy with that revelation.

My parents used to give me curfews that I would abide by but once I had the older guy in tow and they knew about it, they did their best to destroy that. That was the final nail in the coffin of me leaving home because that was when my mother called me the biggest 'whore' and 'slapper' under the sun, and it wasn't long after that that I left.

The sixties had been and gone and it was a new era. It's not just rose tinted spectacles because there were issues. Vietnam was still going on. But there were also opportunities and London was such a fantastic place. I got a job in a design agency and a flat in Notting Hill and the world was my oyster. It was like coming alive. It was bloody wonderful.

It was also the era of Spare Rib, the women's movement was big and Germaine Greer was at the height of her power. I was a feminist but I was my own feminist. I never saw the point of giving up your femininity and hating men. Later on, I had a *studio at London Bridge and it was full of artists and writers and dancers. A lot of them were fully paid up members of the feminist movement and they were so horrible to the men in their lives, and the men that hung around them were so wimpy and wet. That wasn't liberation to me. It was another set of rules and I wanted to write my own rules.*

At the time, I had the body and the face to die for and the belief that I could have any man that I wanted. I was so proud of who I was that I decided I wanted to be a Penthouse Pet. The women's liberation movement was horrified by that kind of thing, but I loved it. I got paid bucketloads of money, had an absolute blast and there wasn't a pervert among them. I did Penthouse, *I did calendars, I was even a 'Page Three girl'. The feminists said that those magazines were exploiting women but I didn't see it. I was out there doing what I wanted to do and loving the fact that my mother would have hated it.*

Young women's needs are actually not any different through the generations. They still want basically the same things but it's not so easy to achieve now because so much more is expected of them. There is this incredible pressure on girls to be everything and I don't think they know who to be. A career girl? A mother? A ladette? A feminist? A 'Sugababe'? When I was young there was nothing that was desirable for a young woman to be except herself.

When I asked our fifteen-year-old son last weekend, 'What are your hopes, wishes, dreams and fears for the following week?', his words were, 'To get laid.' I did laugh, we all laughed, but for our daughter, my heart would have cracked in two if she had said that. She's twelve years old.

It scares me because sometimes I look at her and think, oh my god, she's me, because she is so mouthy and 'out there', and then she looks like a child again. But then perhaps I would have done that if I'd had a mother that I could have curled up with. I don't know. I believed I was invincible at that age. I only see now that I was vulnerable. Losing your virginity is a loss of innocence but I never perceived it as that because I think I lost my innocence an awful lot younger through various family circumstances. I never saw it as that at all.

Sherrie's story travelled full circle. She began by taking us back to her own virginity loss and finished by pondering the possibilities for her twelve-year-old daughter's future. She also pinpointed an important distinction between girls and boys. Her son hopes 'to get laid'. But she acknowledges that if her daughter had given the same answer, she would have been heartbroken.

Perhaps she gets to the heart of a question that we asked at the beginning of the chapter. Why do we place more importance on a woman's virginity than on a man's, even in an age when, for many, the loss of virginity is a personal choice? Maybe it is down to the way that women are made. A woman is physically more vulnerable than a man. Our anatomy is such that the loss of virginity requires us to allow another human being *into* our bodies for the very first time. You cannot alter the dynamics of that exchange any more than you can stop night from becoming day. Losing virginity for a woman requires a level of trust that a man does not have to heed, whichever way you look at it.

'I was very much the driving force', says Sherrie, but in the end, this is only ever a subjective type of control and an unspoken agreement of trust that exists between two people. Any victim of date rape will confirm this. A woman's virginity is always going to be a more fragile proposition simply because of our physical make-up.

The concept of vulnerability is an interesting segue into the next story: my own. A little like the loss of virginity itself, the sharing of such a personal piece of history requires us to be vulnerable in the presence of an unknown quantity. I was often overwhelmed at the trust that people showed me when they agreed to be interviewed, particularly as most of them had never met me before. I decided to reciprocate. Quite apart from anything else, how could I expect to relate to these people unless I had been through the same experience?

I wrote a list of questions, grabbed my tape recorder and enlisted the help of a trusted male friend. What emerged during this session amazed me. My virginity loss story had often been reduced to its essential components around a pub table – it had elements of slapstick to it – but I had never discussed the emotional nuts and bolts with anyone. Viewing this story through the lens of a 37-year-old woman's experience shed new light on my teenage motivations.

I had often wondered why I had sought such a sexually pedestrian experience with a boy I barely knew at the age of fifteen. It was one of the least satisfying sexual encounters of my life. Having listened to the stories of hundreds of different people for this book and my blog, it now seems obvious why, but at the time, it irked me. Was there something wrong with me? It sounds nuts to say it, but I had unconsciously carried this question around with me for years.

As I let my words hang between me and my interviewer, everything fell into place. Hormones did not drive me at the age of fifteen. That came later. I was motivated by something more powerful than lust: the desire to be included. The idea that I might get left behind while my best friends marched towards womanhood snookered me. I wanted to be in the driving seat of my life. I wanted to become a woman. Losing my virginity was the fastest way I knew to do this. It all made sense to my subconscious mind at the time.

There was another ingredient in this potent cocktail of confusion: I needed affirmation. Being desired by an exquisite French boy was as intoxicating as any drug. I didn't require a physically satisfying experience at that stage, but I did need to know what it was like to be desired by a very handsome man. Like many fifteen-year-olds, I didn't have an overabundance of confidence. My partner's beauty made me feel better about myself. Perhaps I thought it might rub off on me if I performed the ultimate act of sharing.

Kate Monro. Born 1968. Lost virginity in 1983 aged fifteen

I would never have said in a million years that I was an unconfident fifteen-year-old, but looking back, I can see I was. Because losing my virginity to an absolute Adonis was the icing on the cake as far as I was concerned. The fact that this incredibly good-looking boy wanted to have sex with me, and only me, was the most important thing in the world. The quality of the experience didn't even cross my mind.

I remember feeling quite alarmed when I first found out what sex was. I was sitting on a bench at school when this loud, annoying boy who was a couple of years above me made that really crude gesture where you stick a finger through a circle made with the fingers on your other hand. I didn't really understand what he was doing and I wasn't even paying that much attention, but then the penny dropped and in that moment, I suddenly understood what men and women did together. I was amazed and grossed out at the same time.

I remember the first boy I went out with because he really, really liked me. Back to the confidence thing again. I think I thought that was how it was. If a boy liked you then you went out with him. I didn't give my own feelings a lot of consideration. Perhaps I felt guilty because he gave me his Echo and the Bunnymen LP. I don't know. But whatever the reason, I still have this mental image of us lying together on my friend's bunk-bed with his hand up my jumper and feeling hideously wrong about the whole thing. It never occurred to me that I just didn't fancy him.

Which is a shame when I look back, because if I had had the wherewithal to wait until it felt more 'right' with someone then I could have jumped straight into the very lovely sexual adventures that I had with my first proper boyfriend; but I was hellbent on losing my virginity at the age of fifteen and I rushed into the experience without thinking about it.

I was on holiday with my two best friends and their parents, who had a nightmare trying to keep us under control because we were like a bunch of escaped zoo animals. It was an amazing moment when I look back, not so much because I lost my virginity but more because of what it symbolised to me. Being abroad for the first time without my parents was the biggest rush of freedom that I had ever experienced in my life and I was totally hooked on that feeling.

We were entranced with everything. The beach, the sea, the drinks and the boys. Jessica's parents let us out at night and we would always come home at the appointed time, but we would sneak out again as soon as we heard them snoring. We would spend all night in a proper 80s disco with flashing floor lights and piña coladas, being chatted up by hairy Spaniards who looked like members of Wham. We were having the time of our lives and then he walked in, this incredible man-boy. He was French, he was charismatic and he was on holiday without any parents. I was like a moth to a flame.

I figured out pretty quickly that this was my big opportunity to lose my virginity. Underneath it all, I was apprehensive but Claire and Jessica had both lost theirs recently and that was the irony really, when you think about it. I always thought I was such a maverick with my spiky hair and ripped jeans, but there I was, about to take a big step with no real thought as to whether it was something that I actually wanted to do. My friends had done it; therefore I wanted to do it. And quickly. I couldn't stand the thought of being left behind.

The big night came and the girls and I did our usual sneaking out routine but this time it was different, because after we had left, Jessica's dad woke up and discovered that we were gone. He stormed down to the village to find us but I was long gone by this point. Up into the hot Spanish night, all ready to lose my virginity.

I remember the heat and the scent in the air. I was nervous but I didn't say anything to him. It wouldn't have occurred to me to tell him that I was a virgin. I wanted to pretend that I was a grown-up. We wandered around, trying to find somewhere to do it and finally settled on a garden with a swimming pool. It was all so calculated. It wasn't driven by passion at all, at least on my part. I just wanted to get rid of my virginity.

We got down to business. I had no idea what I was doing. And although he might have been a year older than me, it was still a bit like the blind leading the blind. He made little attempt to get me in the mood and I was no better. Somehow, before I knew it, we were doing it and my absolute first thought was: 'Oh, this feels like three Tampax instead of one.' Nothing more. It felt like what it was, like having something inside you for the first time, which is an odd sensation.

I don't think I even wriggled around so that it might feel better, I just let him get on with it and it didn't last long. I had this bizarre idea in my head that because he was so good-looking, obviously it was going to be the greatest sexual experience of my life, and it wasn't. But then, in many peripheral ways, that night is full of very evocative memories for me. It happened on this pine-scented hillside overlooking the sea and it was on one of the best holidays I ever had in my life. I still only have to smell pine trees on a warm summer night to transport me straight back to that time. I can't tell you how much excitement I felt about everything at that point. I just knew that I was going to have a lot of fun in my life and I couldn't wait to jump in and start experiencing it all.

It was done. I'd stepped through the door. As far as I was concerned, I was now officially a woman. I was delighted with my new-found status. You may just as well have given me a shiny, spanking new passport to adulthood. That was how I felt. It could have been anything in a way, like running the fastest race. What had actually happened was immaterial to me. It was the fact that it had happened that mattered.

Afterwards we walked back down to the port and I said goodbye to him because he was leaving in the morning. On the one hand I felt gutted because I'd just shared something very intimate with someone and now we were going to walk away from each other, but as I skipped across the square, I also felt like I had something in my pocket that nobody could take away from me.

When I got back to the apartment, Jessica's dad had locked the door so I had to ring a bell to get in. I must have looked like something that the cat dragged in but he never said a word. He just stood there and looked like the angriest dad in the whole world. He wasn't my dad but it didn't matter. The sentiment was clear. He was hopping mad.

I didn't tell anybody the truth about what had happened that night until I got rumbled a couple of days later, and I couldn't have planned it better. There was a girl on the beach called Danielle who used to tell us the most amazing stories about her nightly sexploits. She was a couple of years older than us and she'd come and find us every day and recall, in THE most lurid detail, exactly what she'd got up to the night before. We would sit in rapt attention, loving her for thinking that we understood even half of what she was talking about.

One day, she suddenly piped up, 'So which one of you three is still a virgin then?' We must have looked like rabbits in the headlights and Jessica said, 'I'm not', which was true, and then Claire said 'I'm not either,' which was also true, and my moment of glory had finally come. 'I'm not a virgin,' I said. I could feel Jessica and Claire glaring at me as if to say, 'You what?' But I didn't say a word. They didn't say a word; nobody said a word until Danielle had walked away, and then came the questions.

My cup of happiness was pretty much full at that point, even though my actual experience had sucked. And later on, in the back of my mind, I think that always bugged me. Why didn't it feel good? Why hadn't it felt sexier? Or more exciting? Did I not 'work' properly? My tendency to look to myself for the answer to the problem instead of considering external factors suckered me every time. It took me a long time to find confidence in my own feelings.

Now I think that each time you meet someone new, it's a bit like another 'first time', especially if it's someone that you really like. Because it's not like we ever stop learning. Every lover that you encounter is going to take you to a new place in your head. Sometimes it might not be such a great place, but even the less interesting places have their value. Because learning what you don't want is a lesson in itself. I had no idea at the age of fifteen that sex was something that you practise at and get better at, and that if you pick the right partner it can be life-changing.

And that's my story. A few days later we began the long drive back to London and I knew that I was a different person. Jessica's dad didn't speak to me for ages after that and looking back, I can see why. Taking someone else's fifteen-year-old daughter on holiday to Spain is an awesome responsibility and like a typical teenager, I never even considered that for a moment.

Somehow, though, the experience bonded us. We often laughed about it in later years and while I never told him the truth about what happened that night, I think he had a pretty good idea. And for me, in the absence of my own parents, having someone to be cross with me about it made the experience more complete.

This story casts the loss of virginity in a new role: as status symbol. Can you imagine Edna itching to tell her school friends that she had popped her cherry when she came back to school after the summer holidays in the 1940s? I don't think so. Women of her generation had plenty of opportunities to lose their virginity, and had they not been so petrified of getting pregnant they probably would have jumped at the chance, but they would never have breathed a word of it to another soul.

The eighties were different. As women, we were one of the first generations to grow up with very little concept of the idea that we might not be equal to men. I watched my mother go out to work every day, and in the evenings she studied for a degree. My sister, in between hiking through the Peruvian jungle and sailing down the Amazon, was studying to be a botanist. We had opportunities on a plate and that also included the opportunity to have sex. There was very little standing between me and my virginity loss besides my own desire. But desire for what?

My virginity had no fiscal value to my parents but that didn't mean it had lost any of its power or significance. A young man wrote to me recently via my blog and asked if I thought that people looked different once they had lost their virginity. 'Don't be ridiculous,' I thought to myself. 'How could that be possible?' But then I remembered how I felt the day after I lost my own virginity. As I sat on the sandy beach of a Spanish coastal resort, I didn't feel it necessary to tell anybody what had happened the night before because as far as I was concerned, it may just as well have been written across my face in permanent marker. It was obvious that I was now 'a woman'.

I hadn't been convinced about the idea of going 'all the way' but it was a small price to pay for the kudos of becoming an adult. This was a conflict for me then and for many young people that write to me, it still is. The pill had removed a significant barrier, but some might argue that the barrier had protected us from having to make grown-up choices while still technically a child. More specifically, it protected women from making adult choices. Twenty-one-year-old Shanice agreed:

I did feel under a lot of pressure ... no one wants to be the odd one out. I didn't want him to go talking about me like, 'Shanice is frigid.' I don't know if you heard about that word but you don't want to be called it.

In a few short decades, virginity had lost its power to control us in the traditional sense. But it still had the power to control us in others.

The good news is that for every young woman who writes and tells me that she lost her virginity because she felt like she should, another will write and tell me that she has no intention of losing it until she feels like it. As we step into the 21st century, I see increasing evidence to support the idea that women are more single-minded than I was in the 1980s. I even began to encounter young women who took much the same approach to the selection of their first partner that their mothers had about choosing a husband. Our mothers often chose dependability and kindness over sexiness and good looks. I have seen young contemporary women approach the loss of virginity in the same way. My next interviewee is no exception.

Sunita decided to lose her virginity to a man that she didn't love. In truth, she didn't particularly fancy him either. 'It was not a lust thing,' she says. 'It was more like "let me get this over and done with. And let me do it with someone really nice".'

What this strategy lacks in passion and impulsiveness, it certainly makes up for in sensible forward planning. It is almost as if she acknowledged that deep down, 'the first one' could be the blueprint for all subsequent lovers. If you get it right first time, do you not have a better chance of succeeding further down the line?

There are so many different stories that I could have chosen for this final slot. I have stories from all sorts of thoroughly modern women. Sunita is one of these women. She lost her virginity in 1993 when she went away to university. In between meeting boys, raving and drinking pints of cider, she also found time to study and now has a successful career in account management; but Sunita is also something of a red herring. She says: 'My mum was seventeen when she first came to England. She thought the Eiffel Tower was here and that she'd be able to wear flares all the time. On the basis of one photograph of my dad, she flew to Heathrow. She married my dad two days later.'

Sunita is a Punjabi Indian by origin and as such, she still has the shadow of a bygone era hanging over her head, one that her parents consistently remind her of, despite the fact that the 'motherland' has developed much faster than her parents have: 'The funny thing is that when I go back to India now, I use really old words. People my own age go, "You freak! Where did you learn that word?" Because it's fallen out of their language and they don't use it any more. It's become English instead.'

While Sunita's heritage clearly plays a part in the choices she makes, nonetheless her story prompts the question: after all the changes that women have seen, post-war, post-pill and post-feminism, how much do their basic needs differ from generation to generation? What point have we arrived at as women? And where are we going?

Sunita. Born 1975. Lost virginity in 1993 aged eighteen

We were brought up in a way that was a very loving house, but it was not free in any way. Because you had to preserve this idea of India. To the point that there was no way I was going to have my hair cut short. In India, people were cutting their hair short in order to be a little bit more 'modern', as they call it, whereas I was going to have two tight plaits.

But I would say the same level of pressure was on my brothers as well. I remember one time my brother came downstairs in this suit, like he was Sonny Crocket from Miami Vice. *It was a bit like that Lenny Henry sketch where he's coming down in his new threads, and his mum goes, 'Just go upstairs, take those ugly clothes off and go to bed!' It's the same thing. Except my dad was like, 'Where do you think you're going? You're not going anywhere!' I love them. They're the best people. I would never have it any other way, but there were massive expectations put on me and my brothers.*

We never spoke about sex at home. Except once when I was in town with my mum and we saw this Indian girl who wore quite a lot of make-up and my mum said to me, 'Oh, you can just tell her character's changed. She's obviously been bad', and from that, I just took this whole thing that my mum would know. The moment I had sex, my mum would know, because my character would change and my legs would look different. Now, don't ask me where I got this bit from, but I thought my legs would bow. The moment that I walked through the door, my mum would go, you've had sex because your character's changed and I can tell from your bowed legs.

I lost my virginity when I was eighteen and I remember preparing myself for it. I mean like really doing the hair removal cream, and thinking, oh my god, what if he doesn't like me, or what if I smell funny? All these things really cross your mind, but the biggest one was: am I going to lose my character?

It was with this older guy. I was living in halls of residence and for the first time, I was really living the life. I was out all the time, doing the things I couldn't do at home like drinking and taking drugs. It was a massive liberation. I think he was a bit like, shit, do I really want to get involved with this girl that's ten years younger than me who's never had sex before? But I had made up my mind that it was going to happen.

It was one of those weird Saturday afternoons when you close the curtains and stay indoors all day. It all felt wrong in a way and it wasn't like there was this huge build-up. I don't even think I was properly wet when we actually did it, but then I didn't know what I was supposed to feel like because I'd never even had a look there. You know how for some women they've gone and got a mirror and had a look? Well I don't think I ever did that, till maybe after my second or third sexual experience.

To me it was just like this act. It wasn't like a real sexual, oh-my-god thing. Afterwards, he was doing the over-hugging thing, like trying to make it a tender moment for me and I don't think I felt like that. I just felt relief. And then I looked at myself and thought about the character thing. It's funny how that keeps coming back but I was a bit like, shit, she's gonna know. And then I quickly realised that no, actually she isn't gonna know.

I've been with my husband John for nearly ten years now. We got married two years ago but we were actually together for six years before I told my mum and dad that I wasn't going out with an Indian boy. It was really awful but at the same time, after I had confessed, my mum's family phoned her from India and said, 'You've got to be proud about this or you might just as well just walk around with your head held down. You've got to accept this if you all want to lead happy lives.' And they did, but it's been a massive journey for them as well.

Our expectations of everything are so big now and I'm all for that, but I hope that if I get pregnant, my expectations on what my life needs to be will change, you know? Because it's not all about the new Prada shoes every week. I get a lot of confidence through my work but lately I've started to think about the effort I put in and how it has compromised other parts of my life. I have started to ask, how far are we really capable of having it all, and actually wanting it all? Because I'm a lot more content when I'm not just the woman that works really hard.

There's part of me that just doesn't want to be superwoman. I'm not saying there's a right or wrong way, but there are certain instincts from day dot that are primal. I think we have to keep remembering that we are women and that we can bear children and grow them in our bodies. I'm all up for choice but I don't want to have to be in control all the time. I still want to feel vulnerable.

Going to university and losing my virginity was a liberation. I was a woman and I knew that I was in control. But meeting my husband changed everything. He was so wicked. A wicked guy, a wicked mate and a wicked personality. He was all those things that I wanted but for me, and this is going to sound really old, companionship is the most important thing in my life.

I love this photographer called Martin Parr and I love his pictures where you see the old couple at the seaside having an ice cream. I think there is something really great about that. It's the conversation and having a wicked time. That's the bit I really missed when I had a break from John. I was doing really *well in my job and earning loads of money but I thought: what's it worth if you don't have anyone to share it with?*

The distance that women have travelled in 50 short years is awesome. Two world wars and the contraceptive pill catapulted generations of women into a world that our great-grandmothers would not recognise. But does the freedom to make our own choices change what we are? As Sunita herself said: 'There are certain instincts from day dot that are primal. I think we have to keep remembering that we are women and that we can bear children and grow them in our bodies.'

This sentiment has resonance for me. I don't know if I will have children, but as I pursued this project I realised that no matter how much time has elapsed, we cannot help what we intrinsically are. I may have lost my virginity in a vastly different way to how my mother did, but twenty years down the line, I still have the same hormones. It doesn't matter how ambitious we feel or how much money we earn; you cannot ignore the most basic of human instincts. This isn't about going backwards or attempting to undermine feminism. It is an acknowledgement that no matter how independent we have become, women have the ability to create life, and as such we will always have big decisions to make, no matter which decade we are born into.

'Young women's needs are actually not any different through the generations', said 52-year-old Sherrie. 'They still want basically the same things but it's not so easy to achieve now because so much more is expected of them.' Choice has given us freedom but some might argue that women have short-changed themselves by attempting to excel in too many different areas. We want to be identified by our trailblazing career but at the same time, most of us have an underlying urge to be the best parents that we possibly can be.

Where does this leave our virginity in the modern world? I had an interesting email from a 23-year-old woman in America recently. She made an obvious but thought-provoking observation: 'When I was eight years old, I learned what the word "virgin" meant and I was shocked that there was a word for the "default" state.'

This is a visceral description of what it is like to realise that one is not just an eight-year-old child but that one is also a 'virgin'. You have barely taken your first breath in the general context of your life, and yet you have already been labelled and defined. Perhaps, then, for as long as a word exists to describe the state of being a virgin, being a virgin will be an issue, particularly for a woman.

The difference is that in the Western world, as these stories have so beautifully illustrated, we have arrived at a point where women can make their own choices. They might not be easy choices, but unlike our mothers and grandmothers, we do not need to concern ourselves with other people's reactions to them. However, we are in a lucky minority. For many other women, this remains a luxury they cannot afford. A comparatively small proportion of the world's population labels itself as 'non-religious', and while virginity has cultural ramifications as much as religious ones, the fact remains that for millions of women, the importance of virginity extends far beyond the confines of the bedroom or the back seat of a car.

In many parts of the world, virginity is still a political issue, it is a religious issue and it is an issue of honour. The loss of a woman's virginity can still cost her at best her reputation, and at the very worst her life. Even now, in the 21st century, women are being brutalised for 'losing' something that is almost impossible to quantify or to define.

It is also worth remembering that in the scheme of things, the footsteps of the women I have interviewed are fresh. Fifty years is but a blip. It would be interesting to come back in 500 years and to see how much further on women's lives have moved. But the fact remains that women will still have wombs, even in 500 years' time – though they may not need to use them.

Tantalisingly, at least for women today, the qualities we traditionally recognise as being 'feminine' and possibly a hindrance have become the power players of the future. Sunita articulates with touching precision what she wishes for in her life: 'I'm all up for choice but I don't want to have to be in control all the time. I still want to feel vulnerable.' She acknowledges what she is. She is female and when she has babies, she wants to rely on the support of her partner, emotionally and financially. But what would once have made her weaker is also becoming a bankable attribute.

In a commercial world that now relies so heavily on communication, tact, diplomacy and intuition are the skills that will push us forward into the future. Men had the advantage in the past. Tact and diplomacy did not fuel the Industrial Revolution, technical innovation and brute strength did. But the tables have turned. If you can communicate well, you are valuable. Women are beginning to compete with men on an equal footing while packing an arsenal of attributes that would have hindered their progress in the past.

This is all the more interesting when you consider where we are going with the next chapter: men's stories. Because if you think that women are stepping onto male territory, what do you think men might be doing? Let me put it to you like this. If you had asked me when I began this project if I thought that men would have the patience or the motivation to sit down and talk to a stranger about their virginity loss experiences, I would have said you were quite mad. I was wrong.

Men talked to me, not just about virginity loss, but about feelings, emotions and all that touchy-feely stuff that we associate with women. Sometimes they did it for hours on end.

We women like to think that we differ from men emotionally as much as we do anatomically.

I beg to differ.

3

Boys Don't Cry

I expected men to hold back, to be economical with the truth. I assumed they would be reticent and reluctant to talk to a woman about one of the most revealing moments in their sexual history.

Reader, they sang like canaries.

Not only that, but they did it with extraordinary sensitivity and honesty.

From a pure nosiness point of view, this was thrilling. I felt like I had a backstage pass into the minds of the opposite sex. Women talk to each other the whole time. We understand each other's worlds because we have a constant, comfortable dialogue with each other but, in my experience, men don't generally share this fluidity. Perhaps it was because I was a member of the opposite sex, *and* one with whom they were not intimately involved, that men took advantage of a rare opportunity. Either way, it was fascinating – and endearing – to listen to men lay themselves bare.

So much is now written about women's history. The last chapter was testament to this fact. I loved the way in which the women's stories had proved to be the perfect showcase for the huge structural changes of the last century. But what about men? Hadn't their lives changed too? Did they not have stories to tell? Or had they remained immobile and unaffected by these developments? As I delved into the minds of the opposite sex, it became apparent that men have *had* to change and it hasn't always been easy. Furthermore, they were more adept at talking about it than we ever give them credit for.

From a traditional point of view, men and women do not share the same history. Men have not spent centuries being castigated for their so-called sexual transgressions in quite the same way that women have. Men are not in the same league when it comes to the consequences. If a man loses his virginity, no one blinks. From this point of view, I really understood the urge that women felt to tell their stories. They had a rock-solid reason to get something off their chests. So what made men so willing to spill the beans? Perhaps this willingness was less to do with virginity loss and more to do with a world that has changed at lightning speed.

In metaphorical terms, men have had the rug pulled out from under their feet and herein lies the irony. Women are so much better equipped to deal with flux. Most women spend their working days multi-tasking like mad, switching quickly between a variety of communications: emailing, texting, talking and in many cases managing homes and families at the same time. Women are built to flex and change in a world that is flexing and changing. They have an advantage in the modern world that doesn't come naturally to most men.

I often spied confusion in the faces of men whom I interviewed, not just about the bewildering speed with which our lives appear to have changed but also about how to react to this new species of female. What does she want? How is a man to gauge the sensibility of every woman that he encounters? I have seen this in action when a man holds a door open for me. Occasionally a look of panic will flash across his face and I can see the thought occurring to him: 'Is this door going to get slammed in my face?'

For what it's worth, I love having doors held open for me but I understand the dilemma. Modern woman can open her own door, thank you very much. She can be economically independent. She can control her own fertility; she can get herself educated and buy herself a house. She can even put babies in that house if she really wants to, all, in theory, without the aid of a man. The truth is that women don't need men to survive in quite the way that they once did and frankly, that must feel strange.

In December 2007, I wrote about these issues on a post for my blog, The Virginity Project. I wanted to express something about the bizarre dance that men and women appear to be doing as we figure out where we belong in relation to one another. I talked about an incident that had inspired some of these thoughts.

One evening, as I walked through Cadogan Square in London, a pair of well-spoken but rather inebriated young men fell into step behind me. They were discussing (loudly) the 'hotness' of a female work colleague and lamenting the fact that she clearly 'masturbates way too much'. I was all ears. What did they mean by this? 'Yes,' they continued, 'she's just not having the cock is she. She'd much rather go home and masturbate ... but she's still blaaddy hot.'

I resisted the urge to turn around and ask them to elaborate on this point and instead, began to consider what might really be worrying them. In their eyes, there was a worrying possibility that they were now surplus, not only to Hot Girl's requirements but perhaps to those of *any* girl. And all because 'Hot Girl', allegedly, was perfectly adept at having a nice time by herself. She could drive her own car, so to speak. 'Women,' I wrote later on my blog, 'have found their own power. And they are not afraid to use it.' In a strange twist of fate, I was about to receive an email that could not have illustrated this point any better if it tried. It was from Paul Ewing and it began like this:

Hey Kate, I just ran across this post and wanted to compliment you on it. I'm a househusband, my wife is a banker, and it's finally dawned on me that, as you put it, 'Women have found their power, and they're not afraid to use it.' It's uncomfortable and a bit surreal at times (I never thought I'd be a 'banker's wife'), but we're both doing well.

Paul Ewing. Born 1964. Lost virginity in 1980, aged eighteen and again quite recently

If Paul had had a successful career as a banker, his wife's could only be described as stratospheric. Georgina was promoted through the ranks faster than her husband and in the end it made more sense for him to stay at home with the children. Over a series of emails, we established that Paul had raised their young family while his wife had become the breadwinner. Mostly we chatted about the weather but in between, Paul gave me a glimpse of their very modern set-up. Gems such as these were never far off:

We threw an Xmas party last year and Georgina and another banker were chatting about work. They're gabbing on about stuff, and I'm of course standing there, drink in hand. Eventually my mind starts to wander to thinking about the baby, whether she's going to wake up, the shopping to be done and cleaning up after the party and I realise that I'm not really part of the conversation and no one expects me to say anything anyway. For goodness' sakes, it may as well have been 1957 as 2007, and I may as well have been the trophy wife with a cute pair of buns and an acutely limited horizon.

We all understand the old adage 'men are from Mars and women are from Venus'. But quotes like these made me wonder whether we are actually that different, or whether we are just products of our individual environments. Paul presented a compelling case for the latter when he wrote the following:

My wife spends most of her time with sharp, aggressive, type-A people. I spend most of my time with people who are good but totally inward-focused and dependent. The mere fact that I'm writing this to you while my wife is undoubtedly negotiating some complex matter illustrates the point. Here I am, blathering on about our relationship and basically contemplating my navel. There she is, totally focused on something else and achieving in the outside world.

This was a scintillating window into a new world. We continued to email backwards and forwards until one day, Paul dropped an even bigger bomb. 'May I bring up a sensitive topic?' 'Of course,' I said, curious as to what it might be. 'OK. Here it is. I lost my virginity well before I met my wife. However, about three years ago, she took my anal cherry. I've never breathed a word of it to anyone and I thought it might be cathartic to write about. Just a thought.'

Well now. Just when I thought I'd heard it all, there was something new to know about virginity loss. One story was about to rewrite the balance between the sexes in the most unexpected way possible. A couple of days later, his completed story landed in my inbox:

I am not exactly sure what qualifies as losing one's virginity. I suppose that it's commonly thought to be when one engages in sexual intercourse. By that definition I lost mine when I was eighteen. But that's not what I am writing about here.

I have been married for more than ten years and was dating my wife for four years before then. I took her virginity (if that is the right way to put it) when we were each in our twenties. But that's not what I am writing about here either. Instead, I am writing about an experience that, even as recently as five years ago, I'd never thought I'd have had, and until very recently I'd never thought I'd ever mention to another person, let alone write about. It was the time, two years back, when my wife and I engaged in anal sex, with me as the receiver.

We have two kids, Georgina works, and I stay home full time. It's been a hard adjustment for both of us, although I complain louder and longer. Even today, when the world has become so much more progressive and accepting of alternative lifestyles, being a househusband has, let us say, its down moments. These changes have carried over into other areas too. Georgina became much more confident and assertive, especially at work. Her world expanded as mine contracted.

Things changed in bed too. Georgina became more assertive, not in an S&M way or anything, but rather more willing to experiment and, quite frankly, more willing to have a good time. Part of that I chalk up to her maturing and shedding past bad lessons and part of it to her outward-directed life. Years ago she would giggle or cringe at an attempt to give her oral sex. Now she loves it and is appreciative of a good effort.

So, two years ago, while we were in bed, she first brought up the idea of anal. I was, to put it mildly, petrified. Visions of 'being gay' ran through my head. She assured me I wasn't but I tried to let the topic die. She wouldn't. She brought it up again and eventually we made a date to go to a sex-toy store, just to look.

We went, we looked, and I was astounded as to how many toys and videos there were about woman-on-man anal. We both laughed and I found myself going along with things, retreating from a 'no way' attitude to one in which I was saying, 'but that's way too big'. Eventually we settled for a harness with a dildo on the small side. The salesman nonchalantly rang up the sale.

That night I was about as nervous as I'd ever been. We took our clothes off and kissed. There was no turning back. She looked at me. 'Ready?' I went over to the bed and lay down. She went over to a closet and finally reappeared, fully harnessed. I must have gasped. The sight of that missile protruding from her, and meant for me, brought everything home. This was real. I was about to get fucked.

She smiled, sensing my apprehension. 'Don't worry,' she said, 'there's nothing to be afraid of.' She lay on top of me, pushed the tip of the dildo to my face and asked me to lube it up. I did, thoroughly. We'd talked about this moment and I remembered the rules. Be calm. Resist the urge to tighten up. It will be fine.

She looked at me and the next thing I felt was a plastic, sticky object rubbing up against my inner thigh and balls. In hindsight, this was funny: Georgina was a total amateur with the harness and dildo. But at the time I tensed up. 'It's never gonna work if you're so uptight,' she said, 'just relax.' I tried to. She guided the head with her hand and the next thing I felt was the tip touching me. Then, slowly, it began to enter. I tensed up and felt horrible. She withdrew, quietly applied a bit more lube, and returned it to just outside my rear end. 'Try again,' she said, 'and trust me.'

I did. I put my arms back and the pushing returned but this time I did not resist. Slowly, slowly, the dildo pressed in and then all of a sudden it just slid forward.

I moaned and gasped, 'Ohmygod.' With that, she pushed in even further. Another 'Ohmygod' from me. Then the thrusting began. 'Keep with me,' she said. I did, mimicking what she'd done for me hundreds of times before – bucking my hips in rhythm to meet her thrusts. I couldn't believe it.

Then she slowed down, stopped bucking and began to manoeuvre the dildo deeper inside me. She hit the spot after a while and then I rolled my eyes. Ecstasy. Ready to come. But she moved away. 'Now,' I said, 'do that again.'

She did, but moved again, and repeated this several times. I got the picture. No demands from now on. Finally, after what seemed like an eternity, she hit the magic spot and stayed there.

It was a mind-blowing orgasm, the likes of which I'd never experienced before. I was joyful and ashamed at the same time. What an odd sensation. It was so impersonal. It was as though my private parts were just there to be used by her. She lay atop me, eyes half glazed, staring into space or at the wall or something, but not at me. After some time, she again stopped, looked down, kissed me, and put her head on my shoulder.

We said nothing for a while, just holding each other tightly. Georgina hadn't removed the harness, so the dildo was still on her, pressed up against my stomach, a silent reminder of all that had just happened. And what had just happened?

The physical act had been one thing, and a weird one at that. But the psychological effects were just beginning to waft in. I'd just come about as close as I ever will to experiencing what Georgina had experienced the first time I had screwed her. This was not like my first experience all those years ago, from which I took away feelings of power and exhilaration. On the contrary, this mostly involved powerlessness – being pursued, penetrated and under the control of another person.

All my life I had been the penetrator and even when the woman was aggressive, there was no doubt as to who was doing what to whom. But now, as the one being penetrated, I was on the other side. She'd gotten me to give it up. She'd probed, thrusted and done any manner of other things, all of her own urging and without regard to what I wanted. She had been cool, under control, self-assured, while I'd been emotional, afraid and out of control. And yet, I'd experienced great orgasms, real rock 'em, sock 'em ones. My mind had reeled at the experience; my body had enjoyed almost every second of it. Even the pain (and there was pain) was rewarded in the end by pleasure.

I told her all these things. She hugged me all the harder and explained how it had been great for her. She told me how she loved being in charge for a change and how great it felt to be able to control me, as opposed to usually being under my control. She said that what really surprised her was how protective she became of me when she realised that I was now vulnerable to her. (Yeah, I thought sarcastically, you really acted protectively.) She said that she felt like she'd conquered me but at the same time wanted to make sure that I was OK.

She also said, mimicking a cornerstone on which patriarchy is based, that she felt surprised at how easily I'd let her do what she was doing and in a way had lost some respect for me. I nodded. I was surprised by that too and a little angry that that was how she felt. After all, I'd just done what she wanted me to.

Paul's domestic setup had spilled out into the bedroom in the most dramatic fashion. In doing so, he revealed a shattering crack in tradition: 'All my life I had been the penetrator and even when the woman was aggressive, there was no doubt as to who was doing what to whom.' In one neat sentence, Paul summed up the pleasure and the pain, literally and figuratively, of our changing gender roles. By relinquishing control and letting go of the idea of being the 'giver' and instead becoming the so-called 'receiver', Paul found himself in a unique position, in every sense of the word.

Everyone who read this story had a reaction to it. It was almost as if people needed to assess their *own* position in relation to this startling monologue. Men had to ask themselves if they were capable of 'giving it up'. Women wondered if their boyfriends had a secret desire to be penetrated, and more significantly, how that might alter the dynamic of their relationship. 'I can't believe you put that story on your blog, Kate,' said a friend, 'it's like pornography.' But tellingly, she followed it up with: 'I couldn't stop thinking about it all week.'

I doubt that Paul is the first heterosexual man to lose his anal virginity to a woman but he was certainly the first one to admit it to me. We could draw all sorts of parallels between the 'bedroom' part of this relationship and their domestic setup, but for me, the really compelling part of this story is the insight it gives into just how close a man can get to *feeling* what we *traditionally* believe to be 'female'. At times this was hilarious:

One thing that occurs to me as I write this is how BORING the whole thing can be. It's like the same thing every time, or at best a variation that is similar to all the other times. And even when the foreplay is different, the screwing part doesn't vary a whole lot. Right, girlfriend? You're probably nodding in agreement.

What Paul doesn't know is that in sharing his story, he endeared himself to the opposite sex for all the right reasons. 'I love that guy who let his wife use the dildo on your blog,' said another female friend. 'Only a man who is really confident in his masculinity would allow himself to do that with a woman. He is definitely a real man.'

My next storyteller would have had no idea what we were talking about because Arthur Perks was born in 1924 and as such, he was absolutely clear about the roles that men and women play.

Arthur was a rarity because, on the whole, men of his generation were not the slightest bit interested in talking to me. It was different for women. They had led comparatively repressed lives and wanted the opportunity to redress the balance, but their male counterparts didn't have the same urge at all. They came from the strong but silent era and on occasions this made for some interesting, if slightly excruciating, interviewing situations.

One man in his late sixties put up a wall of steel as I tried every trick in the book to try to get him to open up and express some emotion about his story, but he held firm. He stuck resolutely to the facts and wouldn't discuss how he felt about them. 'How's it going?' his wife asked as she entered the room towards the end of our interview. 'It's VERY hard,' he spluttered, and it was only then that I realised how much pressure I was putting him under. It wasn't that he didn't want to be helpful; he just came from a generation that didn't express such sentiments. Another man looked like a rabbit in the headlights as I asked him about his first sexual dalliances. If I had been his doctor it would have been okay, but I wasn't. I was a (comparatively) young whippersnapper asking a 70-year-old man some impertinent questions about his sex life.

Arthur Perks was a different kettle of fish. 'Don't worry about Arthur,' my contact had told me, 'he'll talk to you about anything.' And he did. I spent an unforgettable afternoon at the English coast with a very charming man. He was old enough to be my grandfather, but not so old that he couldn't remind me why he had been such a hit with the ladies.

Arthur Perks. Born 1924. Lost virginity aged approximately nineteen

I had no idea at all about sex. Not at all. I never even saw my mum and dad kiss each other. It wasn't heard of. Oh, I had erections and things like that. My mum used to tell me it was 'PP'. Piss-proud. 'Oh that'll go away son, now that you had a pee,' she used to say. Which it didn't. I used to go to bed with a hard-on, and I'd think to myself, well, I'm not bloody piss-proud now, am I?

Later on, I did get an idea about what an erection was for. You might have rubbed yourself against the sheet and it erupted that way and you're thinking, cor, what's wrong here? But how to manipulate it was another matter. I did think of going to somebody to show me how to do it, and that would have been a prostitute. But I didn't pluck the courage up to do that sort of thing.

In 1942, I went to the recruiting office and joined the army. When I got home, you'd think a bomb had dropped there. He went berserk, my old man, but I wanted to go so I did, and I got wounded and saw a lot of what I didn't want to see, naturally. But I never had time to go with women because I was a front-line soldier.

The only time I started was when we went into Austria. We annexed a couple of hotels on a lake. It was beautiful and I used to row round the lake at night and one night there was this girl, Sabine, standing on the jetty. 'What do you want?' I said. She wanted to go over to the hotel to see her grandfather who owned it. I took her over there and got to know the old boy a little bit. He didn't like me all that much, but she took a fancy to me and I began to get a stir, know what I mean?

We were in Austria well over a year picking up the pieces, so we started getting into romance. One night we had a nice night of rumpity-pump and it happened. Just like that. And the unfortunate part of it was, there was nothing splendid about it at all, nothing splendid at all. I got the erection and Bob's your uncle. Away we went, and plenty of times after that. Of course they weren't so adventurous in those days. You didn't try positions or nothing like that. They would have been embarrassed in those days, course they would. Women are more forward-going today than they ever were back then.

Eventually she asked me if I'd like to get married. 'No, thank you love,' I said. I wasn't interested in getting married at all. In any case, we got a red alert to go to Greece and I was gone *for a year and a half. You can't keep love going in letters, we tried, but it's impossible. I did go back to look for her afterwards because it was bugging me, but she had gone. Of course, you always think the worst don't you, with the war.*

I got demobbed in 1948 so I decided to travel. I went to Canada, Italy, met a few birds down there. Dodgy women, Italians. When I say that, they're lovely, but you get friendly with the Italian women and it's marriage or leave her alone sort of antic. Then I went to Tasmania, Aussie and Denmark. I had plenty of crumpet because women were becoming more forward. There was never a drawback after a kiss and a cuddle, but they never lit a fire under me. It was just getting dirty water off me chest. I was looking for a friend, someone who's emotional, who likes you for what you are, and I had found symptoms of that in the Austrian girl.

I'm coming to Audrey, my wife now. My wife was 36 when I met her, born in 1925, right? She'd been brought up by her mum and three sisters. Spinsters all the bloody lot of them! So work it out for yourself. Every time there was a grope or something like that, up went the shutters. She had no idea what sex was. She didn't even know what a menstrual stream was. At 36 years of age. You wouldn't believe it, would yer?

I knew I was on to a good thing straight away with Audrey. You just get a feeling. It happened one night when I said, 'Don't you think this is silly love, just kissing and cuddling?' And she said, 'Well, I never had it before.' So I said, 'Well, nor have I,' you know, I didn't let on. So I stayed the night and that was it. It was good. I'm not joking. It was if something exploded inside you and you thought to yourself, cor, dear. It wasn't like that before. And then you just know. I've never understood when someone says they're in love with somebody, as opposed to someone loving somebody. But there is a difference. One is when you're infatuated with someone, and one is when it's sincere and deep.

Eventually we did get married, nine months later actually. Which was just as well, because we had a bloody baby. We went to Paris for our honeymoon. 'Let's go up whilst they're at lunch,' I'd say, 'instead of walking around the town.' 'No way,' she said, 'you're not having any.' 'Why not?' I said. 'Because I can hear them next door so what do you think they'll hear from us?' She wouldn't wear it. Give her time; and this is what I learned with her, you see. I've always been spontaneous. But with Audrey, if she had something wrong, there was always this invisible wall that would go up all the way round her, but I knew she would come round eventually.

We used to go away on holidays twice a year and this is the part which is ironic. We go back to Austria, don't we, for our holidays. I've got two boys by now, one seven, one four and we're walking down the main street one day and we walk straight into Sabine. Do you know what? It was as if I was transported back into uniform, to 1942. I said to Audrey, do you mind if I take her out for a meal and talk over old times? No, she said, and it all got a bit dicey. Sabine told me she'd never stopped loving me and all that old stuff so I kept my mouth shut.

When we came home, I was getting all these letters from Austria telling me she wanted to come over here. 'No,' I said, 'you're not. I don't love you any more. It's the past,' you know. But it didn't stop and after the wife found one of the letters I said, 'Well, I'll have to go over there and sort her out.' So I got in me car and Audrey said, 'If you go, the locks will be changed after a week, alright?' 'I'll be back in 24 hours love, don't you worry about that.'

Off I went down to Austria, and she's working in one of these bars, you know. Big steins and all that, so I'm sitting there with all the yokels and I looked around me and I thought to myself, what the bloody hell am I doing? I've got a wife and two kiddies, I own my own bungalow and what have I got here? A couple of shirts and that's it. I got in me car and come home. I never even saw her. Coward if you like, and she called me all the bastards under the sun but I loved my wife and that was it.

I once said to Audrey, I said, 'Do you enjoy intercourse, Audrey? Do I light your fire?' She said, 'Yes, you light me fire alright, but I just can't gel with it at times.' And then all of a sudden she fell into place, and that was between the first boy and the second. She loved it after that. She was quite a goer, actually. She wasn't the type to just lie there and say nothing. You get some birds like that, you know, might as well read a book while you're having a go. And that's what I mean. I can't envisage having sex if there's no feeling.

I think with the Austrian girl, it was the fact that I learned what an erection was for and that made me feel that I was a man. But I think there's always a first time which is the best time. What I had with my wife was something different. It was sex, but it was a loving sex, you know what I mean? That's it, you see, it's intimacy. You can tell somebody you love them, it's only words isn't it? It's what you show. My sex life has been pretty fair on the whole, I mean now of course I'd probably be called a right old bore. Probably they do bleeding hanging from the ceiling by now. They'd certainly have you believe that, yes.

Articulate, emotional and wide open. It was difficult not to love Arthur. His honesty was appealing but it was also extremely un-British. When I quizzed him about this, he told me that his blue eyes and sandy-coloured hair had come from his Swedish parentage. Perhaps this was a worthy explanation for his candour, but the fact remains that most men of Arthur's age wouldn't have gone 'all the way' with me. It wasn't standard issue for that generation. Women 'did' feelings and men went to work.

External life was to change the internal lives of men. In Arthur's day, a man stood firmly in charge of his family. Today, families come in all sorts of shapes and sizes. Whereas the older generations were bound by law to try to make their marriages work, the Divorce Reform Act of 1971 created the concept of 'irretrievable breakdown' as grounds for separation. For better or worse, unhappy couples were able to end their unions and as a result, a new type of family was born: the single-parent family.

Marcus Price. Born 1961. Lost virginity in 1978 aged seventeen

If the 1970s created a new kind of family, it also created a new kind of child, specifically a new type of boy. Marcus is as manly a man as you could hope to find. Rugged, hairy and handsome, feminine is not a word that would spring to mind were he standing in front of you now and yet, as Marcus says, 'Women have always said they feel comfortable with me, it's always been, you know, you're one of the girls.'

Marcus was raised by a woman. The new divorce laws pushed women into the foreground. For Marcus's mother, this meant taking over a role that would have traditionally been played by her husband. A generation of children watched their mothers take the reins and run a household. Whether they knew it or not, men and women were beginning to step closer to each other.

Feminism was also on the rise. Women had been fighting for decades, even centuries for basic equality but the 1970s saw feminism enter the mainstream. It wasn't just for radicals now, but for the woman in the street. Women like Marcus's mother. When Marcus was a baby, his father had an affair with another woman and decided to leave his young family. Marcus's mother reacted by adopting feminism alongside a very understandable anger. Marcus begins his story by describing the result:

It's a story of a boy being emasculated by his mother. It's an extreme story. It's like a Greek tragedy, because basically my mother took out all her rage against my father on me.

And because her anger never abated, I had to learn everything on my own. She never gave me any help in understanding women (which is ironic when you consider that she called herself a feminist), so I grew up thinking women were this hypersensitive, untouchably erotic, unknown quantity that you could only relate to from a distance. My mother and father were divorced by the time I was two and my mother went pretty well bananas from that point on. It was really difficult growing up with this woman who was perpetually angry and quite often violent. It wasn't easy at all.

And then there were things like getting taken to women's camps with hardcore feminists, dykes and real man-haters and I'm, like, twelve years old. That was pretty bizarre. Once we went on holiday with Erin Pizzey [the founder of Women's Aid] and all these poor women and their kids who were getting beaten by their husbands and we'd have to look after them! And the whole time my brother and I were getting beaten up by our mother, but no one knew about that. They all thought she was a saint.

So, you know, my relationship with women was difficult. I had no father around to guide me from a male perspective, like, 'It's alright son, don't worry about women, they're all fucking mad!' And there was no sense of any loving appreciation of sexuality from my mother, so all my information came second- or third-hand, from fiction, from boys at school or porno mags. Bizarrely, I had this idea that women were fragile little princesses who didn't even really like sex. I was very confused.

Despite all that, I did have a tenuous sense of wanting to respect myself and not surrender to the peer pressure to do all the things you were supposed to do, like lose your virginity. It was such a huge bloody thing at school. If you hadn't lost your virginity, there was something wrong with you. It wasn't cool.

I had my first girlfriend when I was about thirteen but the thing is, at that point, I just wanted a mate that was a girl. I wasn't that interested in sex. Later I discovered that she dumped me because I didn't fuck her. She was dying to be fucked and I just thought we were having this innocent relationship, taking our time to get to know each other. How naïve I was! Only later did it dawn on me that all of the girls I met at that time were up for just about anything. When my own sexuality kicked in around fourteen, it was weird having this thing in your life, which kind of took over. Suddenly sex was everywhere, in everything, in every woman I saw.

I really liked the girl that I eventually lost my virginity to. I thought she was beautiful. I was seventeen and she was fourteen, but fourteen going on twenty, and the whole thing had a fumbling inevitability about it. The opportunity finally arose one night when I stayed at her house. I was sleeping downstairs on the sofa and after she was sure her parents had gone to bed, she crept downstairs and got into bed with me. I'd had sexual intimacy with a few girls before, you know, kisses and a bit of a fondle here and there, but this was to be the first penetrative act for both of us. I think we were both nervous and it wasn't sensual at all. I felt like I was on auto-pilot. I can't remember kissing her, or even any foreplay. I just had to get past this virginity thing. What I didn't expect was that her hymen was still intact. I had to push really hard to get inside her and there was this terrifying cracking sound when I went inside and all this blood came pouring out. All over me, all over my legs. That was quite a shock.

So although it was kind of dramatic, it was also an anticlimax. I think that's what everyone says, but it really was. I thought that it was going to be some kind of earth-shattering emotional experience, some kind of new dawn rising. But I didn't feel anything. It was just like a mechanical operation.

I also had this very clear feeling that I hadn't honoured myself. That I wasn't ready for this. It was like I was just paying lip service to all those things you're meant to do as a teenager instead of following my heart and doing it at my own speed.

After that, we'd be screwing each other all the time, whilst her mum was cooking downstairs and she'd try to burst into the room and try to catch us at it. So it was kind of funny, but it wasn't exactly enjoyable.

I don't know about this for a girl, but as a young man, you've got this fucking great big pressure to perform, because you're so concerned that you won't be good enough. Sex was never great for me until I got into my thirties because then it was about *being old enough and wise enough to appreciate a woman and it not being such a fucking big act.*

It's great that it's more equal between men and women now. It's much more open for my daughter. She's got a much more confident, self-assured outlook on life and boys in general. Plus, you can be gay, you can be lesbian, you can be bi, whatever, it's not such a big deal, whereas when I was a kid, it was a HUGE thing. If anyone even sniffed that you might be slightly camp at a boys' school, you'd had it. Because of that first girl I went out with, who I didn't fuck, I got called all sorts of names at school. She'd only bloody told another kid at school that I wasn't interested in sex, and my entire class revelled in it. That was a harsh thing to have to deal with as a sensitive young lad with no one to back me up. So of course, as soon as I'd lost my virginity, I had to tell them straight away, the next day, just to prove to them that I was virile, I was normal, I was as good as they were.

I think this concept 'virginity' is a social pressure mostly. It's like another form of initiation into society. You do your driving test, lose your virginity, smoke your first cigarette. You have to do these things; it's all part of a process. But sometimes I think it has gone a bit too far compared to the past; now sexuality is just another consumer item, another thing on the shopping list. Yeah, fuck, shag, get drunk, whatever. I mean, there's very little respect for ourselves or other people in this modern world. There's no real sense of honouring. Which was what I felt when I was a teenager. And I think that's really missing, even more perhaps now than ever.

It was an extreme story. Lots of young men had mothers who discovered feminism but perhaps not with the fervour that Marcus's mother had. It had a huge impact on her young son.

On the one hand, it created a compassionate man: 'I have a huge amount of sympathy for the suffering of women,' he told me later. 'I feel very angry about the horror of what women often have to endure.' But this had come at great personal cost. 'I feel "human",' he said, 'as opposed to exclusively male or female. I don't come from a stylised pre-packaged male point of view. I come from my own perspective but it's been a shattering journey to go through. I had to rebuild my male psyche much later in life because it had been bashed out of me, quite literally. I had to start going to football and doing bloke stuff.'

To me, Marcus felt like the connecting fibre between two very different generations of men. Your 'Old Man', the flat-capped gents of Arthur's era, and 'New Man', the type who is just that little bit more inclined to embrace his feminine side. Speaking of which, the 1980s were just around the corner.

In 1982, life as we knew it ground to a halt when a band called Culture Club got to number one with a song called 'Do You Really Want to Hurt Me?' As a beautiful person of indeterminate gender opened his or her mouth to sing on *Top of The Pops* one Thursday night, the population of Great Britain descended into debate. Was it a boy or a girl? Welcome to a decade's worth of hairspray and make-up, not just for the girls but for the boys as well.

Boy George made the general public question what it meant to be masculine. He also made us realise that boys can be beautiful too. Marcus agreed. When he and a friend first saw a picture of David Sylvian, a pop star for whom the media coined the phrase 'the most beautiful man in the world', 'we could barely get down to Boots the chemist fast enough. This was it,' said Marcus. 'This was the future. David Sylvian wore make-up and we wanted to be beautiful too.'

Bands like Culture Club, Duran Duran and Japan were pretty boys and they sold millions of records. For the first time, a different type of masculinity was being celebrated. As if to really drive the point home, Great Britain was being governed by a woman. While the boys were getting to grips with a mascara brush, Margaret Thatcher was busy redefining what it meant to be feminine.

But what did this mean for my next interviewee and his virginity? 'It was never going to be a huge macho trip for me, the virginity thing,' said Toby. 'It was going to be about not hurting anybody, and making sure you both got something out of it.' Toby fell in love with a girl who expected equality, not just in the bedroom, but from life in general. As Toby left college and went on the dole, his girlfriend signed up for a degree course. That summer, she took the decision for both of them. They were going to lose their virginity together.

Toby. Born 1969. Lost virginity in 1986, aged seventeen

There was a big element of politicisation in the eighties. CND was a big thing. The Smiths happened and wearing daffodils in the backs of your pockets became fashionable, which was really important because it wasn't just about the music. It was a celebration of the fact that there's nothing to be ashamed about if you're not a great big muscled rugby player.

I stayed on at school to do my A levels and there was a girl there who I had become very keen on. Fell for her completely. Our first date was a CND march in Birmingham. The Beat were playing, so we took the local CND bus and I think we snogged permanently for five hours. On the way home, we went down a gated farm road and that was where the first fumblings-in-the-pants experience happened which I always remember as being the really magical part of virginity loss.

Without being too crude, I really remember the earthy smell. Because I'd been reading Tess of the d'Urbervilles *in English Literature at school and all the stars were out and it was all linked into this earthy experience. It was a pretty potent combination. It was also the first attempt to get to grips with a woman or with somebody physically. Because you don't touch anybody else, apart from your mum and dad, do you, for most of your life?*

Anyway, we went out, and this was coupled with the fact that I was living on a council estate and she lived in a mansion. Three floors, swimming pool, classic cars out front, ponies out back. I remember when I first went round and she brought me some boiled millet with artichokes, where you peel off the leaves and dip it in the sauce. I told my dad about this when I got home and he said, 'They're feeding you bird food. What sort of place is this?' I thought it was great.

Then it got a bit messy. There was such a culture of intelligence. They went to the opera and I wasn't like that. She went away to university and I signed on the dole and did a lot of shitty jobs. Then halfway through her first year she said, 'Why don't we go hitch-hiking around Wales?'

When you live in the city, you don't smell anything apart from dirt and grime, whereas everything you smell out in the country, you remember it so much more vividly. You can't help but get involved in that when you've been reading Tess of the d'Urbervilles *and you're going to lose your virginity. Halfway through the trip, she decided that the time had come, so we spent three or four days just trying to find a chemist which sold* condoms, which meant that the tension was building up and we were both getting pretty excited.

One night, towards Snowdon, we pitched our tent in a field off the main road. A storm was brewing and it started to rain, so we got the tent up and decided to walk to a nearby pub. Now, I still try to describe this pub, because it's a bit like Brigadoon, I don't actually know if it existed because it's a pub which appeared to be backing onto a cliff face. So whilst you're sitting in the back room drinking your pint, people are climbing up a cliff face behind you. Very odd. Coupled with some bloke who kept putting 'A Song for Guy' by Elton John on the jukebox.

So we have our drink and we've got the condoms and we finally decide to go for it. Outside, all hell has broken loose and the rain is coming down in sheets. We make a run for it, dash across the field, obviously shitting ourselves about the farmer whose permission we don't have, make it to the tent and we do it in three minutes flat.

The next thing I know, she's crying. I'm bawling my eyes out because she's crying, there's a storm raging around us and there's blood absolutely everywhere. The amount of it was just staggering. The condom came off as well, because my penis shrank to such a small extent when all the crying kicked off.

We'd done everything else. We'd done oral sex, we'd done 69. We'd done the whole list. It wasn't as if this was the first physical time, but it was the first penetrative time and it was the most bizarre experience of my life. It was the combination of the storm and the blood and the rain and this pub, which I've been desperate to find ever since just to see if it's really real, that I have never been able to get out of my head.

It was done. The goal had been reached, but I was under no illusions. I knew it was a one-off. Even though I was madly in love with her, a new life was opening up for her at university, whereas it wasn't for me. Yeah. It was an event in my life of which virginity was just one part.

It's funny because I spoke to her afterwards many times and the big thing for her was when she had her first orgasm, which was way before that. She certainly didn't have an orgasm when she lost her virginity. For me, the first hands-down-the-pants experience was far more significant. That was earth-shattering. I mean, there is a hole there. How bizarre is that? For a man, that is an amazing, staggering thing. You're this thing which sticks up, and then there's something which isn't there. It sounds a bit hocus-pocus-y, but because there is a hole, it's almost like there is a universe in there.

That was the biggest, most tumultuous part. I equate that much more with losing my virginity. Because you never forget that heightening of the senses, so perhaps it's not the virginity that you lose, but the heightening of the senses. And then you think, thank God I'm not going to go through that again!

I always say to people who are just starting off, you've got to get in there. Make an idiot of yourself. Have sex. Do it really badly. Don't give a shit about it, but just get stuck in and learn. You've got to dive in and make a mess of things, but what you can't do is put someone on a pedestal. I know a lot of people who are really obsessed with trying to marry the perfect woman, but it's never going to happen. You've got to get involved in the nitty-gritty of love, and lovemaking and relationships.

It took a while to get to the fun bit. Because you've got to be relaxed with the person you're with, otherwise it's too much hassle with the power struggles, and you don't want any of that. When you're more relaxed, sex is so much more fun. And it is funny. Well, I find it funny. The way you've just been grunting *and groaning, and then you stop and you think, I'm making stupid sounds, why were we just doing that?*

All this time spent listening to men talk so honestly about their lives began to have an effect on me. I felt I was beginning to really understand life from the perspective of a bloke. It was impossible not to, because men's virginity loss is fraught with a whole host of considerations that most women don't even think about. Will I get an erection? Where do I put it? Will she even *like* it? I had never considered for even one moment just how nerve-racking an event this must be for the opposite sex. Men are road-testing a highly visible piece of equipment for the very first time. Can you imagine how petrifying that must be? What if it all goes horribly wrong? Rob from Scotland knew only too well how this could feel. Born in the same year as Toby, he made his first attempt at losing his virginity when he was still at school in the early 1980s:

Losing my virginity was one of the most humiliating experiences of my entire life. Partly because I was a wide boy at school and I had set myself up in this gang as the guy that ran this group of kids. I was supposed to be the boss-type character and I had put myself into a position of high visibility. So, for the image, I had to do it. It was with a girl that used to hang around with our gang. She was called Tracey and it was a disaster. I was with this girl, shitting myself, absolutely fucking terrified in case I wouldn't be able to perform and then because of that, I couldn't. She told everyone I was gay. It literally could not have been any worse.

It was so bad that it almost put him off on a permanent basis. 'That was the last time I dared to go anywhere near a girl for about three years. I was absolutely terrified. When I finally did it again, when I was about seventeen, it worked and all I remember thinking wasn't, "Great, I've lost my virginity, I'm a man." It was more like, "Thank fucking Christ, I can do it."'

Rob's story spoke volumes about the intense pressure that men felt to 'perform' and, even worse, the misguided assumption that they should automatically know what they are doing. They don't. 'You're supposed to somehow satisfy the person that you're with,' confirmed Rob, 'even though you have not got a clue what you're doing.'

I often wished that I could gather the young men and women who wrote to me in one room and knock their metaphorical heads together. Communicate with each other! Tell her you are nervous! Tell him you are scared! Unfortunately, youth doesn't always equip us to articulate ourselves. Via my email communications with them, I tried to endorse the rather radical concept of choosing somebody that you actually *like* in order to avoid some of the calamities mentioned above. This was easy for me to say, but the reality is that for lots of young people, particularly men, virginity loss is something that they must do 'alone', if only in spirit. Which is ironic, really, when you consider that the experience involves being in the closest physical proximity that you can be to another human being for the very first time.

For all our modernity, men are still not generally given to the idea of talking in quite the same way that women are. 'They talk,' said a 30-year-old interviewee, 'but it wasn't like with girls, who would talk about it properly, like, was it any good? Or how long did you last, because that's just far too intimate a question for a bloke. Blokes ask stupid stuff, like, how big were her tits? Raw facts, like football scores.'

From an evolutionary point of view, this makes sense. Being candid has the potential to weaken your position in 'the pack'. How do you know that sensitive information might not get used against you at a later point? This is perhaps where I came in, because men clearly do have something to say about virginity loss; they just don't always have someone to say it to. Whether it was via my blog or during face-to-face interviews, I provided a 'get out of jail free' card for my male correspondents. I wasn't a pack member. They could say what they liked with no fear of repercussion.

The problem was that sometimes they told me things that would have been much more beneficial had they been aimed at the correct recipient. At sixteen years old, Gwynne lost his virginity to a girl he barely knew at a party, despite the fact that he was in a loving relationship with his partner of eight months. As a man of 24, he wrote and explained something to me that he should have told his (now ex-) girlfriend eight years previously:

My girlfriend and I were almost identical in age and sexual experience. We could spend hours in her room snogging and playing around. Over the eight months we eventually progressed to the point of some genital touching, but were happy to take our time.

A couple of times during our playing-around sessions, it had got very heated and she would ask me if I wanted to have intercourse with her; I said no. This was for several reasons. I felt like intercourse should come further down the line when we were much more comfortable with each other's bodies. I was a little scared too and protective of my virginity. While I would have been happy to do lots of other things, I wanted losing my virginity to be something really special.

There was a party organised for a friend from school's birthday at their house and my girlfriend couldn't make it. This wasn't a problem; I had previously had no problems with restraint but was more than a little flirty and got on well with people from school. At the party I got chatting to a girl I didn't know very well. She was a little quiet but I had always found her sweet and more than a little cute. She was a bit upset as things weren't going too well with her boyfriend, and I was happy to comfort her about it. I was happy to do a bit of hugging as it didn't seem like I was breaking any rules (although of course I was!).

After a short while, she asked whether we could go upstairs to talk about it some more. I was enjoying being close to her, and my naïve brain didn't put two and two together. I said 'Of course'. We went into one of the upstairs rooms, it turned out to be a darkened spare room with a double bed taking up most of the space and we lay on it side by side still talking about her boyfriend.

After a while, the way she touches me changes. No longer is she wanting comfort hugs from me but instead, she is stroking my chest. After a while we are kissing, badly, and my head is reeling. I had never even contemplated cheating on my girlfriend, and had previously always felt in control of situations but I seem to be passively sleepwalking into it. She asks if we can lie naked next to each other and I agree. I still did not have any idea that anything other than a bit of snogging/hugging was about to happen, as strange as that sounds looking back on it.

As soon as we are both undressed, she climbs on top of me and pushes my penis into her. I lie there in shock, thinking how I don't want this. As she starts moving her hips she tells me to 'pull it out before you come'. I do not understand fully what this means, as I had never ejaculated before (except in my sleep), and lie there silent and still. As she continues to move her hips I blankly watch what she is doing, shocked at what is happening.

After a minute or two I come into her and my penis becomes limp. She stops and looks at me angrily. 'What the fuck, did you just come in me?' And all I can get out is 'Sorry.' A few seconds later, she realises that I am petrified. 'Oh, you're a virgin?' she says with a mixture of anger and surprise. I nod. She turns on the main light in the room, hastily gets dressed and heads back downstairs to the party. After about five minutes I get dressed and wander outside to be alone. I manage to pull myself together to pretend nothing had happened and get back to the party.

The next day I arrange to meet with my girlfriend, she knows something is up due to my urgency on the phone. We meet in the park and I decide to tell her that I slept with someone at the party and give no details about it. She is distraught and runs home. With the help of my sister, I phone the girl from the party and ask her to take the morning-after pill. I'm really grateful for my sister's unquestioning support.

I asked Gwynne if he ever attempted to explain what really happened to his girlfriend. 'No,' he said. 'My thinking at the time was that it would be easier for her to think that I was a complete bastard and forget about me rather than try and explain the (potentially implausible) situation. Perhaps it was a bad approach,' he concluded, 'but such is hindsight.'

Gwynne's story shed new light on the mystery that is the male mind. He also did me a personal favour by casting a much kinder hue over some of my own teenage dating disasters. Perhaps there was now a logical explanation for some of my personal disappointments? Either way, Gwynne had given me a first-class example of how ineffectual men can be when it comes to the art of expressing themselves.

He was a tender, confused sixteen-year-old boy at the time so I think we can make allowances, but a darker side of his story was about to emerge, because as we passed emails back and forth, he began to reveal what had really controlled the outcome of his story. Fear.

'If the genders in my story were swapped around,' he went on, 'it would read differently; i.e. if a more experienced boy forced sex on a girl in an identical way and it wasn't consensual, I would perhaps think of this as rape, even if she did not physically fight the person.'

Gwynne brought a taboo subject into the spotlight. Very little is written about this issue, probably because we don't really believe it could happen. How is it possible for a woman to take advantage of a man? Surely an erection is a sign of consent? Not necessarily. When I did a late-night radio phone-in show, listeners were invited to call in with their stories. One of the most memorable, for all the wrong reasons, was that of a young man who had lost his virginity because he was too scared to put a stop to it. He cried as he told his story live on air. His body might have given the green light, but his mind had not.

Slowly but surely, stories like these began to emerge, their owners reluctant to tell them because they sounded so improbable. This, as I came to see it, is one of the hardest parts of being a man. We women love our New Man, the one who puts the rubbish out, picks up his own socks and isn't afraid to express himself, but at the same time there is part of us that will always expect him to be indestructible. No matter how much the sexes have absorbed of each other's sensibilities, a man will always be expected to be *a man*. And it would be really difficult for a man to admit that he got into a sexual scenario that he felt unable to control. Men are every bit as vulnerable as women. Just in a different way.

My final man also wondered how much of an effect virginity loss had had on him, but for a totally different reason. Of his own volition, 30-year-old Damon lost his virginity to a sex worker.

Damon. Born 1980. Lost virginity in 1997, aged sixteen and a half

I searched high and low for a man who had lost his virginity to a prostitute. Whatever your feelings about this type of transaction, it has been occurring since the dawn of time. For this reason, I needed to ensure that it was in my book. It wasn't an easy story to find. I knew it was out there but it wasn't exactly advertising itself. I came tantalisingly close at times. 'My little brother lost his virginity to a prostitute,' someone at work once told me. 'Do you think he would like to talk to me about it?' I asked. 'Probably not,' he answered. 'He lost it on a scout camp trip to Amsterdam when he was fourteen years old.' I couldn't think of a reply to this statement because I was too busy scraping my jaw up off the floor.

But as a result of my blog, many would talk about it. I got sent some extraordinary stories from men, all of whom appreciated the anonymity of the internet. In a scene that could have come out of a movie, 28-year-old Jordon proved that women are every bit as good at fetishising virginity loss as men are. Jordon wrote and told me how, as a teenager, he had lost his virginity to a prostitute who 'offered to fuck me on one condition and that was when we were done, she would get to shave my pubic hairs'.

After the job was done, Jordon's partner showed him her collection of 'conquests'; each one of them in a sealed envelope that was named, dated and contained the pubic hair of every young man whose virginity she had taken.

Who needs to retreat into fiction when reality is this weird? Not for the first time, I found myself wondering how my own life had come to be so *odd*. At one point, I had three different email conversations on the go with three different young men, all of whom were exploring the idea of losing their virginity to a prostitute. To all intents and purposes, I babysat them through this decision-making process. As if I knew anything about the world of sex work. But by this point, I did know a lot about young men and the pressure to shed this most unwanted of burdens. Frustrated, lonely and confused, many of them decided to take drastic action. The least I could do was to support them in an unjudgemental manner. Some of them felt wretched about their choice. One said: 'I lost my virginity to a prostitute. I am not proud of it. As a matter of fact, I am ashamed.' Nothing I could say to this particular man would make him feel better about it but in the end, most of them conceded that it was a practical solution to a solvable problem.

Of all the stories I could have chosen for this last slot, I picked this one because it made me laugh. Its owner writes comedy and it shows. It is beautifully told. But what really gets me about this story is that after all our talk about the architecture of masculinity and femininity, its protagonist is the last person I ever expected to have lost his virginity to a prostitute. Damon is a pretty boy. He is also ever so slightly camp. Some people think he is gay. As it happens, he is anything but.

Get the violins out. I was the last of my group of friends to lose my virginity. In the world of the teenage boy there can be nothing worse. My problem wasn't aesthetic, I may not have been Johnny Depp but I wasn't exactly Andrew Lloyd Webber either. I was the 'safe' one. The funny one. The one that girls would tell their problems to. That's right, I was the 'we're such good friends' guy. I swear if the wind had blown the other way, I would have been gay but despite the rumours and an unhealthy obsession with show tunes, I wasn't.

There were occasions when being charming, funny and polite got me somewhere, but it was never far enough. Once at a party, the girl everyone – in particular me – had a crush on got drunk and said she wanted to sleep with me. We kissed and canoodled but when it came down to it, we did nothing more than that. She had a boyfriend who was a shit. They kept breaking up and getting back together and I didn't want her to get more confused so we talked and I stroked her hair until she went to sleep. In the morning she blanked me. I thought I'd done the right thing. Maybe the 'right thing' didn't work. Then and there on a cold North Yorkshire morning the 'right thing' ceased to be the thing I wanted to do.

What better thing to do for a sixteen-year-old with a tsunami of lust washing over him than to go away from his small town and small life? I went to the big city to stay with my big brother. Those two weeks, or rather the one weekend smack in the middle, changed me – more than I realised at the time, as what happened would have an effect on every relationship I would have from then on.

My brother is dodgy. No two ways about it. He hangs out with dodgy people and does dodgy things. We say that he is the rough diamond and I am the polished 'set in a ring' one. It's actually more the case that I get away with things and he doesn't. It'd be easy to say he corrupted me during my two-week stay, but the truth is that any corruption was more than encouraged by his saintly little brother.

The action began on a Saturday afternoon. Having dabbled with speed and weed, I was keen to try some 'city stuff'. After much arm-twisting we scored some party powder from a guy who only the previous night had stabbed someone in the neck over a debt, in a crowded bar, and continued drinking as nobody said anything. He was a good friend of my brother's and I only found out his previous night's story when he went to the loo and my brother suggested I stop taking the piss out of his hat.

We hung out in cool bars, met new people, chatted up girls, drank, ate, party powdered the day away. It was cool. The sun went down and the music got louder. What to do next? My brother's axis of evil stretched to the door staff at a well-known Manchester club which is no longer with us. On the night in question some soap actor was having his birthday there and so the question my brother posed was this: 'Do you want to go hang out with wotzisname or do you want to go somewhere and pop your cherry?' He didn't need to ask twice.

Armed with a pocket full of cash we made our way to a delightful establishment that offered massage, sauna and steam. *After we were buzzed in we walked up the dark stairs with an aroma of damp around us. We entered the 'reception' where there was a tiny, middle-aged, sweet-looking woman with glasses. She greeted us and told us that her name was Pam. She then asked us what we wanted. I didn't know! 'It's £35 for massage and full personal service,' she smilingly told me. 'Personal service?' I asked. 'Look, love, we're a brothel!' she answered.*

Two girls appeared wearing sexy underwear. One looked like a Page Three model and the other was amazing. Long, dark curly hair cascaded down her body. Full pouting lips, gorgeous green eyes and perfectly formed breasts. It's like someone had reached into my head, pulled out some instructions and given them to someone who'd made this fantasy come to life. She was my bespoke bird!

I pathetically handed over my money, hands trembling and said, 'I'll go with Tanya if that's alright.' Of course it was. They weren't there to tell me what a good friend I was. Tanya wasn't there to ignore me. She didn't care that I was funny, charming and polite.

Tanya took me by the hand and led me into a back room. It has a massage table in it and for one moment I thought I was actually going to get a massage and nothing else. I was actually relieved. Then Tanya told me to strip and lie face down on the table. She unclipped her bra and removed all of her underwear. I didn't know where to look ... actually I did and I probably stared for too long.

I did as Tanya said and lay down. She started to massage my back; she rubbed her breasts over my back, kissed down my spine and cheekily bit my bum. She asked me how old I was.

'Sixteen,' I said, 'and a half.' She said I was cute and had a good body for my age. Then she told me to turn over.

She slowly caressed and kissed her way to my crotch and still to this day I've never seen anyone put a condom on the way she did. She climbed on top of me and eased me into her. Thoughts swirled in my head. 'Don't come too soon,' 'What do they do in porn?' 'How do these places get away with it?' 'Is £35 a fair price?' 'WHAT DO THEY DO IN PORN?'

Half an hour later we were done and getting dressed. 'You're a sweet guy, you should get a girlfriend,' was Tanya's parting shot before kissing me on the cheek and patting me on the lower one. I went back into the reception area where Pam and my brother were finishing off the party powder. We said our good-byes and went home to bed. The rest of the two weeks wasn't as eventful but when I returned home, people knew something was different, something had changed.

That one night opened a floodgate. I was now the original rampant rabbit. The sex just kept coming (no pun intended). I got a girlfriend, got another one, got another one, got caught, got another one. I'm not a bad person but I do bad things. I'm very sexually active and often blur the lines of what's right and wrong. I don't think being faithful is in my programming, my make-up. For me there is no such thing as too much sex. I get it where and when I can at the risk of relationships and such. Why? I don't know. Is it because I was the last to do the deed and am still making up for it in my head? Is it because I paid for my first time and see sex as a transaction? Or am I just a greedy bastard?

I'll never know if I would have turned out the same or different depending on that 'first time' experience. I didn't give it away to someone I was in a relationship with. I didn't develop *a style or technique over a period of time with someone. That came later. Maybe I did it so I could practise so that I would get it right and be good by the time I got into a relationship. The fact that I actually made the decision to lose my cherry in this way surely says that I would always have been a horny 'up for anything' kind of person because I wanted to do something, so I did it. I still do.*

I didn't expect such an effeminate man to lose his virginity in what is often seen as a traditionally masculine manner but this just goes to show how much gender roles have evolved.

'Don't be such a girl,' I overheard a friend saying recently to his crying six-year-old son as he fell over. This is ironic because when this same man's tiny two-year-old daughter falls over she stands up, dusts herself down and continues on her way. Phrases such as these are redundant in 2011 because our notions about gender are not just changing, they are interchange*able*. Women can be 'like' men. Men can be 'like' women. As we also know, at our most extreme, a man can have a genuine understanding of what it feels like for a woman to lose her virginity.

And both sexes have benefited from this process. Listening to men recount their tales made me see that while feminism changed women's lives, it had given men more choices too. My male friends have more time to observe the differences between their growing children because they spend more time with them. In 1960, British fathers spent an average of fifteen minutes a day with their children. Post-millennium fathers spend an average of two hours a day getting to know their kids. During the World Cup in the summer of 2010, I saw a well-groomed man in my local pub during lunch.

He was holding a pint of lager in one hand and when he turned around, he had a tiny baby strapped to his chest in a sling. His partner was nowhere to be seen, but it didn't matter because he looked more than capable of attending to his child's needs should the occasion arise. He was the perfect poster boy for the many ways in which men have embraced, and enjoyed, our ever-evolving gender roles.

We have a more egalitarian attitude towards beauty too. I had to pinch myself recently when a male friend extolled the virtues of a popular brand of organic face cream 'because it makes my skin look dewy'. These words could have come from the mouth of any of my female friends. It makes me happy to know that my male friends are comfy enough in their 'dewy' skin to embrace what are traditionally seen as feminine aspirations. Women no longer have a monopoly on them.

The truth is that men have always had a feminine side but it hasn't always been fashionable to express it. The courts of Louis XIV were full of beautiful men who adorned themselves with make-up, hair extensions and couture clothing. It was *à la mode*. It was a way of expressing their financial mettle because men who looked 'dandy' were communicating an important message: I have the time and the money to do this. I am *someone*. In 2011, men have swapped the hairpieces for some chunky bling but the sentiment is the same. I am a man of means. I have status.

It is also a great way of saying: I am so confident in my masculinity that I am happy to embrace my femininity. Remember how impressed my female friends were with Paul, the man who gave a special kind of virginity to his wife? They found his willingness to expose his vulnerable side appealing.

But there are other reasons why modern man wants to buff up. There wasn't a section for male grooming products in my high-street chemist five years ago. There is now. Men are getting manicured, massaged and waxed because they can. But they are also doing it because deep down, they know that they need to raise their game. Contemporary woman is getting her fulfilment from so much more than just her relationships. She has a career, opportunities to travel and lots of other single friends to do it with. 21st-century woman feels little compunction about delaying partnership and motherhood, because her horizons have broadened since our grandparents' day. Just as my two toffs suspected at the beginning of this chapter, women are independent creatures and men need to work a little bit harder to get included in their lives.

At which juncture I feel I must share a critical piece of information with my male readers. Bearing in mind the sheer volume of stories I receive from women, stories that contain as much hope and ardour as they ever have done, there is little evidence to suggest that women are going to get bored with men any time soon. Or, in fact, ever. Women might be wealthy, ambitious DIY experts but money can't buy you love. Women don't *need* men in their lives in the way that they might once have done, but they do *want* them. There is a critical difference between these two verbs. Nothing will change that.

But where did this leave modern man and his virginity? He values it. There is no doubt about that. Men got increasingly expressive and emotive about the loss of their virginity as the decades ticked by. 'I remember playing with her hair afterwards,' said 31-year-old blog correspondent Donnie, 'as we lay together panting and hot. And most of all I remember the feeling much later, as the sun was rising. Everything in the world was different. As though everyone had been speaking in a foreign accent and now suddenly switched to my own.'

Men had been given permission to place more value on their virginity. Once again, words tumbled out of their mouths that we would typically think of as feminine. Some were even prepared to forgo sexual opportunities in order to hold out for something really special. In all cases, men surpassed my expectations when it came to the sheer intense recollection of first-time love, lust and romance. I didn't think they had it in them but they did.

I cannot deny that many of them were also riddled with hormones. For obvious reasons, I get lots of desperate emails from frustrated young men. But aside from the physical pressure to copulate, men feel a pressure to lose virginity that has got nothing to do with hormones. While women have often felt stigmatised for losing their virginity, men feel stigmatised if they don't. This is because, for many members of the opposite sex, the loss of virginity is inextricably linked to the idea of 'becoming a man'.

This was the phrase that motivated guys to write to a total stranger and reveal their tender spots. This was the phrase that motivated men to get over a moral dilemma and seek the services of a sex worker, and this was the phrase that was the cause of joy, frustration and in some cases, profound unhappiness. Lots of people don't lose their virginity. We are about to meet some of them, but as you will see, in a debate that has occasionally caused stand-up arguments on my blog, virginity is still a far harder burden to bear for a man than it is for a woman.

4

The Invisible Virgins

It is interesting to note that after all my explorations, interviews and random conversations at social events, family dinners and water-coolers, there is one story above all others that brings the conversation to a standstill. It is the story of a 38-year-old virgin … who is married. No other story has messed with people's minds in quite the same way that this one has.

No matter that I encountered this man at a 'Submission and Domination' evening. I was in search of a story from a disabled person for this book at the time. In pursuit of this perspective, I met a gentleman who ran what he called 'an interesting monthly talk group'. He was vague about the subject matter but I decided to check it out. Things became clearer when I arrived at a venue called 'Coffee, Cake and Kink'. Thankfully, as he promised (and despite my knocking knees), it *was* an interesting talk. A more affable and ordinary bunch of people you couldn't hope to meet. Afterwards, we went to the pub and some of them offered me their details and the opportunity to interview them at a later date. Simon was one such man. Was anybody ever interested in the fact that Simon liked to be dominated? No, they were not. All they wanted to know was this: how could a person have been married for ten years and not have lost their virginity?

When I first began my blog, I put a line of text under the heading that read: 'Virginity loss. It happens to all of us.'

'Does it?' came a slightly irritated email soon after. 'I find this to be a generalisation and somewhat presumptuous. Surely you don't believe that everyone on the planet loses their virginity? You could drop that opening sentence,' my wake-up call continued, 'or replace it with something less … antagonistic.' That told me. I duly changed the offending line of text and so began my correspondence with a largely invisible bunch of people who just happen never to have had sex. Simon was not alone.

We often assume that virgins are lank-haired, social outcasts who could be picked easily out of a crowd. I am here to tell you that this is not the case. The virgins I have encountered are articulate, attractive people who just happen never to have had sexual intercourse. You might be sitting next to one right now. You wouldn't know it because this is hardly a person who is going to advertise his or her status. 'There is no room in this society we have created for people who aren't doing it,' wrote 21-year-old Claudia to me recently, 'especially not young people. So they have to hide it, and in turn this reinforces the idea that everyone else is having sex but them.'

Despite the fact that the entire point of this project was to interview people who *had* lost their virginity, those who hadn't clearly had stories to tell. Quite apart from anything else, they raised an interesting question. How have we arrived at a point where to be a virgin has almost become the most perverse lifestyle choice that you could make? How could it be that bondage and domination hardly raise an eyebrow but a 38-year-old married virgin causes a metaphorical mental roadblock? What has virginity come to represent to us? And what does it represent to the people who possess it? Are they sad and lonely? Or empowered about a way of life that can seem rather antiquated to the modern Western eye?

Cast your mind backwards and it's not hard to see where this began. Sandra Jones described reading the problem page of her grandmother's copy of *Woman's Own* in the late 1950s: 'We had to do an awful lot of reading between the lines to guess what they were talking about.' You wouldn't have to guess what they are talking about now. We live in a world where nothing is hidden and that includes sex. Can you imagine our grandparents' generation talking openly about pornography? Today, words and images that would have been considered legally obscene 40 years ago are ten a penny. Not only that, but you only need a broadband connection to view them. The gap between everyday life and sexually explicit material has never been smaller.

And the change continues. We would have been embarrassed to talk about female masturbation when I was at school in the 1980s. Now, thanks to the ubiquity of Ann Summers and TV shows like *Sex and the City*, most women wouldn't think twice about heading to a high-street sex store for a guilt-free purchase. The pursuit of sexual pleasure for both sexes has become a culturally acceptable pastime and if you are not pursuing it, why not? Sex is not just plain old sex anymore. It is part and parcel of a *lifestyle*. A lifestyle that includes exciting partnerships, a beautiful home *and* a hot sex life. We have placed sex upon a very public pedestal, but in the process we have attached a stigma to virginity.

Despite the subliminal pressure to conform, 21-year-old Claudia was unconcerned about her virginal status: 'I do believe that virginity is something to be valued,' she said, 'and

I am content to wait for a relationship that's worthwhile.' Not everyone I encountered felt the same way.

For many of the people who wrote to me via my blog, virginity was not a choice; it was something that they felt had been foisted upon them. For my first storyteller in this chapter, this is entirely understandable. Ash is a 36-year-old man who cannot move his arms or his legs. He has a physical disability. Having sex, unless carefully orchestrated with the assistance of a helper, is a logistical nightmare. However, as we shall see, it is not a complete impossibility.

Ash's story might seem an odd inclusion in a chapter about virgins, given that it is an explicit description of a loss; but I defy you not to feel moved by it, because not only is it a story about virginity loss, it is a story about one human being's first intimate contact with another. The only form of touch that Ash has ever encountered up until this point is that of his parents, doctors and carers. For Ash, losing his virginity represents the separation between the 'unattractive, defective lump' that he feels he has become and his discovery of himself as a sexual being.

From a purely practical point of view, his virginity loss had to be planned and prepared for in advance. To that end, the services of his trusted assistant and a sympathetic sex worker were required.

Ash. Born 1974. Lost virginity in 2010 aged 36

This is the story of how I, a severely disabled man in my thirties, recently came to lose my virginity to a sex worker. Having had a neuromuscular disability from birth, my life has taken a differ-ent path to most able-bodied people. I have a graduate degree and an ongoing professional career, and given the debilitating nature of my disability this is a decent achievement. I am also well liked by most people who meet me. However, I have never had any positive attention from the opposite sex that would suggest that I was fanciable, despite getting on with girls when I am in their company and making them laugh. Any time I have found the confidence to make my interest in a girl known, I have been met with polite rejection.

Over the past few years, the gradual deterioration in my physical abilities has accelerated. Abilities such as moving my hand across a short distance have become more difficult and in some cases impossible. I often lose my balance and flop over to one side of my wheelchair. Eating, even breathing, is a struggle. As bit by bit I lose each of those skills, I face up to the fact that in all probability I am in the final few years of my life. I do not fear death itself, and I have never expected to live to a ripe old age. But I feel incomplete and lonely, and that is not how I want to be when I die. In recent months I have found myself trying to troubleshoot this problem, and have come to the conclusion that before I can succeed in forming a connection with another person I need to find a way to better connect with my own humanity. To do that I need to embrace myself as a sexual person; not the unattractive, defective lump I usually identify with, but as a unique and desirable individual. My virginity was making this impossible to do – without a sexual or sensual experience to draw upon I wouldn't be able to move forward with this plan.

After much deliberation and research, I decided to pay an escort to help me with this. I emailed a girl called Ruby to introduce myself and received a very positive response. Over the next few days I thought about it further and considered the practicality and even the morality of this decision. I plucked up the

courage to speak to my personal assistant, David, whose sup-
port and understanding I would need. This I got. Fast-forward
through the excruciatingly anxious intervening period to the
big day ...

I was sitting on my bed waiting when I heard the doorbell
ring. The anxiety turned to nervous excitement. She was here,
and moments from now I would get my chance to experience
being with a woman. I knew that within the hour, assuming
my body didn't fail me yet again, I could stop identifying as a
'virgin'.

After maybe 30 seconds that seemed like an eternity, Ruby
popped her head through my bedroom door, smiled and came
in, closing the door behind her. She was wearing a pretty black
dress and came in laughing because David had told her: 'He's
all yours!' She gave me a brief kiss on the lips to start with and
from that point on I was completely ready for anything – as
that kiss was the most intimate moment I'd had in my life up
to that point. It felt so pleasant and natural; and the sensation
was unique.

After talking for a few moments and breaking the ice she
said I would probably want her to get out of her dress so I could
see the goods! With a sexy little shake she slipped out of her
dress to reveal her lingerie underneath. She then started to
unbutton my shirt and, with a bit of instruction from me as
to how to move my arms, she took it off. I thought this would
be more difficult and had intended that I would keep my shirt
on, just unbuttoned so she could caress my chest. But I was glad
it was off. She then slid down my trousers. I was now com-
pletely naked, and loved this. It's not like I haven't been naked
in front of women before, but they've all been nurses or carers,

or my mum. *This time it was different. I was naked to receive pleasure. Ruby then began to get out of her lingerie.*

First she removed her bra, revealing beautiful round breasts. They try to teach you as part of sex education on TV that a 'real woman's' breasts are not like you see in porn, symmetrical and firm with small and perfectly round areolas. Well, Ruby's breasts were exactly like that. Just like in my fantasies. She brought one of them towards my mouth and I rolled my lips and my tongue over it.

Next she slipped out of her briefs and introduced me to her clitoris. I mean to say she actually, verbally announced it to me – 'and here is my clit!' That was another strange moment. It was like I was getting a commentary. Once again I missed having a perfect view, but I wanted my time with her to keep developing and didn't want to pause for a freeze-frame.

Back on the bed, she picked up my hands and guided them over her body. It was so lovely to feel her, yet so frustrating to not have the motor control to do this myself, or the strength to squeeze her and pull on her like every instinct I had was commanding me to do. She took my hand and pressed it up against her vagina, then put two of my fingers inside her. In their natural position, my hands make a loosely clenched fist, and if you try to straighten out my fingers then very soon they start to close up again. So it took some concentration on my part to keep my fingers straight. I tried to press my fingertips against the sides, and generally just feel and explore as much as I could before my fingers curled up again. I had literally a few seconds to enjoy this but it really was magical for me.

After a couple of minutes she shuffled down the bed and began to kiss me again. She worked her way down my neck and onto my chest, as I started to breathe more deeply in an effort to open myself up to the pleasure. She gently sucked on my nipples, which was something I enjoyed the sensation of more than I would have anticipated. She climbed off the bed again and continued downward ...

Now it's probably quite hard to imagine how I wasn't already hard by this point. I'm sure that had this been a year or two earlier it would have been, but I had been feeling depressed and hollow and hadn't had an erection in ages, not even the slightest 'stirring'. It had started to feel like nothing was working down there any more. I used to think it would be a blessing if my erections would stop; after all, what use were they to me? I can't masturbate to get any enjoyment out of it because my hands don't work properly. So erections and any sexual urges whatsoever just felt like the bane of my life. However, in recent weeks I had come to realise that without those urges, I was not 'me' any more. I had no smile and no spark. As Austin Powers would say, I had lost my 'mojo' and I needed to get it back. That is basically why Ruby was here right now. I needed to test if it had gone forever so that I would know what I was dealing with.

She locked her lips around my cock and got to work on it, and unsurprisingly it felt very nice. I was very nervous about whether it would have the desired effect, and it might sound cheesy to say it, but it felt as if she was literally breathing new life into me. Then I experienced what was quite possibly the most pleasurable act of the evening, and obviously therefore of my life, when she sucked on my balls. It was ecstasy for me. Like most things it only lasted for moments, and I regret not asking Ruby to do that for longer. It was like it had started everything within me whirring into action.

She asked me rhetorically if I wanted to be inside her, and I nodded. She climbed back on to my bed, and briefly stood upright before the inevitable comedy moment when she almost lost her footing and had to scramble to avoid falling off. But she was fine and she sat down on me, facing me, and with her arms stretched out behind and her hands pressed flat on the bed. She gently rocked her pelvis, but I was disappointed that I was just not feeling very much at all. I had wanted to have intercourse ever since I stumbled across its definition in a dictionary at primary school! And I had questioned for so long if it would even be practically possible for me to achieve. I then asked the question that, as soon as the words came out of my mouth, sounded like another of those embarrassing things I was sure I'd heard before on the TV: 'Is it in?' Three tiny words, but if I could have bashed my head against a wall I would have done. She confirmed that it was, and suggested it might be the condom dulling the sensation. That was a very good point, not that there was anything that could be done about it. But I realised the bigger problem was that my bed was not completely flat. I figured that if it was flatter, I could get deeper inside her. Ruby grabbed the controller and pressed the button to lower the backrest … NO! PLEASE NOT NOW! My bed has been very temperamental; every now and again the controller stops working, and of all the times it has failed me this was by far the most inconvenient. David can usually fix the problem quite quickly by unplugging the controller, jiggling the connections and reconnecting it. I asked Ruby to try this so she got off me, found the plug and tried to pull it out, but it was fitted just too tight. Seriously, it is only as I am writing this that I see the irony of the problem! There was only one thing for it. Ruby pulled the blanket up over me and, slightly embarrassingly, left the room to summon David. While she was spending a few minutes in the bathroom, David entered with a peculiar grin and I told him the problem. He fixed it, lowered the bed flat and left. Ruby returned to continue from where we had left off but in the time that had elapsed, my erection had started to fade. She removed the condom and set about restoring me to my former glory with her mouth.

It only took a few moments, but this time I knew I just couldn't contain it any longer. I felt that amazing burning sensation that I don't get to experience nearly often enough as I ejaculated hard and for the first time in months. I managed two respectable bursts and Ruby exclaimed: 'That's a lot of cum!' I told her I wasn't surprised considering how long I'd had to wait for this release.

What happens now? I wondered if Ruby would just excuse herself and leave. What was the protocol? I hadn't really given this any thought. She sat on the edge of my bed again, moved in closer to me, and just talked to me. I can't remember what we talked about exactly. She told me a little bit about her life in London, her close friends who knew about her life as an escort, and her own difficulties in starting a relationship over the past few years. I told her some stories about my own heartbreaks and about the love I have inside me that I don't know what to do with. In truth, it didn't really matter what we were speaking about. It was just beautifully intimate to be naked and to look into her eyes and to see her looking into mine, and to sense that she actually did care about what I was saying. It was unforced, affectionate and rounded off our encounter nicely. She covered me up and got dressed again. We thanked each other and I asked her to tell David to give me a few minutes to myself. And with that she was gone.

I am proud of myself that I was able to engineer an opportunity to explore myself sexually, however brief it might have *been. I think I did it with dignity and maturity, and I have no regrets. Obviously this is not how I would have planned to lose my virginity; I will always yearn for a deep sexual connection with a partner in a loving relationship. But time is running out for me, the likelihood of that happening is remote, and it was up to me to make something happen sooner rather than later. I am relieved that I succeeded, and hope I will be able to find the strength from this adventure to continue my journey of self-discovery and ultimately find contentment.*

Ash is a unique man with a unique story but he highlighted a universal truth. Sex is about so much more than physical pleasure or the ticking of a box. We crave emotional closeness too. Ash had never experienced either. When, at the end of his hour with Ruby, he said she 'sat on the edge of my bed again, moved in closer to me, and just talked to me', I got the feeling that this was the intimate encounter that he really needed. This was when he felt affirmed as a human being, as a man and a naked man at that. Boys need this assurance just as much as girls do. But for Ash and many others like him, his physical limitations had prevented him from getting anywhere close.

But what if you do possess the ability to reach out and touch another human being at will? What if you do have control over your limbs? And what if you are an eighteen-year-old male virgin living in a society that sees no reason why this should be the case, at least in your mind? By far the largest volume of email I receive is from able-bodied men who feel hideously self-conscious about their virginal status. From eighteen to 58, men feel the stigma of virginity in a way that women rarely do. A recent male correspondent summed it up in brutal fashion: 'Most people view virgins as pathetic losers who should just make more of an effort.'

This might sound melodramatic but these words are far from unusual. Men feel a sense of powerlessness that is peculiar to them, and there is a reason for this. Generally speaking, and as the law decrees, the buck stops with women when it comes to sex, i.e. women get to control when they lose their virginity in a way that men don't. Allow me to explain.

Assuming that I still had virginity to lose, if I stepped out of my house one evening and took a walk to my local pub, the chances are that if I asked around, I would probably find a member of the opposite sex who was willing to relieve me of my virginity. It is perhaps difficult to imagine a man getting a similar result.

If I walked further down the road to Holland Park, and assuming that its famous feathered inhabitants could speak, the male peacocks would confirm everything I have just said. Female peacocks have far plainer plumage than their male counterparts because they do not *need* fancy feathers. The female peacock decides whether or not courtship will proceed. In fact, a female will probably check out the plumage of several males before she makes her choice. The buck stops with her.

No matter that a decent sexual experience begins in the head for most women and that as such, women require a degree of chemistry to be present, even if it isn't sexual. No matter that generally speaking men can, if they choose, have a physically gratifying sexual experience with far fewer emotional consequences than a woman usually can. It can be just as hard for a woman to lose her virginity. I have the emails to prove it. Lots of women have checklists as long as their arms and thereby reduce their choices before they even begin. But in a man's mind, and possibly a peacock's too, the female of the species holds the cards. If nothing else, this is a *psychological* impediment.

My next correspondent – or 'Bench-press Guy' as I like to think of him because, as he points out, he can dead lift his own body weight twice over – has all his faculties in full working order. He has two functioning arms and legs and while I can't help thinking that he'll probably laugh a woman into bed pretty soon, he may just as well have Ash's physical disability because he *thinks* that he can't get a girl to sleep with him.

'Bench-press Guy'. Born 1990, still a virgin

Hey, I am eighteen years old and I am from Alabama, USA. I just returned home from my first year of college and I am still a virgin. Here are my thoughts on that.

I hate it. I hate everything about it. I hate the word 'virgin'. Whenever I read it or hear it, I cringe inside. For me, it symbolises my inability to do the one thing that humans are here to do. I can juggle. I can do a handstand. I can dead lift over twice my body weight. But the one activity that is infinitely more human than any of those, I am incapable of. I can't have sex.

I don't care how functional your sperm cells actually are, if you can't get a girl to engage in intercourse with you, you are, effectively, sterile. Nature has not selected you. Your genes will not be passed on. You didn't make the cut. You're a fuckup. You're a B-side, not to be included on the album.

In high school I was OK with my virginity. It rendered some good jokes and I was perfectly happy with it. I didn't feel angry with myself for not losing it because I thought 'just wait till college'. In my mind college always seemed like this paradise where you can get laid by accident. Almost as if you could just trip up and fall into a girl. I figured that when I arrived at my dorm room to move in, there would be a beautiful girl lying in my bed waiting for me as if it was included with tuition. I was wrong.

Some of my religious friends are waiting until they're married. They tell me about their decision. 'I really want to wait until I'm married but it's SO HARD!' Really? Is it hard? Is it a challenge to NOT get laid? If so, I must just have a natural knack for it. Throw me into a room of horny girls with a few other virgins. Guarantee you I'm the last one left. It would be like the opposite of porn or something.

Masturbation used to suffice. It was like a drug and I was a heavy user. Whenever I started thinking about sex and getting turned on, I could run off to my room and trick my poor body into thinking it had gotten what it wanted. But there was still something missing. I needed human contact. I wanted somebody to snuggle with, post-orgasm. A girl, with whom I could discuss how great we'd just made each other feel and how, in twenty minutes, we'd do it again.

Bench-press Guy embodied what I have come to think of as the 'self-fulfilling prophecy'. To this day, at any given time, I am corresponding with at least one Bench-press Guy. Being a virgin is a lonely business. Not only do you not have anyone to 'snuggle with post-orgasm', but who can you share the burden of loneliness with? Stigmatised virgins are unlikely to reveal their status because they feel too embarrassed about it. 'Nature has not selected you,' said Bench-press Guy, 'your genes will not be passed on. You didn't make the cut.' That's some heavy baggage to carry around. The trouble with keeping this sort of baggage to yourself is that pretty soon, it begins to assume a disproportionate amount of importance in your head. That's when you've got a problem on your hands. That's when the self-fulfilling prophecy comes into play.

The self-fulfilling prophecy decrees that what you think about the most, you become. People who feel self-conscious about being a virgin tend to behave like one. They become shy and nervous around the opposite sex and in doing so, they repel the very people they want to attract. They become a self-fulfilling prophecy.

It's such a tired old cliché, but it's true. Losing virginity has got so little to do with looks and almost everything to do with attitude. Some of the most ordinary-looking people I have ever encountered are the most successful at getting laid because they believe in themselves. They have confidence, and confidence is like catnip to the opposite sex.

For every man that has ever emailed me with a sad, lonely tale, I offer the next by way of redemption. And while I don't expect everybody to get as lucky as Dan, take note, Bench-press Guy: I take your eighteen years of age and I raise you eleven. The owner of this story was a geriatric 29 years old when he finally lost his virginity.

'I am a decent-enough looking guy,' wrote Dan in his first email to me. 'I'm not crazy or weird in a way that makes people run away. I was pretty popular in school and even had a girlfriend but I just turned 29 and somehow, I am still a virgin. As 30 looms large on the horizon and I feel like more of a sexless freak, I have been considering the possibility of paying for sex … I dunno if I'd have the guts to do it but virginity is such a pointless burden.' I wrote back and made sympathetic noises but I heard nothing more. Out of the blue, several months later, I received this email:

My name is Dan and a few months ago I wrote you an email about my situation, which you then replied to. I really want to update this for reasons that will become obvious. I was at a nightclub with friends recently when a female friend who I had always thought was stunning but out of my league, drunkenly confessed that she really liked me. I was in total, and I mean TOTAL shock. Before I knew it, we were kissing and she made it clear that she was willing to have sex. I felt quite wary of her being drunk so we left it at that, with the promise of a date. We met a few days later and hit it off right where we left it. We had a great night of conversation and flirting and increasingly passionate kissing, before walking back to her place.

Before I knew it we were on her bed, then becoming naked – a new first for me – and then we were doing all those things I was beginning to wonder if I was ever going to taste. And it all felt so natural. For a first time, I would guess it was pretty good. As we talked afterwards, I told her that that had been my first time, and she was shocked. She said she never would have guessed. I feel different inside. I feel like a weight has been lifted off my shoulders and I find a new courage to look forward in life with hope and confidence.

I was delighted for him. I was also curious. How had his female companion reacted to the news that she had 'taken' a 29-year-old man's virginity? He replied:

Well, it's funny, because she is moving overseas at the end of July. We both knew this when we hooked up so the whole thing has been on a sensible no-long-term plans basis. Meanwhile, we have been meeting up without the pressure of 'is this going anywhere?'-type questions.

So I asked her how she feels about me being a virgin to start with and she said she felt a bit bad for 'corrupting' me – but not really because I am so obviously happy with the 'corruption'. So after a little shock and embarrassment, I think she was pleased that I could be so open. And the best bit? She has decided that as this is the case, it is her responsibility to leave the country having equipped me with as much new experience as possible by introducing me to all the different elements of sex and trying everything to see what feels good.

It's really cool to have someone be totally open and honest, showing me things and asking how it is, helping me find what I like or don't like, encouraging me to explore everything ... she always asks if there is anything I want to know, to just ask. Everything is completely relaxed and curious. To be honest, it's like a guy's dream come true.

Dan had hit the jackpot in a big way. His story also proved a point; sometimes the wait is worth it. Not long afterwards, I read a line in a newspaper article that reminded me of Dan: 'In an ideal world, you would wake up already in your second relationship.' These were the words of Dr Malcolm Brynin as he attempted to explain why puppy love was best avoided. Having listened to so many gut-wrenchingly sad stories from young people, I had to agree. Sex and love at a young age can be an unbearably intense experience. Wouldn't it be easier if we could time travel past the crazy stage and get down to a relationship that actually works?

Dan had done just that. He had lost his virginity at a point in his life when he was mature enough to keep a sense of perspective about it. Twenty-three-year-old Sarah agreed: 'I can honestly say without a doubt in my mind that at 23, I can make the informed decision to do something I am physically, mentally and emotionally ready for. I know the risks, I know the advantages and I know that it doesn't change anything. I will still be me; the world will not view me differently. I will always be Sarah no matter what physical changes or choices I make.' When Sarah eventually did lose her virginity, she wrote and described it to me as 'imperfectly perfect. I wouldn't change a thing.'

She was able to do this because she had waited for someone decent to share it with. It's a classic piece of agony aunt advice that we almost always ignore when we are young. Don't go out with someone who isn't prepared to make your needs a priority. A decent partner will always move at a pace that feels comfortable for you. In Daniel's case, this had turned out to be a mutually beneficial experience. When he told his partner the truth about his virginal status, he also told her about his email exchange with me. I almost fell off my chair when she wrote to me and explained how this situation had worked out for her:

When I met Dan I had just come out of a very long-term relationship and we had stopped exploring. It was great to meet someone who I felt so comfortable with that I could explore and reconnect those feelings of desire without feeling judged or embarrassed. It was as much learning for me as I think it was for him. But it was fun too and I believe that everything should have an element of fun or positivity to it or why bother! It brings a smile to my face knowing that he will at least be going out there with a few tools that he can develop and have fun with.

People are far more understanding than we give them credit for. The fact that I have an ongoing email exchange with a man who lost his virginity with a willing partner at the age of 54 is proof of this fact. I got a fabulous story recently from a lady in Belgium who searched desperately for a man to lose her virginity to. She had 'even considered hiring a gigolo, because at least that would give me a lot of control'. As it happened, that wasn't necessary. Aged 34, she met her future partner, she told him the truth and the rest is history. They are still together to this day. It's never too late to take a chance. But whether you want to or not is another matter because as I soon found out, not everybody has the desire to lose their virginity.

Laura. Born in 1982. Plans not to lose her virginity

Simon, my 38-year-old married virgin, foxed people. He clearly didn't have a problem attracting the opposite sex because he had successfully lured a partner into the cave, but once he had got her there ... nothing had happened. How could this be? How could a man sleep side by side with his wife every night and not make love to her? To the ears of my frustrated young correspondents, this was beyond the pale. What was Simon's problem? Perhaps that was the problem. He didn't have one, but they did.

In a sea of emails from people who were desperate to have sex for the first time, I began to encounter a small but significant proportion of people who identify themselves as asexual. An asexual is defined as 'a person who experiences little or no sexual attraction'. We might like to believe that these characters are confused or damaged to the point that they can't express themselves sexually, but that couldn't be further from the truth. Asexual people have the same aspirations for their lives as you or I. They want intimacy, they want companionship, they might even want good old-fashioned romance, but sex is unlikely to be part of the picture. Asexual people do not feel repulsed by sex; on the contrary, they do not have any feelings about it at all. How can you miss something that you don't actually want? Laura wrote and explained that her biggest problem was dealing with other people's expectations for her sex life:

I never really thought about my virginity until the summer of the year 2000. I remember the moment clearly: I was eighteen, sprawled on the beach with a couple of college friends. Someone asked me how many guys I had been with and I responded 'none' without really thinking about it. The reaction: total shock. 'Why are you so surprised?' I asked them – 'You knew I don't really date …' My friend looked at me blankly: 'But you don't LOOK like a virgin!'

What does a virgin look like? I suppose that I, with my choppy dyed-black hair, too-short cutoffs and cigarette hanging from my fingers, did not fit the bill. I was not ugly and I was not innocent. I was not religious, I swore terribly, and I had done more drugs than most of my friends combined. But I had no sexual experiences beyond some drunken make-out sessions. Where did I go wrong?

Or had I gone wrong? The reason I had not yet had sex was because I had never had a desire to. I had been propositioned by boys at parties but turned them down due to disinterest. The drunken make-outs I had did nothing for me. I had occasional crushes but I had no urge to have sex with boys or with girls or with myself. I found the thought mostly boring and a bit off-putting. I just didn't care.

My first and only boyfriend showed up at the age of twenty. I felt romantic feelings for him but our making-out sessions left me bored. He asked me for a blowjob once and the look of confusion on my face said it all. Once I confessed just how inexperienced and disinterested I was, the relationship disintegrated.

At 21, my friend suggested that I just go and have sex to get rid of my 'burden' – her words, not mine. We went to a bar and I got very drunk and one young man who seemed rather nice asked me to go home with him. I almost did. But at the last moment I thought to myself that I was doing this for the wrong reasons. It seemed incredibly stupid to have sex solely to fit social expectations when I really did not want to have sex in itself.

Since then, I have made no more efforts to sexualise myself. I am nearly 28 and still a virgin and I am in every way OK with it. I would be willing to have sex in the context of a relationship with someone I loved very deeply, but I am not naïve enough to count on this happening. I'm fine if it doesn't. I've never consulted a doctor about my lack of sexual desire because I don't think I am 'broken' or need to be 'fixed'. After recently reading www.asexuality.org I feel more than ever that it is totally alright to be the way I am. At any rate, I consider myself wholly blessed

in life: I have a great career and wonderful friends and family.
The fact that I have not had the sex I do not desire should not
make me any less lucky.

Society was uncomfortable with Laura's sexual orientation
but she was not. 'I feel like in this day and age happy virgins
really do not have a voice,' she said. 'It's either you get laid,
you want to get laid, or you should want to get laid. So I'm
glad that I can provide the voice of the happy virgin, rare as
we may be!'

Beauty and sexual success were clearly interwoven in the
minds of Laura's friends. 'But you don't LOOK like a virgin!' they would say, mainly because she was 'not ugly'. I got
the feeling that it wouldn't matter how many times Laura
explained the concept of asexuality, they still wouldn't get it.
Beautiful people have choices and for this reason, we can't
– or won't – understand why they are not engaged in sexual
relationships.

My next interviewee would relate to this because she is
what most people would consider beautiful. She also likes
sex, but of her own volition, she decided not to have any
until she got married at the age of 30. Sabina is a Christian.

Sabina Evans. Born 1979. Lost virginity on her wedding night in 2009, aged 30

Several stories consistently eluded me throughout the process of researching this book. The first one was the traditional Muslim story. When I say traditional, I am referring to
the practice of saving one's virginity for marriage. I searched
high and low for this tale. I hung out endlessly at The City
Circle, a group for professional young Muslims in London.

They were lovely to me but every time I revealed the reason for my presence, both men and women began to back slowly away from me. I understood. It wasn't culturally correct for them to talk to me or, indeed, to anyone about such matters.

I got sent several 'out of wedlock' Muslim stories via my blog but that wasn't the story that I wanted, or one that I felt I could include in this book unless it had its more traditional counterpoint sitting by its side. I wanted to understand what it's like to *wait* for marriage in a world where you are consistently being encouraged to get rid of your virginity. Our grandparents saved themselves for their wedding days but this wasn't unusual for the time. Being a virgin in the 21st century is a different kind of challenge. I wanted to know what it felt like to be young, contemporary and chaste in a society that doesn't always expect that of you. How does this work?

Christian organisations gave me a similar response. All sorts of lovely vicars and lay people entertained my strange request. Some were even quite excited about it but somehow, once the initial enthusiasm had worn off, I never heard from any of them again. Until finally one day, at the eleventh hour, just when I thought I would never be able to tell you a single thing about this perspective, I found Sabina. Sabina was the living embodiment of a fashionable, fun-loving young woman, who had also chosen not to explore her sexuality until she found a lifelong partner with whom to make the journey. How, I asked her, did people react to the news that she was a virgin?

The weirdest thing about waiting for marriage these days is that you can say you're anything. You can say you're bisexual or lesbian or gay or this fetish or that fetish and no one will bat an eyelid but if you say you want to be a virgin, it's like, 'What? I don't believe you.' People have actually said to me, 'I don't believe you are a virgin.' Mainly because I'm normal. I've got loads of friends, I go out. I do the same things that other people do. I'm not like a freak that lives in a log cabin in the middle of nowhere. I'm a normal human being.

She then went on to tell me how she had met her husband, a person who, like Sabina, had made the decision to save his virginity for one special person:

I remember the day I first started fancying my husband because I'd handed in a university assignment which I'd been working on all night. I hadn't slept, I hadn't eaten anything and when I finally handed it in at 4pm, I went straight to the bar for a pint of lager and it went straight to my head. Before I knew it, I was flirting my head off with him.

I felt really confused the next day. It didn't seem fair to get involved with a non-Christian so I took him out and apologised. 'I'm so sorry that I was really flirting with you,' I said. 'There really does seem to be a bit of a connection between us but maybe we're just meant to work together or be good friends or something.' I finished up by saying: 'I'm a Christian and I don't believe in sex before marriage and you know, I couldn't, you wouldn't, you'd never ... that's crazy for you right?' And he just sat there going, 'Oh my gosh. Now I'm really interested,' because it turned out he was a Christian too. So then he really pursued me.

I've been interested in the idea of God since I was a little girl. I always felt like there was a presence, something that I was *close to. When I was seven or eight, my friends stopped playing with me for a bit after I told them that I believed in God. They all laughed and said, 'You're crazy'. But even when it was costing me my friendships, I was still convinced.*

Eventually, in my teens, I quietly made a decision with God that I would keep my virginity for marriage. It never felt like a rule or a regulation. I felt that this was for me, for my own benefit. Even if I hadn't been a Christian, that still would have made sense to me. I never wanted to bond, to tie my soul up with someone if I wasn't going to be with them forever because then I was just going to be more broken when I left.

It took my husband and I five years to get married because we were really focusing on our careers. That made it easier for us in a way because we couldn't see each other so much but if you are both committed to not having sex before marriage, you can just switch it off. In the Bible it says 'do not awaken love until it so desires,' until the time is right, and you don't awaken it. You don't look at things that make you feel like that. You don't let your thoughts wander too far in that direction. You don't snog for too long or too passionately; you just don't do things that lead you down that path.

When it finally came to our wedding night, I wasn't nervous. I'd had a good sex talk from some married friends who had done the same as me so I felt like it's natural, it's the next step and I didn't have huge expectations. I knew that we'd get better at it as we went along. I don't think either of us had put our virginity on a pedestal. We were more focused on how wonderful it was to get married, to commit to someone and move into the next phase of our lives together.

We knew it would be a bit crap physically and that it would probably be painful and quick and it was all those things, but as virgins, what neither of us had expected was the emotional side of it. Something really amazing happened in the room that night that was beyond the hedonistic side of sex ... although once you've got a bit more experience, that bit is nice too! I cried, we both cried actually, it felt amazing. I suppose it felt like we had finally united ourselves spiritually. We had become 'one' somehow, we had sealed the deal. He was mine and I was his. I wasn't expecting the feeling of unity and emotional intimacy to be as strong as that, but it was.

I didn't really make a big deal out of my virginity. It's like: you don't just marry anyone, do you? You don't just throw your heart away and commit to signing on a dotted line. We had both thought long and hard about this beforehand. It was never going to be about 'performance' on the night either because I think that sex is much deeper than that. I think sex is deeply emotional and spiritual.

I made the decision to wait based on a deep faith that I have. I actually hate when people say, 'Oh, you're religious.' Because I think, no, I'm not religious, I'm irreligious. I hate religion. Religion says you do this, you have to do that and then you'll go to heaven. That's nonsense. I don't care about those things, I just love Jesus. I've got a living relationship with the God who made the world.

Of course the church is made up of people and some people are wonderful and some people are bigots. I know a lot of Christians who are amazing people and I know some Christians I can't stand because I think: 'You represent me and you do me a great injustice.' Jesus was friends with prostitutes and tax collectors, people who were outcasts of society and he was loving and all-accepting. He showed grace and mercy to everyone. He wasn't a bigot who asked people to leave his church. Jesus said, please, everyone come. It doesn't matter where you've been or what you've been doing. I love you, I accept you and that's the message of Christ.

And that's why, in a way, it doesn't matter whether you do or don't stay a virgin till you're married because God's gonna love you either way, it's just that I decided to wait because I thought that would be best.

Sabina owned her own virginity in every sense of the word. Had she been born 40 years earlier, even if she had not been a Christian, she would have been expected to remain, literally, 'intact'. But virginity and religion also share a long history. In the simplest of terms, virginity has been seen as the most exalted of all states of being. For both men and women, it has been tied to notions of purity and spiritual and moral superiority. At its most dramatic, the loss of virginity had the power to cast doubt on the purity of the individual, the family and even the community. Sabina was unencumbered by such responsibilities. She was very clear about this. Her decision to keep her virginity was a pact between herself, God and eventually, her husband-to-be. No one else was involved.

That didn't mean it was of any less significance to her. Her virginity represented a commitment that few of us are prepared to make in the modern Western world. We have grown up with so many choices that to flit from one option to the next is par for the course. For thousands of couples, cohabitation is the modern compromise between marriage and so-called freedom. If it doesn't work out, we can move on. Sabina and her husband, however, were prepared to take a risk and commit to so much more than just having sex for the first time:

Of course we lived together for the first time so it was every-thing all at once. We were learning how to have sex together and learning how to be married so it was quite intense and amaz-ing. And I think that's why we do have the lack of commitment because it's like, if it feels good do it and if it doesn't feel good, don't do it and that's such a load of nonsense. Sometimes it feels really hard when someone wants one thing and you want another thing and you've got to compromise. It's not easy.

As is always the way, in the week that I finally found Sabina I also found 28-year-old Matthew. Hailing from Belfast, he and his fiancée, both Christians, were eight weeks away from their wedding night. They were both virgins. I asked him how he felt about this:

I think the first time is much harder for teenagers and young people because they have the expectation that sex must be, you know, all action, amazing, best night of your life, six-pack, per-fect body, all that kind of stuff. That's what they are being fed, and anything short of that is going to be a disappointment. Whereas we've realised that we don't all look like Cheryl Cole and we've got a little bit more experience of life so we're going to accept one another for who we are.

If the first time is disappointing, it's not like we're going to get up the next morning and think, you're not for me, you know?

Within the framework of Christianity, these people had the information, the life experience and the free will to make an informed decision about their future. Not everybody I encountered was empowered to make that choice.

Sadie, the 35-year-old daughter of Protestant Christian evangelists, wrote to tell me that her family had asked her to remain celibate for the rest of her life. Sadie was gay. The fact that her family were prepared to forfeit their daughter's happiness in order to support their own beliefs was staggering to me. What a price to pay, and for what? But I soon came to see that people did not require religion in order to wreak havoc upon other people's lives. You will meet Jane in the next chapter. Her parents 'were not particularly religious but they were rabidly opposed to premarital sex'.

Religion was not the problem. People were the problem. In 2005, an organisation called The Romance Academy caught my attention when they featured in a three-part television series called *No Sex Please, We're Teenagers*. In it, a group of young people – some virgins, some not – were challenged to refrain from sex for five months. I was sceptical at first. What was the point? The results, however, were a revelation; mainly because five months was time enough for the penny to drop. It gave the participants the time in which to see that their relationships were defined by so much more than just sex. The Romance Academy is a Christian organisation but part of their charter includes the idea of 'never imposing our Christian faith or beliefs on others'. The Romance Academy had one agenda and that was to equip their participants with as much knowledge and perspective as possible. At the end of the agreed timeframe, everybody was free to make their own choices.

Free will or not, most young people are under pressure. If they are not trying to meet the expectations of their parents then they are feeling the heat from their peers. The sixteen-year-old son of a friend recently confessed to his mother, in much the same way in which someone might confess that they are gay, that he didn't feel ready to have sex yet. He is a confident, popular boy who will never be short of interest from the opposite sex but this was a difficult admission for him. This is a contemporary conundrum because, generally speaking, we don't celebrate the choice to wait.

When I walked across a west London council estate to interview seventeen-year-old Jim, in a moment of unscripted comedy our path was blocked by a pair of Staffordshire bull terriers performing a frantic mating ritual. Poor Jim was nervous enough about our interview without being accosted by copulating dogs. We laughed but they were a canine reminder of the ubiquity of sex in the modern world. It's always been difficult to stand out and be different. Sex is the same. According to Jim:

There are a couple of people that I know who are coming out now because they're my age and they're still virgins. They're proud of it because they're different. Everyone tries to rush into things too quickly. When all your friends are around you and you're going to parties and everyone's kissing each other, you feel like you're weird if you're not doing the same. So you psych yourself up, you make yourself want to do it, you know? But I think it's a better thing if you leave it. Because then you will have those butterflies. You will have that feeling when you wait for the right person.

My 21-year-old blog correspondent Claudia wanted to lose her virginity in the fullness of time, but meanwhile: 'I think it would be immensely refreshing for society to accept, and even promote, that you can be happy not having sex. That there are so many more values and human characteristics for us to judge one another by, if judging is what we must do, and that in fact there *is* a place in the Western world for those who, for whatever reason, choose to hold on to their virginity.'

Furthermore, this choice did not need to be viewed as 'abstention', or the holding back from something that has been instinctive for millions of years. 'Young people are being told about all the choices they have,' Claudia continued, 'including abstinence. But in my opinion, this has always been presented as just that – abstaining from something. Denial. No one talks about celebrating the choice we have to have sex or not. I don't want to have sex yet … that means I'm abstaining? It must not be natural.'

I set out to interview people about the experience of losing virginity. It was never my intention to deviate from this idea, but I'm glad I did because I learned just as much from the people who hadn't lost virginity as I did from those who had. Some people held on to their virginity because they literally could not let go of it. Vaginismus is a condition that affects a woman's ability to engage in any form of vaginal penetration. As you can imagine, this makes the technical loss of virginity more than a challenge. Simon, my 38-year-old married virgin, was not asexual, prudish or secretly gay. He couldn't – or wouldn't – lose his virginity for complex psychological reasons that went way beyond my layperson's understanding of the mind–body connection. He had, as he once told me, the overwhelming sensation that the penetrative act could have huge physical consequences: pain and the beginning of new life being just two. He understood intellectually that he needn't let these ideas stand in his way, but the feeling was such that he was unable to get past it.

The pertinent part of his story is that as he headed towards the age of 40, he still felt his status as keenly as he ever had done. It was an issue in his life. Even though very few people knew his secret, he felt excluded and he desperately wanted to change that. Virginity, even for those who hadn't lost it, was a big story in their lives.

One line of contentious copy on my blog had been all it had taken to connect me to this intelligent, funny and very beautiful collection of normal people.

5

<center>~~~~~~~</center>

Love Bites

'There is nothing like returning to a place
that remains unchanged to find the ways
in which you yourself have altered.'
NELSON MANDELA, FROM *LONG WALK TO FREEDOM*

It is doubtful that Nelson Mandela was thinking about virginity loss when he made that statement, but each time I asked someone to go back in time and recall their virginity loss experience, I couldn't help thinking that he might have been. Something very special happens when you ask somebody to tell you a personal story, and I wasn't always able to articulate what that was. Until recently, that is, when I did an interview for a newspaper.

'Would you be prepared to include your own story in the article?' the journalist asked. 'Of course,' I said. I was always going to put my own story in this book anyway so what difference would it make? I dug the story out and was about to mail it off when I decided to have another read about my teenage self. As I did so, I felt as if I were reading it in a public place with no clothes on. How could I have been so dimwitted at that age, so eager to follow the crowd and take such a big step when I was barely a teenager? Didn't I have a mind of my own?

This is the number one reason that people find this story so difficult to tell. As I hit the 'send' button and dispatched my story to the journalist, I felt horribly vulnerable because it meant revealing exactly who I *had* been at the age of fifteen: an insecure teenager who was desperate not to get left behind.

But via the process of storytelling, I also began to see this tentative teenager in a more flattering light. I began to see a spirited young woman who had never been afraid to grab an opportunity for adventure. Within a year of that experience, aged just sixteen, I would take the first of many adult-free trips to Europe. I wasn't stupid either. It still surprises me to remember that I had the wherewithal to insist that my partner used contraception. Pregnancy was *so* not going to be part of my teenage experience. But what I found most heartening was the acknowledgement that I was relatively indestructible. I had taken the experience in my stride. In fact, here I was almost 27 years later doing something constructive with it. My interviewees experienced similar revelations as they told their own stories. Recounting this episode from our past had helped us to understand exactly who we were, and what we had become.

But my story-sharing friends had an advantage during this process. They had anonymity. For entirely understandable reasons, not one person in this book wanted you to know who they were. Which brings me to one of the most popular questions I get asked about this project: 'Do you think that people lie to you when they tell you their stories?' To which I can only reply, what would be the point?

I care about the outcome of these stories inasmuch as I am a caring person but beyond that, no one knows who you are, so why bother lying? There would be nothing to gain. Besides, the people who ask this question are missing the point. People were drawn to tell me stories not to try to pull the wool over my eyes, but because they had something to say. Storytelling happened to be the perfect vehicle with which to do this.

People have told stories for thousands of years. We tell children stories at night because it paves the way for a peaceful night's sleep. We use storytelling to document our history. We entertain each other with stories – make-believe and factual – but we also tell stories because we want to understand our worlds more fully, whether on a personal level or on a wider scale. The act of recounting personal experiences allows us to do this. As my explorations drew to a close, I began to grasp the really powerful transformational qualities of this age-old tradition. My storytellers were here for a reason, whether they knew it or not. What brought them to the table? What had they come to understand about themselves that they didn't understand before? And what did I now understand about the intimate lives of ordinary people?

Until I began my blog, The Virginity Project, I always believed that the only way to get a decent story was to sit down and interview a person face to face. Virginity loss was too precious a subject, too personal and too private for an interviewer to ever get the measure of a person during a telephone conversation. So much of what we want to communicate is in our eyes, our facial expressions and the tiny tics and movements that our bodies make as we attempt to express ourselves.

I clearly underestimated the power of the internet.

The blog gave me the opportunity to communicate with people whom I would never normally have encountered. Not just from a geographical point of view – after all, I was now being emailed stories from America, South Africa and Australia, all interviews that would have been almost impossible to conduct in person. No, it was the chance to speak with people who would not otherwise have told me their stories in a million years, even if we had been living in the same street as each other.

Sometimes, these were the stories that were harder to tell. Often they involved shame, coercion or abuse. In these cases, the digital realm gave people the extra layer of anonymity they needed to hide behind. The written word was all in these cases. There were no facial tics to observe on the internet, just the carefully chosen prose of a person who really needed to express something.

Jane Bailey. Born 1979. Lost virginity in 1999, aged twenty

It will come as no surprise to you to learn that first sexual experiences can be incredibly influential. Good, bad or indifferent, they have the potential to set the tone for subsequent sexual endeavours. This next story brings home another truth. Difficult experiences have the potential to make us even unhappier if we keep them to ourselves. People keep secrets for years, sometimes decades, because they feel too frightened or ashamed to let them out. My blog became a repository, a place for people to release the pressure and speak to someone whom they will never have to face in person. 'I lost my virginity when I was twenty to someone who I was planning on spending the rest of my life with,' wrote Jane in an email to me one day. 'Unfortunately, although I consented to sex in the beginning, when the pain became unbearable, he kept going.'

Through a series of emails, Jane decided that she wanted to write this story down for the first time. She also decided that she wanted me to post it on my blog so that other people might learn something of value from her experience. This is Jane's story:

I lost my virginity aged twenty to my boyfriend at the time. I was raised by parents who, though not particularly religious, were rabidly opposed to premarital sex. I wasn't really sure what I myself believed. When I mentioned this to my boyfriend, he wanted to know if I really thought we could be together for eight to ten years without making love, and how strange that would be. He wouldn't stop pressing and I was curious, so after a couple of months I agreed to do it with him. However, I was so ashamed of my decision that I was afraid to tell any of my mentors in life about it or ask them any questions in advance.

I was a little nervous about the pain, but he assured me he'd be gentle. We went and got our STD testing done and bought some condoms and lube. I got on the pill (BIG mistake – it gave me SEVERE depression and badly interfered with my ability to think clearly and make good decisions. I didn't discover this until nearly a year later!). At around noon on the appointed day, we went over to my house.

We kissed for maybe two minutes. I had moved the condoms and lube out of the way because I thought we were supposed to make out for a long time first. He moved them back, put on the condom and put the lube on me. I didn't say anything because I figured he was the one with experience. Then he got on top of me ...

PAINPAINPAINPAINPAINPAINPAINPAINPAINPAIN PAINPAINPAINPAINPAIN

I started screaming. He did it again – tried to go all the way in as hard as he could. I was sort of looking over his shoulder at the sunshine in the window and then I blacked out from the pain and I couldn't see or hear anything for a few moments.

When I came to, he gave a happy laugh. 'Wow, you really ARE a virgin!' he said before doing it AGAIN. The pain was absolutely blinding and he started to express frustration at not being able to get it all the way in.

We tried a couple of other positions before he was able to get the thrusting going, though it would be another couple of days before my hymen actually broke. I looked up at a picture on the wall and focused on not blacking out again. After a while, he laughed again, pulled out, showed me the filled condom, said, 'Look what you did!' and went in the bathroom to wash up.

'I feel like a failure,' I said when he came back to bed.

'Aw,' he said, 'you're the best!'

Subsequent 'lovemaking' sessions were not quite as painful as the first, but almost, and by the time my hymen finally broke I was pretty much terrified of the sexual act. My body would tense up with fear, which of course would make it more painful, which would make me more afraid, which would make it more painful, etc.

If I said 'no' he would either do it to me anyway or he would stop for the moment but sulk, complain, or call me names until I gave in, even if it took weeks. All this time, I was still afraid to tell anyone what was going on.

I stayed with him a total of six months, until he sucked me dry of emotional energy, and then I finally got out of there. I was numb for two months before having BIG TIME flashbacks that I now know were symptoms of PTSD (Post Traumatic Stress Disorder). At that point my only alternative was putting my head through a wall, so I told one of my mentors. He was extremely caring and supportive, so I told the other two. I got off the pill, went to counselling and fought the PTSD for about a year and a half before meeting my husband, who is the love of my life. We have now been together for more than seven years. I hope to make a full recovery.

Morals of the story:

1. Don't go on hormonal birth control unless you have a close friend closely monitoring you for signs of depression (you can't do this yourself; you can't tell if your head is being fucked with when your head is being fucked with).

2. Abstinence-only sex education is TERRIBLY harmful and damaging. I would have been FAR less likely to do it, and I certainly would have ended the abusive relationship sooner, if I hadn't been afraid that anyone I told would think I was a horrible person for having sex outside of marriage.

3. 'Sexual abuse' and 'rape' don't have to involve weapons or even fists in order to destroy people. My boyfriend used only words nine times out of ten and never hit me or threatened to hit me. I still struggle with self-loathing that I 'could' have stopped him and didn't. But I have to accept that I didn't have a superhuman psyche. PLEASE, if something like this is happening to you, TELL SOMEONE (you probably know, deep down, whom to tell) and GET OUT.

Jane revealed a truth about abuse. Physical force is not necessary in order to exert control over another human being. Verbal violence can be just as effective. Some of the most disturbing stories I have received involved mental, not physical, manipulation. Jane also illustrated the inherent danger of placing too much value in the preservation of virginity. Though they may never have intended to do so, Jane's parents tied their daughter's sense of self-worth to her sexual status. This was to present Jane with a terrible dilemma. 'I thought I had to stay with him,' she said. 'I thought no one would love me – either romantically or as a friend – since I wasn't a virgin any more.'

Not everyone who emailed me wanted to enter into a correspondence, but in Jane's case, I sensed she wanted help in reaching a more positive resolution. I picked up on something she had said at the end of her email: 'Fortunately I am happily married now.' I gently nudged her about this. Had she, I asked, ever had an experience that was akin to the virginity loss experience she would *like* to have had?

She wrote back to say that she had felt guilty for years because she had consented to her first time, even though there was no way she could have foreseen the outcome. And no, she finished up, 'I have never had an experience of what virginity should feel like. I feel sad and regretful about this but on the bright side, I have had many experiences that were mutually pleasurable and caring.'

I nudged again. I told her that almost everybody I had ever encountered in the last five years had been disappointed with their virginity loss experience to some degree. I also told her that whenever I asked people to tell me about the first time they had sex and *enjoyed* it, I got a totally different response. That was when people got really animated. This did the trick:

Thank you for that, Kate. Because it's true, there are a lot of first times. At 22 I had my first pleasurable experience with intercourse. Shortly thereafter, I met my husband, and the first time with him was REALLY REALLY wonderful, like the heavens moved. And they are still moving seven years later :) I found your blog a long time ago but didn't write to you then because I was in too much pain. I'm so glad I wrote now.

The greatest irony of the modern world is that despite our ability to communicate across a multitude of platforms, we rarely do. Problems isolate people, particularly ones that involve sex. At its best, the blog had the power to blow the lid off isolation. By being brave enough to write her story and asking me to post it online, not only does Jane feel different, but someone else somewhere in the world might be feeling different too.

If people discovered things that they *did* need to know, occasionally this process worked the other way around. People discovered things that they didn't want to know and I was the chump that helped them to do it. 'I can't wait to tell you my story,' said 28-year-old Charlotte on the telephone, 'because I really did have the perfect virginity loss.' As I set off in my car one evening to interview her, I realised that I couldn't wait to hear her tell it either. I hadn't encountered perfection before. I wondered what it might look like.

It started out well. Charlotte came from a liberal Jewish family. Her parents were happily married and she could talk to her mother about anything. She was, by her own admission, 'the last to do everything; I wasn't scared of being intimate; I just knew with certainty that a one-night stand was not going to be my first time. I was waiting for the right time. I remember thinking, oh wouldn't it be great, you know, a real fantasy, if I got to lose my virginity to my first love. And then I did.'

The scene had been set for a meaningful first-time encounter. Her suitor arrived in the shape of Justin, the school football star-slash-heartthrob. The summer that she turned fifteen, 'he put a romantic song on his CD player – he told me that bit years later – and he called me up and asked me out. I was literally over the moon.'

They were together for almost two years before she seriously began to consider losing her virginity to him. Just at the point when their relationship also began to falter. Fearing that she could miss her chance to have the perfect first-time encounter that she had dreamt about, late one night at her parents' house they finally talked about sleeping together, 'with the lava lamp on in the background and the song, "Never Be the Same Again", by Lisa "Left Eye" Lopez, playing on the radio.' She continued:

I think I thought that this was the one thing that I wanted to have with him before he broke up with me. It wasn't just to keep him with me. It was because I thought, he's going to end it with me and maybe this will give him something to hold on to.

Finally, and after four tries, 'bless him. He was unbelievably excited,' Charlotte and Justin consummated their relationship. But she knew, deep down, that the ending of their story had already been written. The next day, he didn't call.

I remember thinking, alarm bells, Charlotte, he is so not good for you, and now you've given this precious thing to him; it's going to be ten times worse. I felt really helpless. I realised that I had given him everything and he still wasn't going to change. That was really bad, that I had thought that maybe I could change him, through sex. The sex doesn't mean anything. It's just a physical act. It's all the emotion that's attached to it that makes the difference.

Charlotte and I talked for two straight hours. The words on this page are the edited version of an epic conversation. As we finished up, she looked exhausted. She also looked distraught.

When you asked me about this originally, I thought, oh yeah, it's going to be such a great story because I lost my virginity to my first love, my first proper boyfriend, and it was the fairytale that I wanted. But it really wasn't. Talking about it reminds me of all the desperation in me, how important it was to me to lose my virginity to this guy, even if he dumped me in a month's time.

I felt slightly rotten. Charlotte had put her virginity loss experience on a pedestal and I had just helped her to knock it off. But it also occurred to me that on a deeper, more sub-conscious level, perhaps this was what she wanted. Perhaps this was another reason why it was never that difficult to find people to interview. Exploring the past at least allows us to step forward into the future.

I encountered a lot of people who sought perfection. Sometimes they were men, mostly they were women. Sometimes religion was involved, but not always. Laura M. Carpenter, in her book *Virginity Lost*, gave these people a name. She called them 'the gifters'. Unsurprisingly, she identified these people as those for whom virginity is a gift. They know that they will only be able to give this gift away once, and as such they want to make sure that they give it to the right person. As we have seen, this exchange is fraught with difficulties. How can we know for sure who the 'right' person is? The parameters of 'rightness' surely change as we get older. Giving invariably involves receiving. Can we guarantee the quality of what we get back in return? And is love supposed to work like that? Is it realistic to have these expectations for our first time, or indeed for life in general?

Derek Carver. Born 1946. Lost virginity in 1959, aged thirteen

I once had a boss who thought that Charles Dickens's novel *Great Expectations* should be re-named 'Variable Expectations' for the younger generation. He was the father of two teenagers and having been in close contact with young people – and recalling my own experiences – I couldn't agree more. I have often been asked if there was a difference between the more senior people that I interviewed and the younger ones. There was. Compared to the older generations, the post-pill generation had the most phenomenal expectations for their first time.

The older generation had a different attitude. Not only did they walk blindly into their first sexual experiences with very little idea of what was about to happen, they expected less because they came from an era of austerity; on every level, not just that of their sex lives. They were the survivors of two world wars. Our grandparents were raised to be thankful for what they had. My generation have very little concept of this idea and it filters through to our sex lives. The older generation understood what rationing was. We grew up in the land of plenty and part of the result is that we have the most amazing sense of entitlement when it comes to our sex lives. It's little wonder that disappointment is a constant theme.

From this point of view, my next story was a winner. Sixty-four-year-old Derek Carver expected nothing when he encountered two sisters in the summer of 1959. After spending the afternoon with them, he went back to the playing fields to play football with his friends and carried on as if nothing had happened. It had never occurred to him to tell anyone, until now.

I had met Derek only once before, via work, and I liked him immediately. When I started looking for men of his age group to interview, I took a chance and rang him up. I fully expected him to tick me off for being so rude and slam the phone down.

'Yes,' he said sweetly as I explained my proposal, 'that sounds like my kind of thing. Come and see me next week.' He followed this up by promising to sue the pants off me if I ever revealed his true identity, but he then went on to share one of my all-time favourite stories about virginity loss:

The problem with school was that nobody was geared up for learning in those days and if you were one of those that wanted to have a laugh or something then you didn't work. I went to primary school near West Ham football ground, which was a good school back then but unfortunately, I was always with the wrong crowd and ended up leaving at fifteen with no qualifications at all.

It was a boys-only school, so as far as meeting girls was concerned, it was whom you met outside of school rather than in the school. In the summer of 1959, on the playing fields near where I lived, I met these two sisters. Any of the girls I'd been messing about with before, I knew them, but not these two. I knew of them but I didn't know them. They were like those girls you see with their hair up on top of their heads, a bit like that Catherine Tate character from that comedy show: 'Am I bovvered?'

I was thirteen years old and they were fifteen and sixteen. Somehow I ended up back at their house one day after school and their parents were out. I don't think I was really thinking about sex that much at that age. You're building up to it aren't you? You mess about with girls and you go a bit further and then maybe they toss you off or something, but I had never been further than that.

I remember that house, I remember that day and I remember being in there with those two sisters. I think the fifteen-year-old came on to me first, she stripped off and we were just kissing and messing about and I didn't expect any more than that, the other sister was in the room as well and she was messing about herself. The fifteen-year-old took my trousers off and sat across me and that's how it started.

We were going further and further and I was starting to quite enjoy it, I hadn't ever done it before but I didn't really think about it too much, I just went along with it. I had already been coming so I knew I could spunk up the pair of them. When the fifteen-year-old was done, on sat the other sister and I had her next. I was in there for about an hour in all and when it was over, I just got dressed and went back over to the playing fields and played football with my friends. I never told anyone about it. I was never one to blab about. The same as now, with anything I do, even if I know it's the best thing since sliced bread. I take it on board and I'm happy within.

I think the experience gave me confidence. The pair of them, messing about with me, they knew more than I did about sex, certainly, sucking me off and everything. It's what every boy dreams about and at thirteen, to me, they were both quite attractive girls. I don't think I actually had sex again until much later and I certainly didn't go chasing. I think it was still toss off and hand up the skirt or whatever until I was about sixteen.

I think young people have shocking expectations these days because everything is supposed to be good all the time, whatever it is, and it isn't. It is half good and half bad and that's if you're lucky. Sometimes people can just be born under a bad sign and they have bad luck all the time. You expect things to go against you; it's the same with sex.

Enjoy yourself, that's what I would say. I think you have to go all the way with your partner. If you're with someone, don't mess about; one at a time, unless you're a free agent. If you're working doing something you don't want to do, stop doing it. You have to have the nerve, you have to go out on a limb, but if you do, something will come of it and it doesn't if you don't try. Definitely don't work for 50 years in a job that you don't like because your life goes and that's the end of it, I don't believe in the afterlife. I think when you're gone you're gone, that's it. You've got 60, 70, 80 years if you're lucky.

Girls like to be liked and be told they look pretty. That's what the girl–boy thing is all about. And if you were with someone who looked good then you'd say they looked good. And then if you made them laugh – and I was a bit of a laugh – then no problem.

Derek was only the third person I interviewed for this book and I felt like I'd hit a home run. I genuinely had not been expecting a little man in a velvet coat to tell me such a big story. I also realised that gawping at my respondent's words probably wasn't helpful, but it was hard not to in Derek's case. He had taken me by surprise. Luckily, I would have plenty more opportunities to practise keeping my countenance. Particularly when I met my next interviewee, Alison.

In order to really understand a person's story, I often asked them to put it into context for me. What was the sexual 'climate' of the time? How had their parents influenced their attitude towards sex? Could they pinpoint a moment in time when they first became aware of their own sexuality? I wanted to understand what impact people's environments had had upon them, where this process had begun and how it had affected their subsequent sexual lives.

Born in 1934, Alison had had a lovely childhood. It wasn't conventional but it sounded exciting and she was well loved by her parents. Her mother had toured with an acting company and in her absence her father, a man whom she clearly adored, raised her. When we got to the sex question, she really surprised me:

I do remember finding out what sex was and it's an extraordinary story. I had this awful itching rash all over my body. It turned out that I was allergic to nickel but nobody knew that, so I went to the doctor. The doctor was there in his surgery, there was no nurse or anything, and he asked me to lie down on the couch and just as he was examining this rash, he asked me, 'What are you going to do when you leave school?' 'I'm going to be an actress,' I replied, which was still tantamount to being a Swedish au pair in those days.

He said I would meet very exciting people and I would probably have alcohol and he was going to show me what to do, because perhaps when I went to parties, I might feel tempted to have sex. I don't think he actually used these words, but that was the general gist of the conversation.

Anyway, he then proceeded to stimulate my clitoris and bring me to orgasm and I really did not know what was happening, because strangely enough, I had never done this to myself. This was something very strange and new. He explained why he was doing this and I suppose I bought into that, but to give him the benefit of the doubt, I do think that he meant well.

I was dumbstruck. I felt angry on behalf of her parents, two people who had known nothing of this incident and were long departed. Not to mention Alison and the utter bewilderment she must have felt about this surreal episode. Alison knew that her story was unusual. She had acknowledged that when she had described it as 'extraordinary'. But she also hinted that as shocking as this tale was, in a curious way the doctor had liberated her. She explained further: 'As a result, I learnt to masturbate and it was a complete and utter revelation to me. I don't know if I would have ever worked that out for myself, but I did that very happily and very successfully for many years!'

Instinct still made me want to search for signs of trauma in Alison's story. I wanted to know if she thought that this experience had affected her in a negative way. I also did not want to disturb her obvious equilibrium. I turned the question around. I asked her how she thought her life had changed as a result of it:

I got a feeling of great relief and pleasure from it but then there were a lot of old wives' tales about masturbation and when I married Roger it was difficult for me to have an orgasm when

he was inside of me. I began to think that this was my fault.
That perhaps because I had become so adept at bringing myself
to orgasm, that I was somehow paying for this. So a lot of pre-
tending went on, on my part.

Thank heavens, a friend of mine who was very sexy and
had slept all over the place, told me about this book called The
White Book. *Has anybody ever mentioned that to you? Well,*
it was an excellent book. It explained that some women have
a clitoris that's very high up, and it's perfectly normal that
they can't come to orgasm internally and have to be brought to
orgasm manually. Everything was fine after that. I'm so grate-
ful to that book, because one felt at the back of your mind that
there was something wrong about masturbation, and the book
put everything right. My husband was always very loving and
careful to bring me to a climax. So much to do with a successful
lover is to do with generosity, in every way. And patience. I had
all that, in my future husband. Damn good choice.

I struggled with the unforgivable breach of trust displayed
by Alison's doctor but at the same time, I had to look at
the facts. She was raised in an era when women were not
encouraged to seek pleasure. It was not part of the equation,
even for those with happy marriages. It's hard to get your
head around this fact when one need only visit a high-street
store in order to purchase an appliance designed purely for
pleasure, but this was a mystery to Alison's generation. The
knowledge that women were able to have orgasms was akin
to discovering the Holy Grail. Whether she had chosen to
ignore the implications of this discovery, or whether she genuinely wasn't troubled by it, it was not my place to decide.
After all, I was sitting in the presence of a woman who had

shared a loving sexual relationship with the same man for almost 50 years. By anybody's standards, this was an amazing achievement.

It was almost impossible not to jump to conclusions about people's lives. I made a huge judgement about my next interviewee before she had even finished her first sentence. 'What did your parents do for a living and where did you grow up?' I asked the then 21-year-old Shanice. I never suspected for a second that she would deviate from the kind of reply that people usually gave. 'I don't have any parents,' she answered. 'I was in a foster home from five until eleven years old and when that broke down, I moved family every six months until I was seventeen.'

My heart silently broke and in the process I decided that this story was going to be a car crash in slow motion. In many ways I was right. Shanice had spent her entire childhood being shunted backwards and forwards within the care system. For sixteen of her 21 years, she had rarely spent more than a few months with the same family. She was, by her own admission, 'the naughty one'. How could this story possibly have a happy outcome?

As it turned out, while I had set out to collect virginity loss stories, along the way I also accrued some priceless pieces of personal wisdom from my interviewees. As we sat perched on tiny stools at the back of a Brixton office block, Shanice obliged me with the practical details I wanted to hear but in the process she inadvertently explained why she was a person who was going to succeed in life, no matter what. Here was a woman who hadn't had a parent to tell her the most basic of facts but somewhere along the line, Shanice had acquired a personal philosophy that could be used to run a country.

Shanice Walker. Born 1985. Lost virginity in 2000, aged fifteen

I was always the naughty one. I was always the one running away from home, drinking, smoking weed and getting arrested and my sister was the good, happy-clappy, going-to-church girl. I think I was aware of sex from a young age. I once walked in on my foster mum having sex and I didn't stand there and watch or nothing; I just opened the door and quickly came out of the room. I knew that boys had willies but I didn't know how babies were made.

Growing up, when everything started developing, I used to think that things were wrong with me but I wouldn't say nothing. I was too embarrassed to go to people and ask and obviously by this point I didn't have a parent either. My girlfriends weren't 'girly' kind of girls. They were more like roughnecks, or tomboys, not the kind of friends you can sit down and ask questions of. They were all having sex anyway, so it was like everyone pretending they know everything about it.

Absolutely all my friends started having sex before me, so that's why I think I kind of rushed into it. I was fifteen at the time. I was supposed to be in school but I wasn't, I was running around with this boy I fancied. Because I was in this foster carer's home and I didn't like her, I disrespected her. I've changed now but I used to disrespect her. I sneaked my friend into her house with these two guys that we fancied and we were all listening to 'Incomplete', by Sisqó. We were playing it over and over again and messing about and then just started kissing and one thing led to another. And then we went upstairs. Done it and I asked him to stop because it was hurting and that was it. And then afterwards I'm so embarrassed and he's running around telling everyone he's got me pregnant because we didn't use a condom.

I fancied him, I really did fancy him but I did feel under a lot of pressure because my other friends were there and I wanted to go with the flow. No one wants to be the odd one out. I didn't want him to go talking about me like, 'Shanice is frigid'. I don't know if you heard about that word but you don't want to be called it.

Maybe he felt under pressure as well, because I've noticed that men think completely different, you know? Maybe he is sitting in his bedroom thinking, if I don't do that, she's going to think I'm an idiot. We did see each other again but it kind of fizzled out in the end.

I think that the way the media portrays women and virginity and sex, it's like, if you do this, you're cool. If you listen to some of the songs, not just rap songs, but pop songs, when they're singing, it's like the ultimate thing that you can give a man is sex, not just holding his hand and spending time. And when you're little and you're growing up in that environment, you know you're not going to think of virginity as a big thing. Back in the day it used to be, 'Oh, a man can have sex with a woman and not care but a woman will always be emotional.' Well, it's not like that any more. There are some girls who will go out, have sex with a man and you don't even have to fancy the guy, because of the way the media has portrayed sex. And you don't realise what you've done until you've proper grown older and you stop being influenced by things around you. That's when you realise – maybe I shouldn't have done that.

When I used to have sex again with someone else, I didn't like it. I didn't have no feelings, and the reason I was doing it was because the guy wanted to. I thought that if you're in a relationship with someone, that's what you do. Because that is what is portrayed around your peer group: he's my man, he wants sex and I have to give it to him. I actually remember lying in the bed, like, freezing. Just lying in the bed, just doing this thing and I would have no feelings. I wouldn't understand it. It was kind of like being raped in a way. Rape is a very harsh word to use. I don't mean that he held me down and raped me but it was like when you're pressurised into doing something, when you're in the bedroom and he's saying, 'Oh come on, come on' – that's pressure. That's force and I still think it's kind of a little bit like rape.

Later, when I was seventeen, I met a guy that I really loved and I was with him for two and a half years. When I first started sleeping with him I liked it but I still didn't understand sex. I used to keep my T-shirt on and not be comfortable. But I think because he was a few years older than me, he just taught me. Then I used to say to him, 'I wish I had lost my virginity to you,' because it was the first time I was properly consenting to it. I guess that's one of the things we lose when we talk about losing our virginity – that chance. I'd say that you might lose a little bit of dignity and self-respect down there as well. Because I did go through a stage, I didn't go around sleeping with everyone or nothing but I did feel that sex was nothing. And that is not how you're supposed to treat down there. Don't let a man enter your body, do what he's got to do and then go, because even though you think it's nothing, you're disrespecting yourself.

It was only a few years ago that I proper opened up about sex and began to talk about it. You could not have been speaking to me about this if I was seventeen or eighteen. When I broke up with my long-term partner, that was when I started to think to myself, 'I'm giving you something'; do you know what I mean?

'You're going like you've got the right to take it from me and you won't.' I am in control and he's got to start thinking it's my body and if I don't want to sleep with him I won't. That's when you realise he's not the king of the bedroom like they make out.

People that have a hard life learn to take things like a knock on the shoulder. The statistics for a girl in care say that she will be pregnant by the time she comes out of care. The statistics for a boy say that he will end up in prison. Things are more against people in care. We're not expected to leave school with qualifications because we're kind of like Oliver Twist kids. I don't feel sorry for myself but some people it will affect, like it affected my sister. She went through some proper emotional stress.

It's a lot to do with how you think and that's why, I suppose, I can come through it. If something happens to me, I don't think, wow, bad things happen to me, I think, OK Shanice, what am I going to do next? Because that's how my brain works.

I think I've learnt that way of being because when I was little, I used to play football which is a good sport to get into. When someone was tackling me, my coach would say to me, 'Shanice, he's not a ghost. He can't go through you.' And even though he's talking about the football, it kind of makes you deal with everything like that. Because people will always try and tackle you and that's why I have always said, you have to try and get round things. If the guy takes the ball off you, you have to team up with your mates and get it off him, or help the goalkeeper so he can't score. That's probably why I've got that way of thinking.

The other day I had a racist boss and he sacked me so I went up to him and I asked if he would like to be my referee for my next job. He just sat there, I think he expected me to cry or something but it was a rubbish job. He couldn't even answer me

straight away, he was so shocked, but I walked out of that place
with a smile on my face.

Shanice stopped me in my tracks. To say that she had had a
hard start in life was an understatement and yet somehow,
she had devised a personal strategy that allowed her to succeed. I turn back to the man whom I quoted at the beginning
of this chapter. Both Nelson Mandela and Shanice share an
understanding of a basic truth: it's not the crappy hand that
you are dealt that matters. It's the way you play it that counts.

Perhaps it was Shanice's sports teacher, a man who via
a straightforward game of football had shown her how to
face up to a challenge. Perhaps it was something that she
was born with – but either way, through a series of difficult
life experiences, Shanice had grasped hold of something
that takes most of us years to understand. Having negative
experiences is part and parcel of the rich pattern of life. In
fact, they can enrich our lives.

I often wanted to explain this to the people who wrote to
me via my blog, but I worried about being too blunt. Was I
running the risk of cutting them off, just at the point when
they really needed someone to talk to? Would they think that
I was being harsh? Or unsympathetic? At the same time, I
felt compelled to share something that I felt to be true on a
molecular level. We need challenging experiences in order
to learn. They give us perspective and eventually we stop
seeing them as isolated incidents and begin to see them in
the context of a whole life. Virginity loss is one such experience. It might not be the best encounter of your life, but the
chances are you will learn something that might be of use in
the future.

I didn't need to tell Shanice any of this because she already knew. 'Breaking my virginity young came out to be a good experience,' she said, 'because I've learnt my worth now and that everything happens for a reason. I had to go through that to start thinking like this.'

She embraced those early experiences because she knew that they were part of an overall, and ultimately more satisfying, trajectory. 'I am very proud of myself,' she told me. And she was. While lots of people were drawn towards the experience of storytelling because they needed to understand something about themselves, Shanice was not one of them. She told me what I needed to know because she is a helpful person but beyond that, she had absolute clarity about her life.

Perhaps it is now clear why I chose to call this last chapter 'Love Bites'. People shocked, surprised and delighted me with their tales but on reflection, what did I expect? If you delve around in people's personal undergrowth, this is what you'll find. This is not unusual or abnormal. This is life. We all have stories like these. Some of us just may not have realised how crazy they sounded until the words came out of our mouths, but the fact remains that these stories are par for the course. The phrase 'truth is stranger than fiction' was invented for a reason.

You could say that I had an advantage during this process because generally speaking, people lose their virginity when they are young. Youth comes with its own set of rules, i.e. none. From a literal point of view, if we are below the age of sixteen, we are considered a 'minor' and therefore not responsible for our actions. We have little comprehension of our limits. We throw ourselves into everything with abandon because we don't know any better. If we tried to live our adult lives with the same intensity we probably wouldn't survive for long. But even if we could, it would be impossible to replicate that feeling because we gain too much knowledge, too much emotional muscle memory to ever let ourselves go again that much. Sadly – or not – we learn the art of caution. But before that, we behave spectacularly badly and hopefully accrue a collection of stories that will keep us going well into our old age.

My last interviewee did this in grand style. This story was a surprise on several levels. Without ever realising it, I had always made the assumption that virginity loss was going to be a disappointing experience. Not just because my own was such a damp squib but because I have interviewed almost 50 people for this book. Many more have written to me via my blog. More often than not, virginity loss fell short of our expectations. So forgive me if I went into this interview expecting more of the same. How wrong could I be?

When Sophie Childs told me that 'losing my virginity was one of the best sexual experiences of my life', she caught me completely off guard. My entire interviewing process was rendered useless. I didn't have any questions about joy and pleasure. I was mute, to such an extent that it was one of the worst interviews I ever conducted. When I got the transcript back, I had to ring Sophie and ask her if I could interview her again. Luckily she said yes, and this time I got the story that I am about to tell you.

This story was memorable for another reason. Sophie lost her virginity to her sports teacher.

Sophie Childs. Born 1977. Lost virginity aged sixteen and eighteen in 1993 and 1995 respectively

I was never really into boys, you know? If they'd have turned around and said, look, you're dumped, I'd have been like, okay, cool! And now I obviously know why. I lost my virginity to a girl and I thought it would be great, but actually it was three hundred times better.

I come from a very happy family and I had a great childhood. I went to boarding school. I didn't learn too much but I enjoyed myself. I was always a little bit on the edge, a wild child, the class joker.

When it finally did happen for real, it was like, Bingo! It just felt right. It was also strange because my first lover wasn't actually a friend. She was my gym teacher.

There was a massive sexual tension between us. For almost a year it was building up. Bear in mind that I did sport every day of the week. She did physio as well, so I was always wishing injury upon myself. There were some situations where I think she knew what I was doing, but tried to act like she didn't. Because she had a lot more at stake than I did. I didn't really care if I got kicked out of school, whereas she had chosen to be there. But that didn't stop anything happening. She could have walked away from the situation, but she didn't.

I was captain of the sports team so I would get to drive to all the matches with her in her car. That gave me the chance I needed to step up my game. It sounds awful but I know my good points. I'm big on eye contact, so I really flaunted that, knowing that it would help me to get my end result.

'It' finally happened during the tennis season on our first away match. We played our match and we won. Great, fantastic, everybody was in high spirits. The team went home in

the minibus, I went in her car and nobody thought anything of it. On the way home, we stopped for petrol and as she got out of the car, I thought to myself, it's 'do or die'. I have to make a move now. Either I've got to get her out of my life, or I've got to act on this impulsion. So I acted on my impulsion.

When she got back into the car, my heart was pounding, I felt so physically sick. I went in for the kill and I took her hand. I didn't say a word. I just thought, if I open my mouth, something awful's going to come out, so I won't say anything. I just took her hand and it was reciprocated. She squeezed my hand tightly and I thought, okay, that's a good sign. That's reassuring, she's not freaked out. Then she turned to look at me and we kissed. I'd waited a year for that. I don't know how long she'd waited, but I'd waited for a year and that's a long time when you're sixteen years old. I think we both knew what was going to happen next. From that point on, everything moved quickly to the experience that I would call 'losing my virginity' and it happened in her cottage, on the school grounds.

For me to get there, I had to do a sort of commando-style dress-up-in-camouflage-after-dark challenge, darting across the hockey pitches. Which all sounds quite comical now, but actually it was terrifying at the time. This was a top-end boarding school. It was really, really strict. If you were even caught talking in the corridors, it was detention. The whole thing was very risky but I didn't think about the consequences. I knew I was doing something wrong, but it just felt right.

I wanted it to be so perfect and I was worried that it wouldn't be perfect. So I got shy when I got to hers. I went from being all, 'Yeah, yeah, yeah, hurrah', to 'Oh my god. Here we go.' I'm making myself feel nervous just thinking about what I actually did. Because I know fifteen- and sixteen-year-olds now and I just can't imagine any of them doing what I was about to do.

We started out talking and chilling out on the sofa then we started kissing and we got very intimate. We did oral together and we tried things, we used things and we both had orgasms. For a first time, it was pretty experimental but it didn't feel like my first time. It was passionate and it was meaningful and it happened very naturally. I don't think either of us felt that it shouldn't have happened when and how it did. I kind of knew it would be amazing. I engineered it that way, you know, she was very beautiful, very confident, and of course older than me.

Perhaps it was one of the bravest things I've ever done, looking back on it. Because I wonder how my life might have turned out if I hadn't taken that chance. I might have got married and had children but I know I always would have had a thing for the girls. Because I need a woman, I need to have sex with women.

I was pinching myself for weeks afterwards. I felt like a woman. I wasn't – I was an absolute prat but I think immediately afterwards, I really felt like, you know what? I'm all that. I felt like I'd achieved what I needed to achieve, and that it had made me who I wanted to be.

Then of course, it happened on a regular basis. At every given moment we'd steal an opportunity, whether that involved locker rooms, cars or anything. She was my main distraction at school. My main distraction. Hence probably not getting very good exam results. I dropped out of pretty much everything that didn't involve a racket or running round a field. But I didn't care. I was so head over heels in love that I just didn't see anything apart from her.

At the time we thought we'd be together for ever, but once I did my A levels and left boarding school, we saw less of each

*other because of location and, I don't know. I was a year and a
half older and I was ready to conquer the world. It was heart-
breaking and it was horrible, but I think we both agreed in the
end that that was how it had to be.*

*I got a boyfriend next. He was really cute, really hot. The
kind of guy that everybody wants to be with, and I was like, oh
God, please don't want to be with me! You're gonna be so disappointed. Of course, he thought I was playing hard to get, when
I was actually playing, 'I'm not really bothered.'*

*When I slept with him for the first time, it was a bit like,
whatever. Which wasn't his fault, and not anything he did
wrong, but I knew that I'd had fucking good sex, solidly, for a
year and a half. That's maybe why I had a bit of sympathy for
him, because girls at eighteen or nineteen years old are hideous.
It only takes one horrible comment and that's crushed a guy
for life. So I sympathised with him, because I knew that I had
been out there pleasuring a woman. I knew exactly what that
involves.*

*For me, sex is not just penetration, at all. All my friends talk
about, oh yeah, I had sex with this guy and he did that and
I'm like, is that all you did? And you think that's sex? I guess I
have a really different view on it, because when I tell them the
things I've done, they're like, oh my God, I didn't know that
was possible.*

*Why was it so good the first time? Had I just found a great
partner, or had the year-long wait made it into a perfect situation? I honestly don't know. But I think there's a connection
between two women that runs deeper than sex. I can say that
because I've been on both sides. I've had good sex and I've had
bad sex with women, but even bad sex with a woman is better
than bad sex with a guy. Because two girls would never do it for*

the sake of it. No one ever feels like, oh God I've got to, or Jesus, I'd better. There's a lot more trust between two women.

Despite the controversial nature of her story, despite it being 'wrong as everyone calls it', Sophie acknowledged that it had changed the direction of her life in the best way possible. As a contented gay woman in her thirties, she now knew that had she not thrown caution to the wind at the age of sixteen, things could have turned out differently:

I'm glad I actually went with my instinct at that early age. It gave me confidence, as I got older, not to conform, whereas a lot of my friends have done that and they're not very happy. I had a choice. At eighteen, I thought, I can stay with this guy, have babies, live in a lovely house with a 4x4 and everything will be fine. But I know I will cheat on him and I don't think that's any kind of life to lead. So yeah, I took a massive leap of faith and thought, I'm going to go down the other route, and at least I'll be in a happy relationship.

Taking a leap of faith or teenage recklessness, as she sat in the offices of the upmarket design agency where she now worked, she was shocked at her youthful audacity. She also knew that it had been a defining moment in her life, for all the right reasons.

She also unwittingly brought us back to a question I asked at the beginning of this book. I asked how people defined the loss of their virginity in the modern world. Do we have one definition to suit all? Or has time eroded the need to stick to a set of specific instructions? As a person who had lost her virginity to both sexes, I was curious to know how Sophie would answer this question:

I think for two people to be naked together and to have an intimate sexual experience, I think that's losing your virginity. But I also think that a major part of it is both of you being pleasured right to the end. The guy and the girl both coming. That's a major factor. If a girl is just pinned up against a wall and a guy has sex with her, I don't think she's had the full experience. It's a mental thing as well.

Sophie was less tied down to the intricacies of 'who did what to whom' and far more concerned about having an experience of genuine value. Because sex and losing virginity are not just about crossing the 'T's and dotting the 'i's. There doesn't have to be a formula. Losing virginity is not a mathematical equation. In Sophie's world, penis + vagina didn't necessarily equal the loss of virginity, but then neither did vagina + vagina. Sophie really got to the point when she mentioned a word that often gets lost in a melee of mixed messages about sex. Pleasure. The concept of pleasure is what we *could* be shooting for in our sexual interactions, and while you might think that this is an obvious statement, it isn't to many of the people who write to me at my blog.

As we spend increasingly large amounts of time worrying about how people might judge us if we have not had sex, or the right kind of sex, or the right *amount* of sex, we move further and further away from the entire point of our closest relationships. Our relationships *should* involve pleasure, whatever form that takes. A foot massage can be an incredibly pleasurable, not to mention intimate experience. A conversation with someone you love can be a deeply satisfying experience. Sophie was the perfect 'love bite' with which to end this chapter because regardless of her gender, her sexuality, her background or her age, she brought a universally good piece of advice to the table. Take a leap of faith and give genuine pleasure. The rest will come naturally.

Epilogue

Is that it?

For all sorts of reasons, virginity loss rarely turns out to be the moment that we expect it to be. From time to time, people would mention this. 'Why are you writing an entire book,' they would say, 'about such an excruciating, potentially painful or embarrassing moment?' That was the point. I wasn't. It was rarely, if ever, about 'the moment' for me. We all understand how 'the moment' works. I don't need to explain the mechanics of virginity loss to you. What motivated me to get off my backside was 'the story'. I wanted to know what *your* story said about you and the era from which you come. I wanted to know what impact your story had had on your life. And I wanted to know who and what had inspired you to take such a big step for the first time. Because aside from the obvious, i.e. sexual frustration, the answers were rarely that simple. But they were almost always one thing: they were interesting.

My own story had been a good starting point. It wasn't what you might call pleasurable. It wasn't even tender or loving, but for one reason or another it was an encounter that I would always recall with joy. Why? Because it symbolised something special to me. It was about finding my feet. It was about shedding my childhood innocence. It was about asserting my right to live my life the way I wanted to live it without asking my parents if that was okay. It didn't inspire me to have more sex. That came later. But I did know from that day forward that I would always be a woman who would travel. Metaphorically and physically. I wasn't just seduced by beautiful boys that summer. I was seduced by the romance of foreign adventures and I would go on to have plenty more. *That* was the power of virginity loss for me.

In the same way, it meant something to other people too. For older generations – and sometimes younger ones too – it coincided with the consummation of marriage. Having sex for the first time represented commitment to a lifelong partner. It very possibly heralded the arrival of children as well.

For Scottish Rob, the self-titled 'leader of the gang', losing his virginity was a political act. A 'boy' cannot be a gang leader. He needed to assert his position of dominance. Losing his virginity, or attempting to, was the most effective way of achieving this. Charlotte slept with her boyfriend because she was nuts about him. She also felt driven to gift him with something of value to her before he left her 'because I thought, he's going to end it with me and maybe this will give him something to hold on to.' Sadly it didn't. While her boyfriend clearly loved her, the giving of virginity had more significance for Charlotte than it did for her first lover.

Virginity loss was generally more complicated than the straightforward desire to make love. And sometimes it wasn't. In 1971, fifteen-year-old Sherrie lost her virginity to a 23-year-old man 'and it was lust. Pure, driven, hormonal lust.' People don't need books, words or pornography to show them how to give in to basic animal instinct. Lots of us lose our virginity because we feel utterly compelled to.

And believe it or not, sometimes plain old romance played a part. As soon as I began to blog in 2007, and effectively handed the floor over to the general public, I started to receive sweet, lovely and highly uncomplicated stories from people who had just fallen in love. The words of one young woman always stuck in my mind:

It wasn't painful. It wasn't awkward. And it lasted quite a long time. Afterwards, I was ecstatic and as we sat cuddling on the side of the bed we opened a bottle of strawberry sparkling wine and ate mandarin oranges to celebrate. We then crawled back into bed and fell asleep smiling and holding hands.

This was not a mythical experience, it actually happened. So who got to have experiences like these? What was the magic ingredient? What made for the so-called perfect virginity loss experience? Because perfection, as we have seen, is often in the eye of the beholder. What constitutes 'perfection' for one person might not work for the next, but over time, I came to see that the people with the endearing stories almost always shared something in common. They had a partnership that involved genuine friendship and they had a realistic sense of perspective. If their experience involved pain, awkwardness or brevity, they were either mentally close enough to deal with it or they were mature enough to know that it didn't matter. After all, they had a lifetime's practice ahead of them to get it right. The first time was just that: the first time.

Great or not, this was the experience that would inspire people to blurt their stories out to me at the most inopportune moments. I could have filled another book full of stories that people have told me at parties and pubs alone. People have shared incredibly intimate details of their sexual lives while balancing a canapé in one hand and a pint in the other. Two minutes into a conversation at a book launch, the wife of the author told me that her virginity had been forcibly taken from her in her youth. She was an elderly lady now. She hadn't been encouraged to talk about it at the time but she took the chance now. It wasn't just that my blog was a repository for these stories, I was too and I took this responsibility seriously. I worried that I might sound flippant or casual as I recounted these stories to you, simply because I have heard them so many times, but they have never lost their impact. The experience of gathering these stories left an indelible mark on me too.

For many of us, our connection to our grandparents' era hangs by a thread. Listening to men and women in their eighties and nineties, and occasionally centenarians, talk about their lives gave me a real feeling for a period of history that is about to slip out of our hands. Our grandparents have not documented their lives on mobile phones and Facebook in the way that we do. I wanted to record these people's stories while I still had the chance. In doing so, I began to understand how history had shaped the lives that you and I now live, particularly if you are a woman.

When Diane Hill asked me if I wanted to take part in a Tantric workshop, I jumped at the chance – despite my fear – because I knew this was an opportunity that my older female relatives could never have considered. We take our modern freedoms for granted and we should treat them with more reverence. A male friend continually castigated me for using the phrase virginity 'loss' during the writing of this book. 'It's so negative,' he kept insisting. Yes, perhaps it is, but first, we all understand what we are referring to when we use this phrase; and second, there is a reason for the use of the word 'loss'. For thousands of years, virginity loss has been exactly that: a loss, sometimes a catastrophic one, but only for a woman.

When Diane Hill had sex for the first time, she didn't just get pregnant; she almost destroyed her family's reputation in the process. She managed to claw it back by marrying a man she barely knew. To this day, a woman can lose respect, honour and so much more through the simple and very natural act of losing her virginity. I felt compelled to tell these stories so that we may understand the journey to get where we are today and the sacrifices that people made along the way.

I also realised that in many respects, despite the passage of time, much remains exactly as it always has been. When people asked me to draw a conclusion about this project, I gave them this little nugget: people of our grandparents' generation enjoyed losing their virginity and discovering sex just as much as we do today.

They might not have talked about it in quite the same way, they might not have referred to it at all, but desire, passion and hormones ruled their worlds in exactly the same way they rule ours now. People are people – and as I discovered, people enjoy having sex, no matter what era they come from. The older generation just had to be more creative about it because the consequences were so much graver.

By the same token, people feel just as insecure now as they ever did. No matter that we have sex education and parents who are willing to talk. People of all ages still ask me the most basic of questions about sex. At first I thought we were being terribly British about it, but then I started receiving emails from America, Australia, Europe and South Africa and the same questions kept on coming. Our hypersexualised world is not analogous to the confidence that we feel in our personal lives. And this is normal. It is entirely natural to need to wonder whether what *you* have is standard issue. Do I measure up? Am I having the 'right' kind of sexual experiences? I still get fixed with *the look* during interviews, the look that says: 'Please tell me that I am normal. Please tell me that I am not the only one who feels this way.'

And I always will, because I deal in a subject that is shrouded in mystery. Virginity loss remains the ultimate private moment and that is never going to change. A handful of people claim not to be able to recall this experience, but for the vast majority, it takes under three seconds to reconnect with an incident that may have occurred over 50 years ago.

It happens every single time I am at a party and I answer that question: 'So what do you do for a living?' 'I collect virginity loss stories,' I reply. 'It's really very interesting because …' – but it's too late. I can see that they are gone. Back to a time, a place, or perhaps even the back seat of a car where they parked their metaphorical childhood. How could it be any other way? Virginity loss is rarely sexy, it's certainly not glamorous but it is an evocative moment. It is a moment that is full of expectation. It is a moment that is uniquely ours, and for this reason alone, I will never be short of something to talk about at parties.

The Happy Ending

You didn't think I'd finish this book without giving you a happy ending, did you? A couple of years ago, just as I began this project, a helpful friend offered me her mother as a potential interviewee. 'I think it's a story that you'd like to hear,' she said. She had a twinkle in her eye. I had no idea what she meant but for reasons that will become clear, when

I eventually spoke to her mother, she insisted that I also interview her husband of several years. This is their story.

Peter. Born 1942. Lost virginity aged approximately seventeen

It's hard to imagine, when one of the problems today is superfluity of everything, that after the Second World War there was absolutely nothing. It was very stark, there were frequent electricity cuts and it was cold.

Everybody spent their holidays at eight, nine years old, doing things which would today be considered anti-social behaviour. The staple diet for reading was escape stories and there were a tremendous amount of guns around. But the biggest difference was that you were turned out of the house at nine o'clock in the morning and you didn't see an adult again until six o'clock in the evening. Totally free roaming, on bicycles, everywhere, because there was nothing else to do.

There was no formal sex education in schools at that time, but then you can tell people a lot of stuff and draw them diagrams but they've still got to actually experiment and get feedback and change the way they behave, so it doesn't really matter. The watershed was learning to dance. Dancing was the basis of night-time entertainment. All the kids went. So you had a hundred people, a band, a ballroom and that was it. That was where you started and if you were good, then girls wanted to dance with you.

The jive was the dance of the time and you very soon got to know what people were like, because it's extremely physical. It's very rhythmic and if you're embarrassed or can't throw yourself into it with somebody, you just can't do it. And it's the most surprising thing, I mean you can have all sorts of very elegant and interesting-looking people, and then you'd try to jive with them and they were hopeless, they hadn't got a clue. So if you found somebody that you can do it with, it's almost a model of sexual activity, which is what made it so popular.

I met Suzie when she was fourteen and I was sixteen. She was extremely outgoing and anti-authoritarian and one thing quickly led to another. Suzie and I jived together a lot, still do in fact, if we get the chance and we can stay upright! She could pass for sixteen and seventeen at any time from her fourteenth birthday. And did. Later on, we'd go to London for a dance and we were meant to be staying with friends but we would go and stay in hotels and get away with it. I didn't realise how ridiculous it must have looked, walking into a smart hotel and announcing that we were Mr and Mrs. Totally absurd. But we got away with it.

Suzie will tell you that at one point her grandfather's chauffeur used to drive her backwards and forwards to assignations. We're talking parents being out all day, maids cleaning the house and the place being empty. I had a whole floor of the house for my records and books and stuff. And so we would go up there during the day, for hours, no trouble at all without any interruption. Nobody thought for a moment what we were doing. They'd have been horrified if they'd known.

It was a big deal to risk getting pregnant and managing the risk was very, very important. I remember when a girl arrived from California with the first contraceptive pills, and thinking, oh my god, you know, after all this hoo-ha, there they are, just this round pack with all these pills in and that's that. If you were intelligent, you knew the anatomy, you knew the biology, but we courted disaster all the time.

I never, ever, conceived of a man as having virginity. Because there was no definition of 'this is sex'. I remember it as a process more than one point in time when you could say, OK, yes, I've done that. We did all kinds of things which fell short of full intercourse and I wouldn't know at what time it actually passed from one to the other. People were far, far freer to set up a regime that went just so far and no further, than they are today. I think virginity is more about naïveté. There's a certain point that you're no longer innocent, and we lost innocence very early on, at boarding school. So it did happen, but not with any sort of medievalism about it, no red sheets and all that sort of thing.

We went out for a couple of years and then my family moved to Cornwall. My parents were keen on splitting from Sheffield and putting everything into this new life and so we saw each other once in Oxford and then Suzie went abroad. You know, it was ultimately my responsibility, but they did break it up, my parents, by not supporting us. We drifted apart and she got married very soon afterwards and so did I.

There's no doubt at all that if you have a very satisfactory first full sexual experience with somebody and you allow that to drift off and then go off with other people, they've not got a cat in hell's chance. It just doesn't work. Unless by miraculous coincidence it's even better than the first one. But I think that's asking too much. No, it was disastrous. There's the awful, awful realisation that actually, that is quite rare.

Suzie. Born 1945. Lost virginity aged approximately fourteen

I think I was encouraged to grow up. I remember my father, when I was twelve years old, looking at me and saying, 'You look awfully dull. Go and buy yourself a lipstick! Put some make-up on. You really ought to make an effort.' And that was at twelve. I was definitely encouraged to make myself look more attractive.

I was born ten days before the end of the war, so I'm officially a war baby. I can remember rationing being over because Mother was so thrilled that you could suddenly get golden syrup again, and of course you were not given articles to play with and toys the way children are today.

The first thing I can remember – how old would I have been? Perhaps seven years old – was getting a scratch on my very undeserved breast and being so depressed in case anybody saw it. That's a huge, I suppose you'd say, sexual awareness because I fancied the boy next door, we used to go climbing trees together, and I fantasised that he would have seen this scratch. Which is rather a strange thing to remember, but it must have been so vivid because that's the first real sexual awareness that I ever recalled.

I was very interested in sex myself, presumably because I didn't have anybody who'd made me feel self-conscious, my parents certainly didn't. My parents were not disciplinarians at all. They allowed you to develop in your own way. But although they were very open-minded, they didn't tell me anything about sex. Not a whisker. Things were only ever implied, as in, if you're going get up to any mischief, you be careful what you're doing. I think it would have been difficult to stop, in my instance. Not because of the boys, but because of the way I felt. You know, I actually wanted physical contact with them, and I found it.

I met Peter when I was fourteen and three months. My sister had asked me to fill in the numbers for a theatre party. So off I went and walked into this private house. I was very shy.

Extremely shy, but you wouldn't have known it because I had a sort of bravado. Peter was in the kitchen; I can see him now, this little thing by the Aga. A very good-looking boy, Peter was. And still is, in my opinion, so there! And he came over to me like a bee to a honeypot and then we went to the theatre, he sat down next to me and took my hand and started tickling my palm. We were drawn to each other very immediately and very sexually. The following evening he arranged to meet me again, I can't remember where, but we stopped in the lanes and that was where Peter and I had a good old tussle in the undergrowth and that was very nice!

I think we saw each other as frequently as we could in those days and it became the chauffeur's job to take me over in the car, sitting in the back, he in the front with his cap on, to Peter's house to drop me off. Peter lived in a three-storey house with a room at the top; I suppose it was called a den in those days. We would be left alone all afternoon to explore and the chauffeur would arrive at the appointed time to pick me up again and take me home.

Peter is absolutely right when he says that there was no defining moment of virginity loss. I remember the house painter – and I would be sitting on Peter's knee and he'd be actually inside me, because you had big voluminous skirts covering everything up – coming to the window and sort of smiling at me. But I absolutely can't pinpoint one moment. Peter would say, 'Oh well, let's just try inside a little,' so it was actually going inside the vagina but certainly no ejaculation or anything. You had to be terribly careful. Lots of little handkerchiefs that could probably have stood up on their own all over the room. It was very funny.

I was lucky because Peter is extremely bright. It wasn't as if I was being bonked by some local yokel who didn't know anything about sex. Peter had gone off to his textbooks to discover the anatomy of a woman, so he knew where all the bits were. We were extremely careful. Otherwise we would really have had a problem because he was going off to university and his parents then decided that they were going to sell the family business and move to Cornwall. It was awful. I was sixteen by this point and we'd been together two years, but his mother was determined to get away from the area and he just said, 'Oh, we're going to Cornwall, it's going to be lovely.' I didn't say a thing. I just said, 'Yes, that's lovely,' and nearly died inside. I never told him. Mmm.

Peter actually says now that if I had expressed the way I felt, he would have reacted differently. But I didn't. I can tell you exactly why; because I was so traumatised by boarding school that I had got into a frame of mind of thinking that I had to tolerate everything. I had this artificial armour of coping. So when he said he was going, I just told myself that this was another thing I'd got to put up with.

So off he went. But we still wrote to each other and I was pretty bloody-minded. I can remember him writing and saying, 'You must come to Cornwall in the summer,' and me writing back and saying, 'No, it's the same distance for you to come to Yorkshire if you want to see me.' I was blowed if I was going to trot after him. I wanted to be padded after and chased by men, because you didn't chase after people in those days.

The last time I heard from Peter was just after I had my first car and his letter came through the post. My sister came running and said, 'Oh, Peter's written to you, Peter's written to you!' and I opened it up and it was to say he was getting married. I nearly died. I had to swallow that one. And that was the last time I heard from him until he rang 32 years later.

He always knew where I was. He had a cousin in the area and he would ask the cousin how I was, and she would always say I was very happily married. Which in a way I was, you know? So he stayed away. But he'd always promised himself that when he was 50 he would get in touch with me come hell or high water. So he went to stay with his daughter in the South of France and went on a diet – although he's never admitted it – and got himself all bronzed up and then he rang.

The odd thing was, he rang and he said, 'Oh, hello, this is …' you know, giving his name. And I said, 'Do you know, I haven't spoken to you for 32 years?' That was absolutely off the cuff. I'd never even thought about how many years it was but it was true, it was 32 years. So subconsciously, somewhere, it was on my mind.

When I went to the station to pick him up, the first thing he said was, 'You haven't changed much,' which I have, so that's a lie! We went back to my home and we sat very staidly in the kitchen and I cooked an omelette and talked in a very stodgy sort of way. Literally, you know. And then he said, 'Well, I've got to get the train.' He was actually going to some conference. 'OK,' I said, 'I'll run you up to the station. I'll just go into the loo and I'll be out in a minute.'

He was in the hallway when I came out and I looked across and I suddenly saw the person from years ago. I literally said, 'Oh, Peter.' And I ran across to him and we were completely back to square one. It was very weird. We got in the car and I have never driven up a motorway at 40 miles an hour before. I was emotionally blasted, as was he. We sat in the car, hand in *hand all the way to the station. Anyway, he was back again the next day and now we are married.*

I do believe that your first experiences are very influential, but it could be badly influential, couldn't it? Actually it could scar you, as opposed to enhance your life or your ideas about men, or women, or sex. So I was just very lucky, but we were also extremely compatible and sex was an incredible experience. Absolutely extraordinary. Yes.

Acknowledgements

I was being serious when I said I never meant to write a book. But the second I had the idea for this one, I knew that my life was going to change in the most delightful ways possible. It has taken me on a fabulous adventure and I have loved every bit of it.

First and foremost, it would not have been possible to write this book without the input and generosity of the many people who allowed me into their sitting rooms, their kitchens and ultimately, the most personal parts of their lives. My heartfelt gratitude goes to you for sharing your stories with me. Ditto the readers of my blog, The Virginity Project. Opening this project out to the digital realm allowed me to connect with groups of people who were hard to reach on 'ground level', particularly young people. Thank you for having the balls to compose and email your stories – many of them so beautifully written – to a total stranger. All of you inspired me to return the favour and include my own story in this book.

In a moment of serendipity, as I began this project, two women were writing histories of virginity loss. My copies of these books are now so dog-eared and marked with pencil as to be almost unreadable. Thank you Anke Bernau and Hanne Blank, and thank you also to Laura M. Carpenter for your book *Virginity Lost: An Intimate Portrait of First Sexual Experiences*. You all helped me to give this project some much-needed context.

Very special thanks are reserved for everyone at Icon Books – Simon Flynn, Najma Finlay, Andrew Furlow,

Duncan Heath and Sarah Higgins, and my agent Diane Banks – you are all an utter delight to work with. Getting a deal on this book took a surprisingly long time but you were worth the wait. Thank you for helping to give this project life. I can't wait to see what happens next. I also want to thank Patrick Walsh for helping me out in the beginning.

Last but not least, a huge debt of gratitude goes out to my beloved family, particularly my parents, Meg and Gareth Lewis and my friends, all of whom have cheered me along the sidelines. I also can't forget the Twickenham connection: Martin Dunkerton – thank you, dear M, Lena Corner and Suzy Lucas, also Richard M. for your guidance, Teresa Stokes and Cliff Jones for enthusiasm and numerous helpful articles torn out of newspapers, Edward S. for company during long hours of writing and editing, Yvonne and her team of charming staff at Karmarama Café and everyone at RKCR Y&R who showed an interest in this project and unwittingly gave me hope on the days when things weren't going to plan. I couldn't have done it without you!

Resources

Further reading and inspiration

Jenna Bailey, *Can Any Mother Help Me?* (Faber & Faber, 2007)

Anke Bernau, *Virgins: A Cultural History* (Granta Books, 2007)

Hanne Blank, *Virgin: The Untouched History* (Bloomsbury, 2007)

Laura M. Carpenter, *Virginity Lost: An Intimate Portrait of First Sexual Experiences* (New York University Books, 2005)

Cate Haste, *Rules of Desire: Sex in Britain, World War 1 To The Present* (Vintage, 2002)

Ariel Levy, *Female Chauvinist Pigs: Women and the Rise of Raunch Culture* (Free Press, 2005)

Marian Salzman, Ira Matathia and Ann O'Reilly, *The Future of Men* (Palgrave Macmillan, 2005)

Jessica Valenti, *The Purity Myth: How America's Obsession with Virginity is Hurting Young Women* (Seal Press, 2009)

Men Speak The Unspeakable
www.menspeaktheunspeakable.com

Practical help

Alex Comfort and Susan Quilliam, *The Joy of Sex* (first published 1972, updated edition Mitchell Beazley, 2008)

Paul Joannides, *The Guide to Getting It On* (Goofy Foot Press, 2009)

Miriam Kaufman, Cory Silverberg and Fran Odette, *The Ultimate Guide to Sex and Disability* (Cleis Press, 2004)

College of Sexual and Relationship Therapists
   www.cosrt.org.uk
   COSRT provides information and advice on finding a
   local counsellor
Em and Lo: Sex. Love. And Everything In Between.
   www.EMandLO.com
The Men's Initiation Programme
   www.sexandrelationshipcoaching.com
   A unique programme for men with little or no
   experience of relationships, sex or intimacy
Shakti Tantra
   www.shaktitantra.co.uk
   Practical, supportive Tantric training for women and
   men in mixed and single-sex groups
London Lesbian and Gay Switchboard
   www.llgs.org.uk
The Outsiders
   www.outsiders.org.uk
   Britain's leading self-help group for people with physical
   and social disabilities
Vaginismus Awareness Network
   www.vaginismus-awareness-network.org
Asexuality Visibility and Education Network (AVEN)
   www.asexuality.org
Sexperience
   http://sexperienceuk.channel4.com/
   Good, practical source of information for teenagers and
   adults alike
Teenage Relationship Abuse
   http://thisisabuse.direct.gov.uk/

ADAM
THE GARDENER

Planning Your Garden

This edition first published in 1995 by
Sunburst Books, an imprint of the Promotional Reprint Company Limited,
Deacon House, 65 Old Church Street,
London, SW3 5BS.

ISBN 1 85778 105 8

Printed and bound in Finland

Planning Your Garden

SUNBURST BOOKS

CONTENTS

IMPORTANT POINTS IN PLANNING A NEW GARDEN

Planning a new garden is great fun. But, like planning a house, it needs a great deal of careful thought and weighing up quite a lot of factors. The first set of factors that affect your planning initially are these:

1. THE CLIMATE OF THE LOCALITY. This alone is many-sided. In the colder areas, such as Norfolk, the North Midlands and much of Scotland, plants must be a good deal hardier than they need to be in the mild south-west or on the coast of Ayrshire. Likewise, moisture-loving plants, such as rhododendrons and hydrangeas, do better in the wet counties of the west coast than on the dry eastern seaboard. Areas of strong wind impose special restrictions and needs, such as shelter-belts, and the seaside has its own problem of winds that are salt-laden.

2. THE NATURE OF THE SOIL. Your designing and plantings will be keenly affected by whether your soil is a dry, light, sandy one, or a chalky one, or a wet, heavy clay one. It will also be much influenced by the soil's acidity. In an acid soil (i.e. one deficient in lime) you can grow a wide range of lime-hating plants, such as rhododendrons and heathers. On alkaline soils you will grow better carnations, irises, clematis and vegetables (except potatoes). Have your soil tested for acidity or do it yourself.

3. ASPECT. This refers to the points of the compass. It is very important indeed to note the approximate compass aspect of all the main parts of the garden, especially the walls. Reserve any wall or fence that faces south for choicer plants of doubtful hardiness or for other plants that need a maximum of sun, such as tomatoes. The north wall or bed, in constant shade for most of the year, is one of the worst features of our small gardens, but there are many fine plants that flourish in this aspect.

4. SITUATION. By this is meant whether you are on a hillside, in a valley bottom, in the middle of an industrial town, and so on, and whether on the flat or on a slope. Valleys do trap the sun, but they also trap winter frosts, and are perilous to fruit. The smoke-laden air of industrial towns is very damaging to conifers and other evergreens, and also to biennials, such as wallflowers and sweet williams. A flat garden has the danger of monotony, whereas a slope offers delightful possibilities in design, though it may also be costly.

5. AVAILABLE SPACE. In small places one must SELECT carefully and thoughtfully. Don't try to cram in too much.

6. THE LABOUR PROBLEM. Never take on more than you can cope with reasonably well, with or without whatever hired help you can afford. Only too often there are cases where the owner finds he has not the time (or perhaps the physical strength) to keep up with his first enthusiastic ideas. In this connection, remember there is nothing that takes up more hours than the lawn.

7. THE MONEY PROBLEM. Alas, only too familiar to most of us! However, don't be put off a good plan because you can't afford it NOW. The golden rule is to take the LONG VIEW, making up your mind what you want to see in the years ahead. Have that firm, then work to your final plan by stages. Nothing is worse in design than casual, unrelated, piecemeal features.

The Plan

Having weighed up all these factors, get out a measuring tape or rule and draw a scale plan of your plot on squared paper. Don't trust to pacing and don't make the scale too small – not less than one square per foot. Mark in the points of the compass. If it is an existing garden, plot in the positions of all trees and shrubs that you want to keep, together with the areas of their spread of foliage, and all paths and other permanent or semi-permanent features. If it is not an existing garden, don't site the trees yet.

Next – and here is the first positive step – decide upon the 'general disposition of the garden'. This means its rough apportionment into vegetable plot, fruit garden, rock garden, and whatever else you set your heart upon – always remembering the long view of things. The very first localities to be apportioned are those for the compost heap, bonfire, greenhouse, frames, potting shed and chicken run, if any. These may be considered by many as of minor importance, but many a garden design has been ruined by forgetting about them until too late.

In locating the vegetable and fruit gardens, bear in mind that, with few exceptions, they should have full sun or nearly so. If possible, plan for vegetable rows to run north and south and keep fruit and vegetables separate.

Having done the general apportionment, decide now on the general style – whether formal in straight lines or informal and 'natural'. In small places the formal style is safest and easiest if not always the most pleasing. The main difficulty as a rule is to get any 'vista' or any impression of distance, but it is not always necessary to put the kitchen garden at the end of the plot, and in broad gardens or plots of irregular shape the vegetables can often go at the side. Avoidance of straight lines is also a help in creating the idea of space.

The next practical step is to decide where your main or essential paths are to go. Have as few as possible, not too narrow, well made and preferably going straight from A to B. No wiggles. Don't make the common mistake of running a path where your sunniest border ought to be – for very obvious reasons!

Now we can get down to something more exciting – the planning of the pleasure garden. Here the first things to get in are the trees and shrubs. They are permanencies and are dominant features, giving background and atmosphere to the whole scene. Stick to trees that are in proportion to the size of the garden when they are full grown. Site both shrubs and trees for these purposes – to give shade where wanted, to give privacy as necessary, to hide some eyesore near or distant, or as purely decorative features at carefully chosen spots.

After trees and shrubs comes the lawn – another dominant feature – and wonderfully effective for giving a sense of restfulness in our gardens.

All else that remains in planning is simply a question of what features you elect to have. You may be a fan of the specialists' flowers, such as delphiniums, dahlias or chrysanthemums, in which case you will concentrate on their special needs. But in general the following few rules will be found of great value in getting a happy result.

1. Plan the general lines of the garden from where most people see it most often – usually the window of the sitting-room.

2. Stick to simplicity, with clean lines and open views. No fussiness. No whimsies.

3. In all flower features, apply mass effect. Don't dot your roses, delphiniums, etc, about indiscriminately. If you have only three phloxes, put them all together.

4. Try to create some element of surprise, so that, walking round a bend or corner, the visitor comes upon some unexpected pleasure.

9

5. Make allowance in whatever way you think fit for the children.

6. The skyline is most important. Consider this especially in your choice of trees and include one or more of columnar shape.

7. Herbaceous borders should be aligned so that, from the house or chief vantage point, you look down along their length, not full in the face. Make them as broad as possible.

8. Give thought to special needs. Roses must have an open position, not closely shut in by fences nor overhung by trees. Rock gardens are best avoided unless they look entirely natural. They need, as a rule, a fairly sunny position.

HERE ARE SOME IDEAS FOR YOUR FRONT GARDEN

This design for a front garden shows the path from the front gate, passing around a squared sunken lawn with bird-bath in the centre, to the porch, before which there is a pergola. A lawn surrounds the path. To the left of this is the path to the side door, with a flower-bed bordering it.

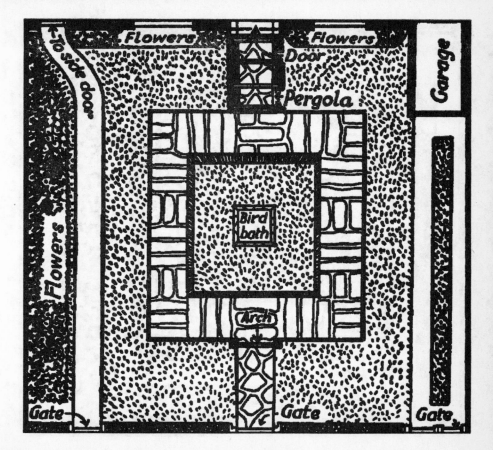

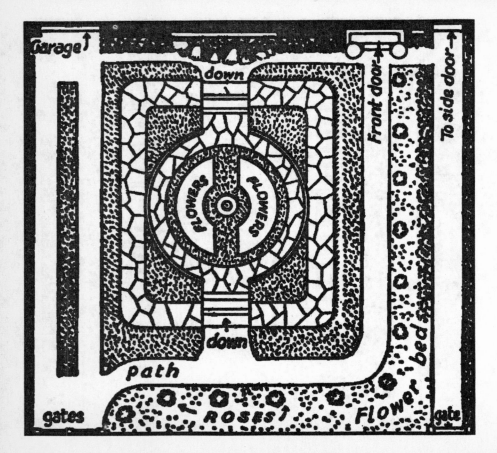

On the right of the path from the gates to the front door rose trees stand along the edge of a flower-bed. On the left of the path a narrow strip of lawn surrounds a path with steps on two sides leading down to a small sunken flower garden, with a central bird-bath. A grass strip breaks up the runway to the garage to good effect.

Here the curved path to the front door is flanked by a narrow flower border which continues in front of the windows and along the left side of the garden. A shaped flower-bed stands in each half of the lawn. On the one near the window a bird-bath stands on a similarly shaped paving, a small path joining it to a strip of the lawn.

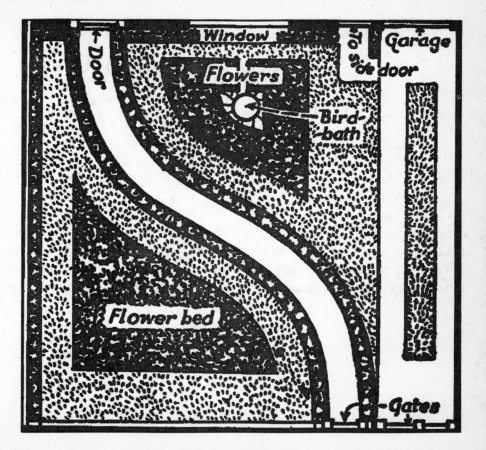

IDEA FOR AN 'ALL-IN' BACK GARDEN

Box trees in tubs on a paved terrace stand at the head of steps leading down to a path skirting the lawn, with two rockeries on the left. Beyond the lawn are steps leading to a paved sunk garden, with seat and pool, around which are laid out the vegetable and fruit plots. Tool-shed, herb garden, etc, are placed behind a trellis across the end of vegetable, fruit and sunk gardens.

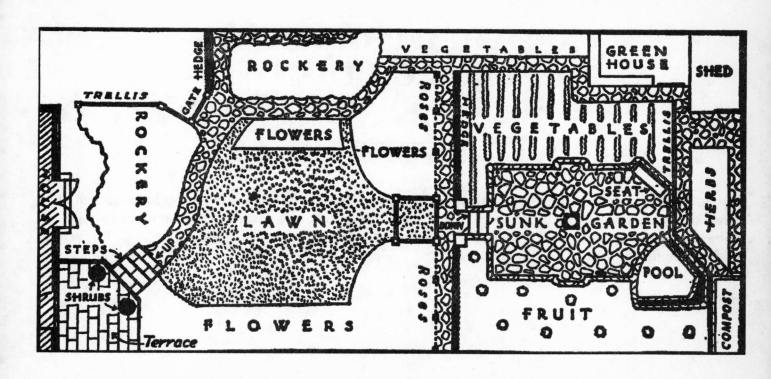

15

ANOTHER PRACTICAL
BACK GARDEN

Beyond the crazy-paved terrace, steps lead down to paths skirting the horse-shoe shaped lawn, in the centre of which stands a pool or ornament. The pathway continues under an arch in the hedge, which cuts off the view of the vegetable garden, to the greenhouse, shed and compost heap. Fruit is planted on either side of the vegetable plots. Each part is reached by paths.

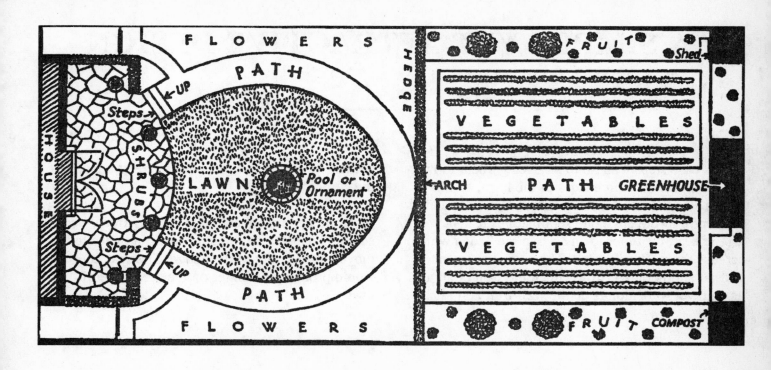

A SIMPLE YET ATTRACTIVE DESIGN

In this case steps lead up to a raised garden. Flower-beds are made on three sides of the lawn, across which stepping stones are placed. From a sundial in the centre of the lawn one set of stones leads to an arbour seat, the other to an arch in the hedge which screens the kitchen garden. The crazy pavement ends at another arch, from which the path continues as a gravel walk alongside the wall fruit and kitchen garden. Toolshed and greenhouse are at the end of the garden.

It should be remembered that if this garden faced a southern aspect, the tomato bed would have to be moved to the front of the hedge. The seat, too, would probably be better on the other side of the lawn.

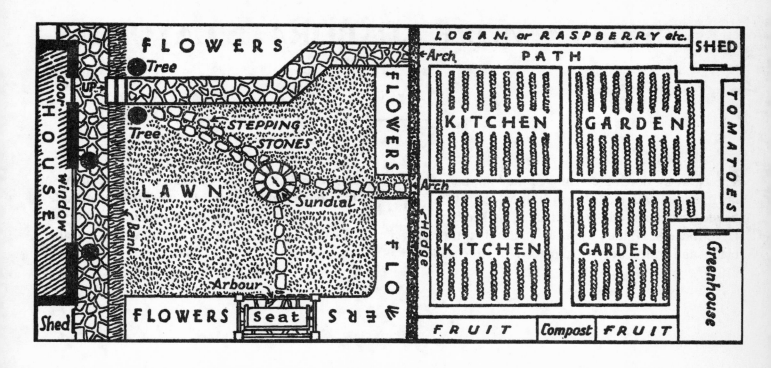

19

THIS IS A MORE ELABORATE LAYOUT

The pathway down the centre of the long narrow lawn, edged with standard rose trees, leads to a paved garden and lily-pool. This is backed by a large rockery. Hidden by roses on a trellis, the vegetable and fruit gardens are placed on either side of the lawn and are reached by gates. The greenhouse, at the house end of the garden, hides the vegetables on one side, while on the opposite side the toolshed serves the same purpose and is shot off by a trellis.

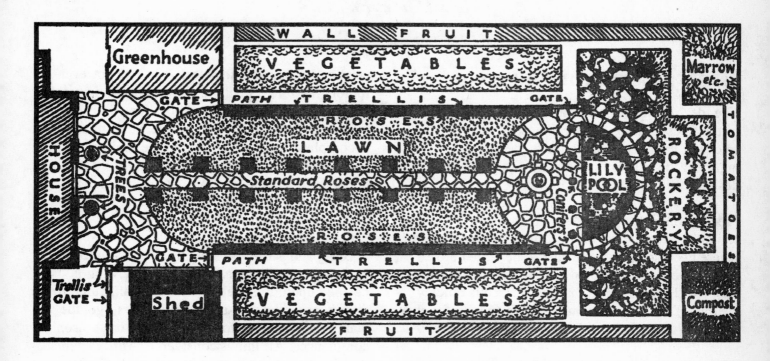

WALL FRUIT

VEGETABLES

Greenhouse

Marrow etc.

GATE — PATH — TRELLIS — GATE

ROSES

HOUSE

LAWN

LILY POOL

ROCKERY

TREES

Standard Roses

Conifers

TOMATOES

ROSES

GATE — PATH — TRELLIS — GATE

Trellis GATE

Shed

VEGETABLES

Compost

FRUIT

21

THE LAWN

Hints on making a Lawn

The ideal lawn consists of a dense compact growth of the finest grasses. This can best be obtained by selecting varieties suitable for the locality, and giving them the cultivation necessary to produce the desired result.

Preparation of the ground – Turf of the best quality can only be produced on well-drained ground, and, where necessary, draining should be done before anything else is attempted. The system of draining adopted should be such that the surface is quickly cleared of rain, and does not remain spongy for any length of time afterwards.

When the draining is completed, the ground should be deeply dug, taking care to retain the best soil on the top. Allow the ground to settle down before proceeding further with the work, because however thoroughly it is rolled, the soil settlement is not so complete as when the ground is allowed to solidify by the action of the elements. After the subsidence is complete, level the ground to the desired surface, and if the soil is of a rough or stony nature it should be sifted to a depth of about 3 or 4 inches. These early cultural details exert a considerable influence on the future lawn.

Seeding and Turfing – Seeding may be done either in spring or in autumn. If the spring sowing is decided upon, it is well to wait until all danger from frost is past, and yet sufficiently early to get the plants established before the summer dry season commences. All things considered, April is generally the best month for sowing in spring. If autumn sowing is preferred, the earliest possible period after the last week in August, when rains have moistened the ground, should be the most suitable time.

The selection of a seed mixture is important. Soils vary from district to district, and a haphazard choice of seed may lead to disappointing results. The advice of a seedsman should be obtained as to the best blend of grass for soil in the locality; he will also estimate the amount of seed required for any size of lawn, thus avoiding waste and uncertainty.

The site should be levelled and rolled. When the soil is dry, firm by close-treading and heeling down the soft spots (Inset A). Then rake to level out any small depressions.

Most sites for lawns benefit from an application of good fertiliser before sowing seed; this will ensure that newly formed roots are well nourished and will produce vigorous healthy grass.
Rake in a fertiliser such as Growmore at about 3 or 4 oz per square yard. Leave for a week before sowing seed at 2 oz to a square yard.

Where it is decided to use turf, the best way is to cut the turf into 1 foot squares, and prepare these to an even thickness by laying them in shallow trays about 1½ inches deep. These trays need to be made so that the turf can slide in and out, but otherwise fit each square, so that there is no room for movement. Then with a sharp two-handled knife cut the underside to the gauged thickness. Treat the soil as advised for seeding, and roll or tread it to a firm solidity. The turves should be laid as soon as possible after delivery. Starting from one side, lay the turf in brick fashion (Inset B).

Then roll the plot once down and once across. Finally using a birch broom, brush in some fine soil to fill in any gaps.

Maintaining Your Lawn

March is a good time to give the lawn a spring clean.

Clear weeds and debris with a wire rake and then roll the grass to flatten any areas lifted by frost. For the first cut of the season, raise the blades of the mower so the grass is just topped. A more severe cut could well lead to unsightly yellowing of the lawn.

Next, tidy the area by going around the edges with a half moon-bladed trimmer. Trimmings can be used to repair any edge damage.

Repair worn patches by loosening the soil and sowing seed. Water well and cover with a criss-cross of cotton or twine to keep birds at bay.

Brush away any worm casts and dress with lawn sand. Make sure you collect the cuttings.

Finally, give the lawn a spring tonic by feeding with a fertiliser high in nitrogen and potash.

THE ROCK GARDEN

A rock garden can give great beauty in a limited space, and can provide an excellent backdrop for many unusual and colourful plants. However this type of gardening is one that the beginner should approach warily. The genuine rock garden should as far as possible look like a slice of natural outcrop. Such outcrops do not normally appear along a sub-urban fence or against a brick wall. The site, there-fore, should be a sunny position away from high walls and large trees. Ideally, the area will face south and will enjoy dappled sunlight filtering through trees nearby. Try to site it so that you can view it from the house for the utmost enjoyment. In nature, rocks normally lie in some sort of pattern, not higgledy-piggledy. The graining of the stones all runs the same way, and each course of stones usual-ly lies in the same plane (though not necessarily horizontal).

In addition to all these factors, genuine rock is very expensive. The beginner, therefore, will do well to study practical examples of good work in the field of rock gardening.

However, we can quite easily enjoy the charms of many rock plants without this ideal kind of rock garden. We do so by FORMALISING it – building dry walls or little stone edgings or revetments of flower borders, or laying down pavements. In such cases we do not pretend to be simulating nature, nor use natural rock. We use CUT stone, usually in flat slabs. In such ways there is a wide variety of charm-ing alpine and rock plants that can be grown, from the queenly gentian to the cottager's humble alyssum and aubretia.

If you choose to build a 'real' rock garden, the site should be well dug and if it is on heavy soil, drained.

The mound should ideally comprise of one part each of moss peat and loam, together with two parts of gravel chippings.

Once this has been laid, leave for a week or so to settle then add a one inch deep top dressing of down chippings. This will help to retain moisture and protect the plants from rotting.

The amount of stone – a local one is best – you will require depends on the size of the plot: for an area of, say, 8 ft x 20 ft about 1½ tons should be ample. The stones should be set into the soil bed in a natural 'lie' (Inset A).

Allow to settle, then check that the top dressing of chippings has not become disturbed. Where soil has become uncovered, sprinkle chippings to make good. Plants must be carefully inserted in the planting spots (Inset B).

Rock plants should be set in their positions firmly. Care should be taken to see that there is no hollow space beneath the roots, which would make it difficult for the plant to establish itself.

Remember that the way of life of a rock plant is to get its roots UNDERNEATH the rock, for coolness and moisture. A few are shade lovers, but most require a good deal of sun. The majority also require a rather poor soil, with plenty of grit but also with a moisture-holding element, such as peat or leaf-mould. A good nurseryman will advise you about any special cases.

Many rock plants are extremely difficult to grow, requiring special conditions, such as a moraine or a scree. Some hate lime. So make careful enquiries. The following is a good safe list for beginners: aubretia, alyssum saxatile, dwarf campanulas, dwarf pinks, true geraniums (especially Geranium sanguineum lancastriense), Lithospermum Grace Ward or Heavenly Blue (if no lime in the soil), dwarf phlox, the dwarf knotweed called Polygonum vaccinifolium, soapwort (Saponaria ocymoides), some of the saxifrages, especially the 'mossy saxes' and London Pride, auriculas, stonecrops (Sedum), creeping thyme (especially for pavements), dwarf yarrows (Achillea), candytuft, sandwort (Arenaria). There are also many charming dwarf bulbs that are entirely suitable. Avoid invasive plants, such as arabis, which soon smother everything.

BRIGHTENING THAT SHADY CORNER OF THE GARDEN

In almost every garden there is a bed or corner against the north wall of the house or heavily shaded by trees that is more or less given up as hopeless. "Nothing will grow there," the owner so often observes. But this is not true. Even the most densely shaded patch can be made attractive by turning it into a fernery. The varying shades of green and other colours in autumn and the delicate tracery of the leaves of the many varieties suitable for such a situation will be a vast improvement on the usual neglected appearance of most sites of this nature. But first of all the site must be improved. Usually it is too wet and heavy for most of the year. If this is so, dig in plenty of strawy manure, compost, leaf-mould, peat, and sand – in fact, anything that will help to lighten the soil, help it to dry and become more friable. Don't, however, include lime in this process as its inclusion would tend to limit the choice of suitable plants.

If the ground is so wet that this improvement would not be sufficient to achieve the desired result, then there is no alternative but to drain the area properly, putting in a complete system of land drains.

This major operation is not necessary in the majority of cases, although one cannot, of course, give any hard and fast rule.

Dig the area two spits deep, so as to break up the sub-soil, as this effects a great improvement in drainage.

Carry out this improvement plan even if the spot is

so cold and wet that you intend to make it a fernery. Select your ferns carefully as not all ferns need such a situation. Moreover, there are a number of other plants that will do reasonably well with the ferns. The Saxifrages, for example, usually will, particularly those in the sections called Robertsonia (which includes London Pride) and Miscopetalum. All the members of the Loosestrife family normally cultivated here are also accommodating in this way. The yellow one called Creeping Jenny can also be cultivated in pots or baskets.

These, suspended from wall brackets or perhaps tree branches, will do much to lift such a corner out of its usual depressing rut. The Periwinkle is also very useful as ground cover, particularly beneath trees, and so too is Cerastium, whose silvery foliage is no doubt responsible for its more popular name, Snow in Summer.

For situations which are not so densely shaded as to justify being treated as a fernery there is a much wider choice of subject for the ground area itself, but first it is often necessary to decide what to grow to cover a north wall at the back of the bed.
It is not necessary to confine your choice to evergreens, as many people believe, but if you do want these, then try Garrya Elliptica, whose long green catkins are difficult to surpass for winter beauty, particularly if accompanied by Winter Jasmine whose yellow flowers appear almost at the same time. Ivy does not arouse much enthusiasm in many people but if you try Hedera colchica dentata aurea variegata (what a mouthful!) you'll probably be delighted with its green foliage mottled and streaked with gold. Then one must not forget our old friends, Cotoneaster and Pyracantha, whose berries are so attractive in autumn. For this situation, order P. watereri or C. salicifolia floccosa.

Roses may seem a surprising suggestion for clothing a north wall, but there are in fact a number of varieties that do well here. They are Climbers, and in recent years several new ones have been introduced which are a great improvement on most of the older ones, although such varieties as Climbing Caroline

Testout and Gloire de Dijon are still well in the picture. Any rose specialist will suggest varieties suitable for this purpose.

Let us now turn to the general question of finding the right subjects for making our shady bed as colourful as possible for as much of the year as we can.

In winter we have to rely on the shrubs for pleasing effects of foliage, flowers or fruit either from those clothing a wall or from bushes in the bed itself.

Then, in spring, we can usually achieve a fine show of flowers from bulbs planted the previous autumn.

I have found that nearly all the popular bulbs flower quite well in a bed with a north aspect, provided that each bulb is planted on a good handful of sand to ensure that it does not rot before starting to grow. The chances of failure are sufficiently small to justify the risk. If you find that in your garden a particular bulb will not produce the desired result, then of course omit it from your plan the next year.

In these difficult corners one must allow for a certain amount of trial and error, as conditions vary so much. In spring, too, we can rely on a good show of bloom from plants such as Doronicum (probably the earliest one to bloom), Primroses, and Polyanthus. Like Pansies, Violas, Violets, and Lily-of-the-Valley, these can be used at the front of the bed. Taller subjects include Christmas Rose, Trollius (Globe Flower), the Plantain Lily (usually catalogued nowadays as Hosta and mainly grown for its decorative foliage).

For the back of the bed you should include Foxgloves (some of the modern varieties are really splendid), Evening Primrose (whose yellow, pink or mauve flowers – some of them fragrant – do not open until late afternoon), Campanulas, two varieties in particular, C. persica, also know as Giant Harebell, and C. glomerata, also called Clustered Bellflower, Japanese Anemones, Daylilies and perennial Phlox, the white one for preference.

These suggestions do not by any means exhaust the choice and by questioning other gardeners you may well find several others.

Quite a number of flowers can be grown from seed sown in a shady spot provided you have worked the soil into a suitably fine tilth. One rapidly growing annual, Tropaeolum Canariense, or more popularly, Canary Creeper, can be raised in this way and is very suitable for a special feature in the bed. If given a special support this plant will cover it in quite a short time and in due course will be a mass of yellow flowers. Sow seed ¼ inch deep in April where it is to grow – a rule applicable to the other subjects in this section.

If you wish to achieve a similar effect with a flower of another colour sow Convolvulus, blue, pink or red.

HOW TO REPAIR THOSE BROKEN FENCES

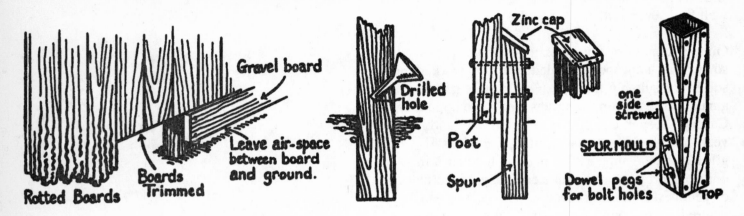

Gravel board

Leave air-space between board and ground.

Rotted Boards

Boards Trimmed

Drilled hole

Zinc cap

Post

Spur

SPUR MOULD

one side screwed

Dowel pegs for bolt holes

TOP

Garden fences are, perhaps, the most commonly neglected items the average gardener has to tackle. Too often we have to cure what we should have prevented. So act as soon as the first sign of deterioration is noticed. This not only saves work, but, what is perhaps more important nowadays, it saves money.

The weakest part of a fence is where it meets the ground. The most common failing is rotting of the lower parts of the boards. This can be prevented by providing air-space between the ground and the bottom edge of the boards. Creosoting or coating with outdoor-quality wood preservative should be carried out at least every three years. But, of course, this is no use if the timbers have already started rotting. Such boards should be sawn off 3–6 inches above ground level, according to the degree of rot. The space is then filled with a horizontal gravel board of ¾ inch thickness. The width of the gravel board should allow a space of about 1 inch between the lower edge of the board and the ground. This board is secured to the fence posts with galvanised nails after coating it with a preservative, and it should be given a second coat after fixing.

Wooden fence posts rot most frequently at ground level too. Regular attention goes a long way to preventing this, provided you clear away the soil around the post as much as possible and flood the wood with creosote or other wood preservative. Nowadays, however, we have an even more effective method of preservation.

A wooden fence post will not rot if the inside of the timber is soaked with wood preservative once a year. To do this, drill a downward sloping hole about 2 inches above ground level. The hole should be large enough to take the spout of a funnel and should penetrate to the centre of the post. Insert the spout and pour preservative into the mouth of the funnel. Leave in position until the preservative has soaked away into the base of the post.

Afterwards plug the hole with a piece of wooden doweling or a cork, leaving sufficient length protruding so that the plug can easily be removed in subsequent years. Plugging not only prevents rain collecting in the hole, but also keeps it clean and ready for later use.

If the base of a fence post is too far gone to save it with preservative, it is still possible to make it good without replacing the post completely. This is done by fitting a spur. The spur can be of wood, using oak for preference, or it may be of concrete. A wooden spur should have a slanting top and this is best covered with zinc. Soak the spur in wood preservative before sinking it in the ground and bolting it to the old post.

Concrete spurs are quite easy to make. These are cast in a mould made of timber of at least ¾ inch thickness. One side of the mould should be screwed for easy removal of the spur. The girth of the spur should be the same as that of the fence post and the length should equal one half of the height of the post above ground. Provision should be made for two bolt holes by inserting lengths of dowel rod through holes drilled in the front and back of the mould.

A good mixture for the concrete is one part Portland cement, two parts sharp sand and three parts ½ inch shingle, mixed dry. Use the smallest amount of water to make the ingredients plastic, turn well and ram the mixture firmly into the mould. Push in an old metal rod as reinforcement, taking care to avoid the dowel pegs. Leave for three days before removing the cast. Keep the freshly made spur covered with wet sacks for at least seven days and store the spurs for as long as possible before use.

If it is found necessary to put up a new fence, careful consideration should be given to the various types available today. Many people automatically visualise a new fence of the same type as they had before and, if this is the close-boarded type, it does not get replaced because it is such an expensive item.

Where for privacy, wind protection, or some similar reason a close fence is required have a look at wattle fencing and interwoven fencing. Both types are almost as effective as close-boarding and yet less expensive. They are bought in ready-made sections of varying widths and heights to suit individual requirements. Erection is then just a matter of siting the posts at the appropriate points so that each post takes the edges of two sections of fencing.

This type of fencing is becoming very popular nowadays but the appearance of it is often spoilt by the use of angle-irons as supports. While they may be practical, they look out of place. Wooden uprights, even rustic poles, look much better.

HOME FOR THE BIRDS – A SIMPLE NESTING BOX

Base fits inside

Underside of lid

This easily constructed nesting box is intended for housing blue-tits or great-tits. It is for hanging from a post or tree, but can alternatively be made to fit on the top of a post. The box can be made from any odd pieces of wood, but it should be weather-tight. Overall dimensions of the nesting box are given in the drawing; these should not be altered to any great extent, those given providing a reasonable cubic capacity.

Cut the sides first and ensure that the lapping corners will fit closely to keep out draughts and wet.

It is advisable to use small-headed galvanised, aluminium or copper nails to fasten the parts together – these will not corrode. Iron nails may be used if the heads are sunk with a nail punch and the holes filled with plastic wood.

Note that the base fits inside the box, and is not nailed below the sides. This provides greater strength and makes the base weather-tight. The roof is hinged to the back of the box and is provided with a centre-piece which forms a rebated edge (as shown) that fits snugly inside the box. The lid is also fitted with a brass hook-catch, and a brass wall-plate is secured to the top and lower edges of the back.

The entry hole is cut with a brace and bit, or key-hole saw before the front is secured to the sides. The diameter of the hole should not exceed 1⅛ inch for tits and the edges should be rubbed smooth with glass paper. If the hole is larger sparrows will soon take up residence!

The finish may be a rustic one consisting of two coats of wood preservative in brown or green. Alternatively, the box may be painted in bright colours. Whatever the finish, the completed nesting box must be thoroughly aired before fixing it in position – and remember to fit it out of the reach of cats.

Having provided suitable free accommodation, it is, of course, essential that it is tenanted. A great help in achieving this is the provision of food to attract the birds. Tits will eat bread scattered on the lawn but it isn't really their line. (I hope I may be forgiven if I digress for a moment here to say that bread should not be thrown out to birds just as it is - soak it in water thoroughly first; this prevents the dry bread swelling inside the bird and giving it tummy-ache at least, if not actually causing its death). Tits love nuts and fat and it is, of course, more important to provide food in winter than at any other time. Having made a habit of feeding in a particular garden all the winter, the tits will naturally inspect and probably approve their new home when they start house-hunting in the spring.

Our design for the box purposely includes a hinged lid so that one can inspect nesting progress at intervals. This does not upset the occupants provided you do not open the box when the hen is known to be sitting on the clutch. Inspection before this period begins affords much interest but it is as well to know by careful observations that neither bird is in the box at the time of opening. If the hen, in particular, is disturbed in this way, the pair may desert the nest. When the breeding season is over, the box should be completely cleared of nesting material. If this is left in during the winter and it should get wet it may cause the wood to rot. Apart from that possibility, tits won't usually nest again on the top of the old material, although exceptions have been known. Having cleared the box, this is the time to give it another coat of preservative, if necessary.

AN ATTRACTIVE SUNDIAL OR BIRDBATH

All dimensions are inside measurements.

COLUMN

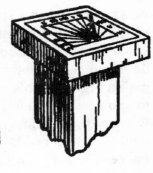

BASE — 15" square x 3" deep.
TOP (SUNDIAL) — 12" square x 2½" deep.
TOP (BIRDBATH) — 12" square x 3" deep.

This attractive garden feature is made of coloured concrete. The three parts – base, column and top – are cast in wooden moulds which are quite easy to make. Use timber of 1 inch thickness for all the moulds to prevent bulging when the concrete is packed in.

The dimensions of the three moulds are given in the drawings. Secure all corners with 2 inch screws, and check squareness of inside angles before use. The corners of the column may be decorated by nailing lengths of shaped moulding inside the corners of the mould, if desired.

Another variation in the design of the column which can easily be achieved by those who are a little more ambitious is to have a tapering column. For this you simply make the column mould wider at the bottom than it is at the top. If you decide to adopt this plan, it would be advisable to adhere to the present size at the base of the column, that is, six inches square, and to reduce the top to four inches square.

A further opportunity for individuality in design is in the base. Some people may like to have a stepped base – that is, another, smaller, concrete block between the base proper and the column. This extra base block could be made, later, in the mould to be used for the sundial top, if desired, although this would delay assembly for a time. If you don't want the delay then simply make another mould the same size.

When assembled, you would have a 12 inch block centrally placed on a 15 inch block, thus giving the base a 1½ inch 'step' all round.

From these two examples of changes in design it will be seen that it is quite a simple matter to adapt the standard design shown in the diagrams to meet individual tastes or perhaps to blend more happily with features already in readers' gardens.

The saucer-shaped depression in the square top is easily formed by burying an upturned kitchen bowl in sand, leaving 1½ inches protruding above the surface. The frame is then placed on the sand with the bowl in the centre and pegged in position. Smear the bowl thickly with limewash to prevent any concrete sticking.

Prepare the casting site before mixing concrete. It must be perfectly level and covered with a thin scattering of sand.

The mixture is two parts sharp clean sand with one part fresh waterproofed cement. Turn the heap at least three times, then pass through a sieve – it is essential that the dry ingredients are thoroughly mixed.

Mix the colouring powder (obtainable in green, red, blue, etc,) according to container directions, in a bucket, then strain into a watering can. Only the minimum amount of water to make the mass plastic should be used, as excess water will weaken the mixture. Sprinkle the water on in small quantities and turn the heap between each watering.

Half fill the base and top moulds, then lay a piece of wire netting over the surface as reinforcement. Shape the netting over the bowl for the birdbath top. Continue filling and level off. When the column mould has been filled push an old metal rod down the centre.

Leave the filled moulds covered with wetted sacks for at least four days. The screws can then be removed to release the casts from the moulds. Leave for at least another seven days, sprinkling frequently with water during this period.

The parts are cemented together with a mortar of one-part-sand/one-part-cement. Wet the joints thoroughly before applying mortar and keep completely covered with wet sacks for about seven days. To conceal any mould marks, paint, while wet, with a watery mixture of equal parts sand and cement. The sun dial is screwed to plugged holes drilled in top. The indicator – or gnomon as it is called – should be sited with the needle pointing due north at twelve o'clock. To be absolutely accurate, the gnomon should be set with the shadow of the needle falling on eleven o'clock (allowing for summertime) at noon on a mid-summer day.

Having made a feature of this kind, one usually has some sand and cement, not necessarily mixed up, left over. If you wish to use this up, make slabs in the mould used for the sundial top. A mix of three parts sand to one of cement is strong enough for this purpose. When thoroughly hardened, these slabs can be used for a variety of purposes, such as edging for a garden pool, as stepping stones for a path through a lawn or for building steps or terraces.

A ROSE-COVERED WAY THROUGH YOUR GARDEN

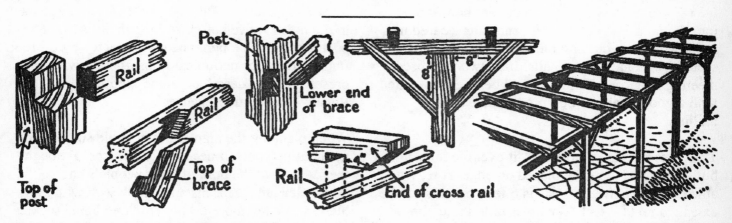

Construction of this pergola is well within the scope of the average gardener. It can be made any size to fit a particular path but there should be at least 7 feet clearance from path to underside of cross-rails.

The posts are 3 inches by 3 inches; the braces, rails and cross-rails are 3 inches by 1½ inches. Oak is the ideal material, but the cost is prohibitive; cheaper hardwood, or softwood of reasonable quality may be used. As the construction is braced, it is only necessary to sink the posts 2 feet into the ground. The post holes should be dug larger than required and the floor of the holes given a 3 inch layer of stones to provide drainage.

The best method of construction is to complete a side section before sinking the posts. Details of the joints are shown in the drawing. The tops of the posts are half-jointed to provide a recess in which the rails rest. The diagonal braces are half-jointed into the rails, and at the lower ends are secured in shallow notches cut into the posts. All parts are secured with galvanised nails. If softwood is used, meeting surfaces of joints should be liberally coated with a good-quality wood preservative before nailing.

The cross rails are notched to fit over the rails, and both these members are placed on edge. A reasonable distance between posts is 6 feet, but this can be extended up to 9 feet. The cross rails should be spaced about 18 inches apart.

The construction described here is a simple one for the not-so-expert constructor. Alternatively, if you have the skill and the tools, all the joints may be mortised and tenoned and then secured by draw dowels.

The finish need not be velvety smooth, in fact a slight roughness of surface will add to the character of the feature. The completed pergola is best protected by applying at least two coats of a good quality wood preserver. The post bases should be soaked in the preservative before sinking them. Also, the post bases may be permanently protected by drilling funnel holes, for periodical impregnation with preservative, as described in the section "How To Repair Those Broken Fences".

When planning the planting of suitable subjects, do not confine yourself necessarily to roses, although they will form the bulk of most people's choice. Some clematises, for instance, look well with ramblers, while the more deeply coloured honeysuckles are most effective. Most attractive, too, are the white plumes of Polygonum Baldschuanicum and the blue of that popular Ceanothus, Gloire de Versailles, as well as mauve or white Wisteria.

Roses would be more effective in most gardens if varieties had been selected according to a plan.

For example, both Climbers and Ramblers are suitable for pergolas but it does not do to mix them indiscriminately. Owing to the varying nature of their habit of growth, they aren't happy bed-fellows. By all means plant both types, but keep them in groups of their own kind. And remember that Climbers will do better if they are on the sunny side and preferably sheltered from cold winds.

When selecting varieties bear in mind not only colour, but also flowering time, so that, for example, you can plant a red and a white variety next to each other which bloom at the same time in order to contrast one against the other.

Any rose-grower's catalogue will give you a good selection of varieties but there are some which should not be missed.

Among Ramblers the old favourite, Dorothy Perkins, would still be difficult to beat. Its large clusters of shell-pink double blooms, however, appear late. The New Dawn is a variety of a more delicate pink with scented double blooms which flowers almost continuously during the season. But it does not grow very high.

For yellow, Emily Gray is perhaps the best. Its large blooms are excellently set off by its glossy, almost evergreen, foliage.

For a colour contrast in one bloom, American Pillar, another old friend, is an excellent choice. Its flowers are single, deep pink with a clear white centre and yellow anthers.

For Climbers consider Gloire de Dijon, which is very hardy, a strong grower, one of the earliest to flower and sweetly-scented. It has large double flowers of a golden-buff shade.

Pauls' Lemon Pillar is very good for pergolas, is early flowering and has large double blooms of a remarkably high standard.

Rose Care

March is the time for pruning roses, a job that frightens many who have not tackled it before. The aim is to 'open up' the plant to admit air and sunshine in order to promote new growth with larger, healthier blooms on more shapely bushes.

All you need is a pair of leather gloves and a pair of sharp secateurs. In the case of established hybrid tea roses, cut away weak, spindly growths and any old or dead wood. Then cut back last year's growth by about half cutting cleanly at an angle and about ¼ inch above an outward facing bud. Floribundas will require less severe pruning, but in both cases remove any growth crossing into the centre. Give the same treatment to standard roses and in all cases, ensure that when cutting out whole stems, the cut is clean and as close as possible to the branch (Inset A).

Newly planted hybrid tea roses should have had straggly side shoots removed before delivery. They will need to be cut back quite hard to about two or

three buds which will produce the new growth (Inset B on page 44).

March is also the time to start to guard against diseases, in particular black spot – by spraying with systemic fungicide.

This will show itself when sooty spots appear on the leaves and which, when severe, will cause early leaf fall – it may then be too late to effect a cure. Start treatment with a systemic garden fungicide.

June sees the advent of many of the problems which spoil your show of roses.

Fast on the scene are the aphids and capsid bugs – both of which cause buds, stems and leaves to become malformed. They can be effectively dealt with, as in the main illustration on page 46, by regular spraying with malathion.

Mildew is another early attacker, covering leaves and young shoots with a white powdery substance which will also distort young buds. Spray regularly with a fungicide.

Also chop off any suckers. Just scrape away the soil from the base (see Inset A on page 46) and with a sharp knife cut away the sucker at its point of origination.

To get the best out of your roses 'dead head' the spent flowers. Always cut with secateurs halfway down the stem at a point just above a leaf bearing five leaflets (see Inset B on page 46).

Hybrid teas have a habit of throwing additional buds. To ensure that the main rose develops fully, pinch out the additional buds with finger and thumb.

Late October is a good time to plant roses.

Dress the soil with bonemeal and add leafmould, peat or chopped turves to a spade's depth.
Dig a hole big enough for the roots to be spread, and deep enough to allow planting to the soil mark

on the stem.

Stand the roses in water for a few hours, trim straggly roots and plant against a stick laid across the hole to mark the correct depth.

To grow roses in containers, crock the bottom of a 9 inch pot, add a layer of peat and bonemeal and plant in John Innes No 2 compost. Firm the soil to within an inch of the top.

MAKING A POND

Have you ever thought of installing a pool in your garden?

There are several kinds from pre-formed contoured plastic, with ledges to take plants, to the basic hole covered with a flexible plastic sheeting.

To set about the easiest method – digging a hole and lining it with a flexible sheet – first select a fairly open site, to allow as much sunlight as possible for pool plants to thrive. Avoid trees, where leaves will fall and eventually foul the water, but choose a spot where it can be seen from the house so that you can enjoy it to the full.

Next, mark out an interesting design, kidney-shaped, for instance. Lift the turf for about 4–6 inches outside the marked area and then start digging out, first to a depth of 9 or 10 inches. This will make the first ledge to take plants. Leaving a ledge about

10 inches wide, dig out the centre.

Firm soil so as to provide a smooth base for the lining sheet. Use the heaviest gauge to ensure a longer trouble-free life for the pool.

To hold it in place put heavy stones around the edge (see Inset A on page 47). Fill it with water so that the liner takes the shape.

When it is full, turn back the surplus liner so that you have a surround of about 6-8 inches around which you can lay slabs (see Inset B on page 47) to anchor the liner.

To keep the water sweet you will need a balance between plant and animal life, and include plenty of oxygenating plants to ensure clear water.

Pond Plants

Where you are not introducing soil into the pond, you can place plants in perforated plastic pots which are filled with soil. The oxygenators will thrive in these, while smaller ones, such as Canadian pond weed (suitable for a depth of just over 2 feet) can be weighted with stones and dropped in.

Plants with larger root-stocks can be grown in plastic mesh baskets filled with soil and there are floating plants which will get their nutriment from that dissolving from other containers.

The end of April is a good time to plant, or replant, a pond.

If planting direct, the bottom of the pool should have a layer of about 6 inches of good soil.

But container growing in plastic laundry baskets, for instance, is more practical. They only need about 3 inches of soil – neutral or slightly alkaline, not peaty. For water-lilies add a handful of bonemeal to a bucket of soil.

Soak the containers. Let them stand for 10 minutes so all air is expelled. Plant water lily tubers at an angle of about 20° and add soil to firm around. Finish off with a layer of gravel.

To fill a pool, don't just turn the hose on – that disturbs soil. Lay a bucket on its side on the pool bed and direct the water into it.

Water-lilies can be grown even in the smallest garden. Several kinds of these charming aquatic plants are suitable for cultivation in tubs, barrels, tanks or even in an old cistern. The best effect is obtained when the tub, which is to form the miniature pool, is sunk to ground level in a hole with a good layer of stones surrounding it and a foundation of brickbats. An edging of flat stones placed around the top will give it a better finish. The tub or tank should have a drain-off plug and be situated in an open, sunny position.

Keep roots moist before planting; set them in wicker or wire baskets filled with the compost. Interlace a few sticks across the top to prevent the plants from floating out of the compost.

Suitable miniature varieties for tubs are Candida, Laydekeri fulgens, Tetragona helvola and pygmaea. They need about 9 inches of soil. Instead of decayed manure a little bonemeal may be used. Don't plant too deeply; allow the crown of the plant to just show through.

In December clear pond edge foliage which may shelter aquatic pests, and remove blotchy or dying waterlily leaves.

Raise miniature waterlily crowns above the water and protect with straw. To 'open' a frozen pond surface, melt with the base of a hot kettle.

THE DRY WALL

A dry wall, made with soil instead of mortar between the stones, is easily constructed.

The best material is rough, unhewn stone direct from the quarry, in blocks varying in size and thickness; but this type of wall may be built with bricks instead of stones.

When making a double-faced wall mark out the site by digging a 6 inch deep trench wider and longer than the wall itself. Put a 3 inch deep layer of clinker, rubble or ashes in the trench, make firm, and cover with an inch or so of soil. Place the first course of stones on this. Then add a few inches of soil before laying the next course of stones, which must be placed so that the gaps between the stones in the first course are bridged. Set each course back slightly, so that the wall is wider at the base than the top. The centre cavity is filled in as work progresses with a compost of one part peat and two parts loam made firm, the plants being inserted in the gaps between the stones so that their roots will reach the centre core of compost.

Climbing plants

It is surprisingly difficult to find self-clinging climbers for north facing walls.

One of them is Hydrangea petiolaris (see A on page 51), the vigorous climbing hydrangea. It is like a lace-cap hydrangea with creamy white flowers in June.

The other deciduous choices for a north wall climber come from the Virginia creeper family.

The true Virginia creeper is Parthenocissus quinque folia (see B), with leaves, each divided into five leaflets. P. triouspidata, Boston Ivy has leaves which can be very variable in form but they generally end up three-lobed on adult plants (see C). The other choice is P. henryana (see D) which has the most attractive foliage, the leaves having broad midribs and prominent white veins.

The other alternative for a north wall is, of course, the ivy. You might as well choose an ordinary green-leaved variety as variegated types lose their variegation if planted away from direct sunlight.

Clematis is an ideal wall shrub for a dry wall.

Fortunately the clematis does not need pruning if it is to flower in abundance. But it is important to tie in tangled growth.

If the plant has become very tangled, cutting back should be done as sparingly as possible. Cut back with secateurs to immediately above a new shoot.

Light pruning is also advisable after the first flowering of the larger flowering hybrids. Nellie Moser (pink), Barbara Jackman (reddish-purple).

The only clematis to be dealt with by harder pruning are the large flowered hybrids which bloom after June, Ville de Lyons and Jackmanii among them.

These can be cut back to within a foot of the ground in February, but no later, to encourage new growth. After a good mulch in spring and a tidy up in May, Clematis should thrive with a generous watering in dry spells.

GOOD GARDENING UNDER GLASS

Cloches

Gardeners who use cloches have several advantages over those who do not. There are a number of makes, differing slightly in construction. The main types are the Tent, large and small, shaped like an inverted 'V'; the Low Barn and the Tall Barn. There are also polythene cloches. To obtain the full benefit from all these types of cloche a few hints may prove helpful.

The Tent type is most useful for covering sown seeds and small plants. It gives seeds protection from heavy rain and birds. The Barn type, being taller and wider, enables two or three rows of seeds to be sown under one cloche row, and allows plants to remain covered for a longer period. The polythene type is most suitable for lettuces, strawberries, etc.

Perhaps you do most of your gardening at weekends. It is exasperating, then, to find that the sticky, wet state of the soil prevents you from doing the job you had planned, but if the ground had previously been covered with cloches, rain would not have spoilt your week-end progress with sowing.

Moreover, the cloches would have served another valuable service by warming the soil beforehand. By the aid of rows of cloches the sowing of many crops can be carried out sooner than their normal time, with consequent earlier maturity.

Cloches are really miniature greenhouses, and, just as you would not have a greenhouse open at each end, so the ends of a row of cloches must be closed. This can be done with boards or sheets of glass, secured with stakes tied firmly to the cloche framework; this is equally important when using odd cloches to form handlights for raising early plants or protecting parsley, mint, etc, during severe weather. Cloches will reduce the risk of attacks from pests and disease.

Provided the soil has been well prepared, watering plants under the cloches is unnecessary; simply draw drills alongside the rows outside the glass and soak them.

When ventilation is needed, remove the glasses at the ends and space the cloches so that there is a gap of two inches between each.

When hoeing or weeding, remove the cloche at one end and put it at the other end of the row. Work the uncovered soil, move the second cloche to cover the first space, and so on. When the end is reached the first cloche is used to cover the last space.

Always keep the glass clean.

As it is unbreakable, plastic is often better than glass.

The Cold Frame

A cold frame is of value in protecting plants during severe weather; for raising plants from seed in spring or from cuttings in summer, and for hardening off tender plants prior to planting-out. When used for housing plants in pots or boxes, stand them on a layer of cinders beaten hard. When used for raising plants, put a 3 inch layer of small stones or clinkers in the bottom, on which place leaf-mould or old manure. Above this put a 6 inch deep layer of turfy loam or old potting soil, with some sand to make it porous. Tread down and rake to a slight slope towards the front of the frame so that the surface is 6 inches below the glass at the back and 4 inches at the front.

Do not over-water your plants. Give sufficient ventilation, especially when condensation appears on the glass. Safeguard pans or boxes of seedlings from soil pests by standing them on inverted flower pots in the frame.

The Cold Greenhouse

The cold greenhouse has similar uses to the frame, but with greater facilities for raising more plants, especially if there is a border on each side of a central path. Early salads may be grown in these, followed by tomatoes or cucumber where there is no staging. Flowers possible to cultivate during the colder months include alpines, early flowering bulbs, pansies and wallflowers, violets, Polyanthus and auriculas. In summer you can grow hardy annuals, zonal geraniums, Centerbury bells and fuchsias, while the blooms of chrysanthemums will make a good display in autumn.

Ventilate the house when possible without creating draught. Keep the atmosphere dry, and water only when necessary and without splashing the staging.

The Heated Greenhouse

The provision of some form of heating for the greenhouse or the frame immensely increases your gardening horizon. You can do almost anything. In particular, you can raise from seed or cuttings all those plants that otherwise you have to buy, notably the half-hardy plants of summer, such as zinnias, petunias, antirrhinums, etc, besides tomatoes, melons, egg-plants and the like. You can grow a host of flowers in pots that will bloom in winter or early spring, either to adorn the greenhouse itself or to bring into your living rooms – cinerarias, various primulas, cyclamen, the indoor azalea and a great many others. You can give an early start to dahlias and begonias.

The old coke-fired boiler is still no doubt the best form of heating, but for the average amateur of today the most practical are the oil stove and electricity. There are advocates of both forms. It is sometimes said that oil fumes are damaging to plants, but oil lamps are used by thousands of gardeners with complete success. Perhaps for the more 'precious' plants oil is inadvisable, but the general run of popular plants seem quite happy, provided certain precautions are taken – use only the best-quality pink paraffin, get a good-quality stove that embodies water tubes or trays, always have a chink of ventilation and never let the lamp burn out.

Electricity, though certainly more expensive, is far more trouble-free, provided you fit a thermostat (which is quite essential). This leaves you only ventilation and watering to think about in winter unless the weather is abnormal. Exact information on costs of current is very difficult to give, as the experience even of technical experts varies.

Costs go up steeply if the required temperature is increased. They fall considerably when the outside temperature rises.

Whatever form of heating you employ, you must get equipment appropriate to the size of the greenhouse – neither too weak nor too powerful – and you must give thought to the amount of heat you will need, which will depend upon what you are going to grow. Perhaps the main advantage of electrical heating is that you can govern the inside heat, day and night, which you can't very well do with oil, the night drop of temperature being the tricky problem; but for the easier plants this is of less importance.

In all greenhouses, bear in mind the supreme importance of controlling ventilation and humidity. Never let the air get stale. When in doubt, give more ventilation, not less, but avoid draughts. As for humidity, the needs of plants vary, but the general rule is to keep the house on the dry side in winter. One quickly learns by experience.

October is the best time to clean the greenhouse. If tomatoes have suffered fungus disease, clear out the plants and fumigate with a sulphur candle. Burn it on an upturned clay pot with the greenhouse sealed. Leave overnight and open the door for an hour before entering.

Next clean glass inside and out to ensure plants enjoy winter light. To conserve heat, line the inside of the greenhouse with clear polythene sheeting.

If you plan to use a heater, remember to keep a roof light ajar to let fumes escape. Or protect plants by covering them with newspaper at night. But do remove during the day.

Other seasonal tips: water sparingly, preferably in the mornings; do not feed plants which are dormant, and allow a flow of fresh air on mild days.

Sowing Plants Under Glass

February and March are the usual months but a few slow growers, like begonias and pelargoniums, can be sown in January provided you maintain the right temperature. This will produce strong, young plants ready for later bedding.

You do not need a glasshouse. You can start them in a frame, a conservatory or even in a pot with polythene over the top, on a window sill.

Your plants will be as good in quality as those from a nursery but you will have to use the proper materials – clean pots and trays, and proper seed and potting compost, not garden soil.

Sow in fairly small pots, later pricking out into large seed trays. Maintaining the right temperature and soil moisture levels is usually the trickiest part.

If you use a seed tray, then thinly layer the bottom with a peat substitute, and cover to within a quarter

of an inch of the top with seed compost. Firm the compost with the base of a flower pot and water it before sowing the seed thinly and covering with a layer of compost. Cover with glass and a layer of newspaper until the seedlings appear.

After germination, seedlings can generally put up with temperature fluctuations but they will need overhead light if they are to avoid becoming straggly.

Use either a peat-based compost or John Innes. Today, you can usually use the same peat-based compost for both jobs, but John Innes has separate types for sowing and potting.

First, ensure your pot is clean and has adequate drainage. Then fill it with compost, lightly firm it to give a level surface, and water it.

If seeds are large enough to handle individually, position them evenly over the surface of the compost (see Inset A). Otherwise shake the packet so that they are only scattered thinly (see Inset B on page 58). Sieve a little compost over the seeds so that they are just covered (see Inset C on page 58).

Tiny seeds do not need covering. To sow evenly, mix them with a little sand which is then distributed over the surface of the compost.

For good germination keep the seeds warm, in humid conditions. Use a propagator, although a polythene bag or sheet of glass over the top will do. As soon as the seedlings are large enough to handle, prick them out 1½–2 inches apart in seed trays or boxed (see Inset D on page 58).

Always handle seedlings by their leaves, never by the stems. Use a peat-based John Innes No. 1 or 2 compost for pricking out.

HOW TO MAKE AND FIT
A SIMPLE WINDOW-BOX

Even if you have a garden, window-boxes will add floral gaiety to plain windows and will enrich the house with the fragrance and colour of a garden on a window-sill.

We explain how to construct made-to-measure window-boxes, and how to fit them securely to different types of walls.

The tools which you will require are screwdriver, hand-saw, brace and bits (or drill), try-square, rule and pencil. As far as the wood is concerned, teak is ideal for window-boxes; red cedar wood is excellent, but you can use deal if the box is well-coated with good quality paint. Cedar costs twice as much as deal, teak twice as much as cedar.

For a box up to 3 feet long and ¾ inches thick timber may be used; if over 3 feet long a timber of 1 inch thickness is recommended. The length of the box should be slightly less than the distance between the brickwork enclosing the window, to allow for fitting hooks and eyes. A reasonable overall size of ends is 8 inches from back to front, 6 inches from top to base.

For a narrow sill, where the box is fitted to the wall under the window, the box may be made longer than the width of the window.

If you plan to exceed these dimensions remember that a box filled with earth – often damp earth – is a very heavy object; keep this in mind if you plan to fix a window-box to an upstairs window. Window boxes must be fitted securely, for reasons of safety, and to prevent them being toppled over.

Make a sketch of boxes to fit your own sills, cut the pieces to size, smooth edges and assemble. As the drawing shows, the ends fit inside the front and back pieces; the base fits inside the four side pieces.

Fasten the pieces together with 2 inch No. 10 brass wood-screws. Use three at each side corner, three to secure base to ends, and space screws at 3 inch intervals along the base edges of back and front. Drill screw holes first, and before driving brass screws, shape the hole with an iron screw of the same length and thickness - this avoids snapping the soft brass screws when driving them. If deal is used, the meeting surfaces of adjoining pieces should be coated with white-lead paint before assembly.

Bore drainage holes through the back, level with the top of the base. Cut two wedges to fit angle of sill and screw them to underside of base. Attach a stout hook at each end and drive screw-eyes into window-frame. Galvanised fitments are recommended.

To secure boxes under sills, plug wall and fit stout shelf brackets. Fit one bracket each end and one in the middle; more if the box is over 3 ft. in length.

To finish off, the top edge of the front may be shaped with a thin saw to provide a decorative finish. Alternatively, make a small picket-fence of thin wood and nail to front of box.

Cedar and teak do not require painting; deal does. Rub down with glass-paper and apply one coat of aluminium priming paint. When dry, fill cracks and holes with linseed-oil putty and apply two coats of a good-quality lead-based paint. Finish with oil paint to match or contrast with colour of window-frame.

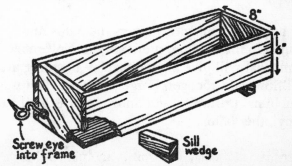

Screw eye into frame

Sill wedge

61

Filling and Planting

In the bottom, place a good layer of broken crocks and small stones. Cover these with a layer of partly decayed leaves, or old turf, grass-side downwards. Then fill to within 2 inches of the top with a mixture of loam, 2 parts; leaf-mould, 1 part; sharp sand, 1 part. If this is not obtainable, fill the box with good garden soil, after sifting it.

If you intend to sow seeds in the box, the soil must be pressed down firmly, and made level. Sow the seeds thinly, cover with fine soil and then sprinkle with water.

For a spring display of flowers the bulbs must be planted in the autumn, preferably in November. Plants that will give a good display in spring are: Wallflowers, Crocuses, Forget-me-nots, Tulips, Hyacinths, Daffodils, and Snowdrops as well as many other bulbs.

There is practically no limit to the plants that can be grown for a summer display. Here are a few that are particularly good: Geraniums both upright and trailing, Dwarf Nasturtiums, Lobelia, Calendulas, Marguerites, Ageratum, Antirrhinums and Violas. If you want a subject that will grow up from the box and around the window-frames, then plant or sow Sweet Peas, Canary Creeper, Convolvulus or Climbing Nasturtiums. Marigolds and trailing Campanula make a brilliant show in a box.

Care must be taken to water the plants and to break up the surface soil regularly. Also conserve moisture by mulching during the summer months, with coconut fibre, lawn cuttings or peat.

If your window-box is on the sunny side of the street you will be reasonably certain of a fine show. A shady box is rather more difficult. In such a situation use Begonia semperflorens, pansies, fuchsia, musk or creeping jenny. Begonia Lloydii, in various colours, is excellent for drooping over the front of the box.

BRINGING THE GARDEN INDOORS

The use of plants in pots – mainly those with decorative foliage – is so popular nowadays, and justifiably so, that we should all learn more about these useful species. They are, of course, used most effectively in contemporary houses with contemporary furnishings, but Mother Nature is so accommodating that they never look out of place in homes with furniture of any style or age. But how much nicer they look than the Victorian aspidistra in the parlour window!

For those who have not yet started this most decorative and fascinating hobby we are suggesting some of the best kinds to obtain, and for those who already have some indoor plants these details may help to identify them, as these plants are very often sold by local florists unlabelled. For beginners it should perhaps be explained that we are not hoping to produce masses of flowers – these plants are mostly those whose leaves are attractively shaped or marked or whose habit of growth is decorative. Don't be put off by the fact that many of these plants have no popular names and must, therefore, be referred to by their botanical names. Perhaps the most useful plant family for this purpose is Ivy (Hedera), as it will climb as vigorously as it will trail and therefore can be used to cover an upright support or hang down from a wall-bracket or similar position. Moreover, it will do better in shade than it will in sunshine.

Hedera Helix Pittsburgh (or Chicago)
Grows strongly and has green, deeply indented leaves whose veins are most noticeable. Can easily be increased by cuttings placed in an earthenware jar of water. (Note, earthenware, not a glass jar as light must not get to roots.)

Hedera Helix Sagittifolia

Fairly similar to Pittsburgh, although the central point or lobe of the leaf is much longer.

Hedera Canariensis Variegata

As its name shows, it comes from the Canary Islands and the green of the foliage is variegated with cream. Can be obtained in several forms. All variegated ivies need more sun than the green forms and do not grow as quickly as the others.

Fatsia Japonica, Aralis Japonica, or Aralia Sieboldii

Popularly called the Fig-leaf Palm or the False Castor-oil Plant. Has large, green, fig-like leaves but can also be obtained in variegated forms.

Fatshedera Lizei

This is the child of a very happy marriage. Ivy is the mother and Fatsia the father and the hybrid off-spring is often referred to as Fat-headed Lizzie! The object of the union was to combine the virtues of both parents in one indoor plant and the hybridists have succeeded. Its leaves are shaped like those of the ivy but much larger – 4 or 5 inches across. It is upright in form, reaching 7 or 8 feet in height unless stopped (in March). It will then develop side growths. A vigorous grower. A grandchild of the marriage is, perhaps, even better. It is a variegated form of FL, has much more attractive foliage and, being a slower grower, is more suited to room decoration.

Impatiens Holstii or Sultanii

Mentioning Fat-headed Lizzie reminds me of Busy Lizzie – no relation. It is outstanding for one reason in particular – it is, perhaps, the only easily grown indoor plant with attractive foliage (green and velvety) that produces flowers for a large part of the year. Holstii blooms are brick-red and those of Sultanii scarlet. This is the Balsam family whose annuals are grown in the borders.

Tradescantia Fluminensis

Of all room plants this is the one most frequently seen – perhaps because it is, in all probability, the easiest to grow. Certainly one couldn't have a plant that is easier to propagate. Push any piece that gets broken off into the soil in the pot and it will grow! Can be obtained in several forms, according to the marking of the foliage which grows on long trailing stems. The leaves are small, medium shades of green and are striped with pale cream, almost white, or pinky mauve and even gold. A thirsty type, commonly called Wandering Jew.

Zebrina Pendula or Tradescantia Zebrina

Some people mean this plant when referring to Wandering Jew and even the botanists are in two minds about its name. It is, in any case, a close relative of the one above, and similar in habit of growth. Its leaves are striped white or silver above and purple beneath.

Very easy to grow.

Chlorophytum Capense (or Phalangium Elatum) Variegatum

This is another flowering subject although the blooms are only small and it is the foliage that is really the attraction. This grows in the form of compact rosettes of leaves that are quite long and striped with creamy-white. It is fascinating to see how miniature rosettes of leaves later form on the long flower stems which gradually bend over in a most graceful way.

Rhoicissue Rhomboidea

This is a rapidly growing climber, covering a piece of trellis in a remarkably short time. Often called Grape Ivy. Leaves small, glossy, dark green, produced in a triple arrangement.

Cissus Antartica or Vitis Antarctica

Botanically related to the above and nearly as good a climber – perhaps the more attractive of the two. Coming from Australia it is, perhaps, not surprising that it is commonly called the Kangaroo Vine. Leaves larger than the above, clearly indented, shiny.

Philodendron Scandens

Justifiably, this is one of the most popular indoor plants. It is easy to grow, is most useful for climbing or trailing and is regarded by many people as the most handsome subject of this type. It likes a warm position, not in full sun, and must be watered regularly. When those simple requirements are satisfied it will grow well and its shiny leaves, something like a heart in shape, will improve the appearance of any room.

Monstera Deliciosa

People often joke about plants' Latin names but for exactness this system of nomenclature is well-nigh perfect, whereas popular names are often misleading. This plant, for instance, is called Shingle Plant, for no apparent reason, while others call it Swiss Cheese Plant, which is definitely misleading, as it comes from Mexico! Perhaps the cheese label comes from its yellow flowers, but as a room plant it is outstanding for its foliage! Anyone can be justly proud of a good-sized specimen of this really handsome plant.

Santpaulia Ionantha

One of the few with an accurate popular name – African Violet – and one that will flower regularly if it has the correct conditions. Coming from tropical Africa, it likes a hot, humid atmosphere, and in most homes it would be difficult to find a better spot for it than in the bathroom or kitchen, if all-electric. Steam won't hurt it, but gas will. Room temperature should always (day and night, that is) be at least 60°. Normally, its flowers are violet-coloured but there are several other varieties such as white (albescens), purple (purpurea) and deep violet (violescens), as well as a number of shades of blue and pink. Not only is there choice of lots of colours but also of leaf forms and some of the flowers are single and others double. To the green-fingered this is a real friend, for leaf-cuttings can be taken from it at any time of the year and they are nearly always successful.

Pilea Microphylla

This is not only an outstandingly attractive foliage plant but it has one amusing characteristic that endears it to many people. The flowers are scarcely worth mentioning, but the unopened buds have the peculiar habit, when in contact with moisture, of popping open and shooting out their pollen. This has earned it the names, Artillery Plant and Pistol Plant. Has an upright, yet bushy, habit of growth that is ideal in a pot plant.

Ficus Elastica – India-rubber Plant

This selection of indoor plants would not seem complete unless one included a few fig leaves! The Ficus or Fig family includes several suitable members and few people can have failed to see an India-rubber Plant somewhere with its distinctive, large, dark-green leaves. Ficus Elastica variegata is not so often seen, but should be, as it is, if anything, more attractive, having variegated foliage, while the same can also be said of the variety, decora, whose red veins can clearly be seen underneath the leaves. Ficus pumila or repens is a most useful variety as it is a small-leafed, self-clinging climber, but it will not climb very well against a smooth surface such as glass or tiles. Even the daintiness of this Japanese subject is exceeded by Ficus pumila minima which has an even smaller leaf. A variety with a most uncommonly shaped leaf is Ficus lyrata or pandurata – it is like a miniature violin.

Cypripedium Insigne - Lady's Slipper Orchid

How many of us would dearly love to grow orchids, if only we could afford to do so. That attitude of mind should now be abandoned. There is a very good chance of succeeding with this orchid and the minimum winter temperature is not very high, only

50°, which is quite easy to achieve in most homes. Naturally, it should be cared for rather more meticulously than most indoor subjects, keeping it out of draughts and not allowing it to stand in direct sunlight for any length of time. A mistake often made is that an orchid often looks as if it needs re-potting when in fact it is better not to transfer it to a larger pot. A certain amount of root cramping is desirable – they flower better then – but, of course, this must not be overdone. This is an aspect of the culture that is not easily taught or described; one can only learn by experience, although regular examination of the plant and the progress it makes will indicate to most people when the point has been reached which makes such action necessary.

Peperomia Caperata

This suggestion will make the owner the envy of all her friends. It is a member of the Peperomia family comparatively newly introduced to indoor-plant enthusiasts. Other members of this large family have been grown for their brilliant foliage for years, but the newcomer is in a class of its own, as it were, because it also bears curiously erect spikes of white flowers which invariably seem to cause comment from one's friends.

General Care

Pot plants do not like a dry, draughty atmosphere or extremes of temperature.

Generally speaking, the care of indoor plants is a simple matter. Watering is the main task and, occasionally, re-potting. It is important not to over-water them but, on the other hand, the job should be done thoroughly at intervals and not in frequent, small doses.

The best way is to stand the pots in a bath or sink of water just deep enough to reach to about 1 inch below the rim of the pot or container. In this way water soaks up from the bottom and when the surface of the soil is obviously wet you know that the whole of the contents of the pot are adequately moistened. Allow pots to drain properly before returning to brackets or other positions in the room.

Having watered plants in this way do not do so again until it is obvious from the condition of the soil that they need it. This is unlikely to be necessary for a week or two, but you must learn to judge for yourself, bearing in mind that some varieties need more water than others. Water less in winter.

Some house plants prefer different watering techniques. Some fare best when their pots are stood on saucers of pebbles, topped up with water to just below the base.

Cyclamen will be happy with their pot standing on an inverted saucer in a bowl of water.

Mist spraying, with tepid water, will ensure plants, such as Christmas cactus, hold their flowers and Solanums, the winter cherry, its fruit.

Other tips: ensure adequate ventilation near gas appliances; keep plants from draughts and do not leave behind curtains at night. Never overwater: wait until leaves start to droop, or the top of the soil is dry.

One final word of warning concerning watering. Do not stand pots in saucers of water.

Indoor plants with large leaves tend to become dusty. Freshen them up, both in appearance and from a health point of view, by sponging the leaves carefully with water that is just warm. If it seems to be necessary, soft soap can be added to this water at the rate of ¼ oz to a pint of water. Mix very thoroughly before use and afterwards clean the leaves completely with fresh water to make sure that no trace of the soft soap is left behind.

For the re-potting of room plants a general mixture is as follows:

Fibrous loam, fairly fine but not sieved so as to be dusty	- 2 parts
Leaf-mould, sieved	- 1 part
Silver sand	- 1 part

Some plants, of course, need a more specialised mixture – Lady's Slipper Orchid is one – and you should consult your garden centre if in any doubt on this point. The best time for re-potting is from mid-April to mid-May, but again there are exceptions.

Cuttings

Taking leaf cuttings is an excellent way of increasing the numbers of pot plants.

For African violets, take a healthy leaf and stem, dip it in a hormone rooting compound and plant so the leaf is just above the cutting compost level.

After rooting, the leaves of the new plant will appear.

The Begonia rex leaf is laid on its front, so veins on the back can be cut. The leaf is pinned, back down, on the soil. Plants appear from cut veins.

With the streptocarpus, cut lengthwise each side of the main rib, the outside pieces can then be planted, with cut edges – from which new plants emerge – in the soil.

CUTTING FLOWERS AND KEEPING THEM FRESH

Few things annoy a gardener more than to see the results of his hard labour not receiving the treatment they deserve. And yet there are remarkably few people, gardeners included, who cut flowers properly or treat them correctly after cutting.

Do you, for example, cut flowers for indoor decoration only in the early morning or late afternoon? Have you not sallied forth with scissors or secateurs between 11 am and 3 pm on a summer's day to gather what you need for your vases? Observe this rule in future and your flowers will last longer.

Again, nearly everyone gathers cut blooms wrongly. They hold them bunched in a hot hand or lay them in a basket. Both ways should be forbidden. As flowers are cut the stalks should be immediately placed in a bucket half full of water. Standing upright in this way, none of the flowers is subjected to pressure from the weight of the bunch. Stalks should always be as long as possible to allow for further cutting as described later on. And it is wise to take a tip from market-gardeners who always cut flowers in the bud stage. We do not need to be quite so early but it is certainly an advantage to cut before the flower is fully opened.

In water in a room blossoms open even more quickly than they do naturally in the garden, and the indoor display is thereby greatly prolonged.

The method of placing cut flowers in a bucket of water is a particularly good one for poppies –a flower many ignore for indoor decoration as the petals fall so quickly. This way, they retain their petals much longer.

Scissors and secateurs have already been mentioned but a really sharp knife is a much better implement for this purpose, even for plants with tough woody stems. Make an upward slanting cut and try to use just one clean cut.

If you can use clean rainwater for your vases, do so. If you must use tap water, try putting a pinch of bicarbonate of soda or salt or an aspirin in the water. Which is best is difficult to say as the effect varies according to the way the water has been treated in your area. Experiment and decide which is best for your district. A little charcoal or a small piece of camphor could also be tried. They are effective in some places.

That part of the stem covered by the water should be stripped of leaves. The regular changing of the water is often an advantage and at the same time it is wise to cut off half an inch of stalk. But this cut-ting must be done under water so that air is not allowed to enter the passages up which the sap normally passes. If it does, an air-lock is created and the flowers are deprived of the benefit of being in water.

The observance of a few simple rules of this kind can make a great deal of difference in the life of the blooms. The temperature of the room is also very important. Keep the flowers in the coolest places you can but don't place them in draughts – or in a room where gas is used, such as a kitchen.

SHRUBS AND SMALL TREES

Trees and shrubs give character and atmosphere to a garden, probably more than any other single factor. They provide the background, they give bulk and density and variety of foliage. They may also serve the utility purposes of screening or of providing shelter from rude winds.

Make them, therefore, your first choice in any new garden, and if you are taking over an existing garden, retain all that are really worth their keep, but uproot all that are gaunt, leggy or otherwise unsightly.

There is a wonderful variety available today, many worth growing for the beauty of their foliage alone. In your planning and choice bear the following factors in mind:

1. The need for diversity of height and shape and foliage. Have some tall and slender, others round and plump, others drooping or arching, and so on.

2. The seasons in which they bloom: you can have flowering shrubs all the year if you have room enough, and you should certainly plan to have something in bloom from spring to autumn.

3. The need for a few evergreens, which may include conifers.

4. The fact that some trees and shrubs, especially rhododendrons and most heathers, hate lime.

5. The ultimate spread of each plant when fully grown: this governs the distance apart that you plant them, and you must accept considerable gaps for the first year or two, which you can fill up with other and cheaper things.

6. Any special requirement of each plant, such as plenty of water or not too much water, together with any query about hardiness.

7. That trees and shrubs appear relatively expensive, but are lasting and well worth the initial outlay.

8. Shrubs provide colour all year round, through bloom, berries or foliage. They are particularly useful in difficult areas of the garden.

9. Plant in bare earth, digging over the bed, incorporating rotting compost and a dressing of bonemeal.

On this basis, the following is a short selection of the best and easiest flowering shrubs for small gardens, covering the period March – October.

EARLY SPRING – Forsythia intermedia spectabilis, Flowering Quinces, such as Knaphill Scarlet, and Daphnes.

LATE SPRING – Rhododendrons (if no lime in the soil) Brooms (Cytisus), the Japanese Snowball (Viburnum tomentosun plicatum), Lilacs, Diervillas, Deutzia gracilis carminea.

JUNE – Musk roses, Philadelphus (Mock Orange).

JULY – Senecio laxifolius, the Hidcote variety of Hypericum patalum, and Hydrangeas – the last two continuing right till the frosts.

AUGUST – Hibiscus syriacus.

All these are first-class and easy plants.

For small trees one thinks first of Flowering Cherries and Crabs, the beautiful Maple called Acer Negundo, Laburnums, Hawthorns and Rowans. Of evergreens the best are Berberis, Holly, Cistus, some Cotoneasters, Ceanothus and Eucryphia nymansensis, besides all the conifers.

Ceanothus thrysiflorus repens, spaced at 4 foot intervals, is a good choice for the middle of the bed.

75

At the front, plant berry-carrying evergreen Cotoneaster dammeri.

For height and colour at the back, a Genista, or broom, is a good choice. Others to put on your list include Lonicera pileta and the variagated Vinca.

If you want your trees and shrubs to look shapely, well clothed with foliage, and generous in flower, you must study a little the simple arts of pruning.

Propagating

Shrubs such as magnolias, rhododendrons and azaleas can be propagated by layering.

First choose a suitable pliant branch of about a year old. Then dig a 3 inch hole below the branch and fill it with an equal mix of peat and sand or a good seed-compost.

Bend the branch down and bury it about 10 inches

back from the tip, having stripped off any leaves at that point and make a shallow nick along the underside which will open as the branch is bent.

Tie the end of the branch to a stake and peg in position with bent wire (see main picture on page 77) before filling in the hole.

Growth at the tip of the branch will show that roots are forming and the new plant should be ready for severing and planting in the autumn.
With shrubs such as Cytisus, Deutzia and Weigala, prune as they finish blooming. Cut back to two or three buds from the branching junction as shown in the Inset on page 77.

By July, many shrubs will provide half-ripe cuttings which can be persuaded to produce roots in a propagating frame.

Among the most popular worth trying are cistus, clematis, cotoneaster, escallonia, lavatera and viburnum.

Pull off a young shoot with a heel of the old wood attached. Trim the heel and remove the lower two leaves. Dip the heel into rooting medium and shake off the excess, before inserting with others around the rim of a pot filled with shrub compost.

The pots should be stood in a cold frame, or covered with plastic bags to maintain moisture.

When roots have formed, the cuttings should be potted up separately into soil. Later they should be transferred to a nursery bed to winter.

Mulberry

If you want an unusual tree to plant in the middle of your lawn, a mulberry is worth considering.

It will provide you with fruit and will spread out to cover an area about 15 feet across.

When planting, leave an area about 3 feet across clear of grass and weeds until the tree is well-established.

The most common variety is the black mulberry, Morus nigra. The white mulberry, Morus alba – whose leaves form the traditional diet for silkworms – is also sometimes seen. The difference is in the colour of the fruit, raspberry red ripening to a deep purple-red in the former, whitish turning to a pinky red in the latter. The fruit (see Inset) can be used both for cooking and dessert.

Mulberries are self-fertile and the trees grow best in fairly rich soils, well-drained but capable of retain-

ing moisture during dry spells.

Although the trees are hardy, there is a risk of the fruits not ripening properly in very cold areas. In such districts it helps to plant the mulberries in front of a south-facing wall.

The mulberry needs no pruning other than to keep it an attractive shape – if you want to thin the branches, do so soon after the leaves have fallen.

Witch Hazel

One of the best shrubs for winter colour is the witch hazel.

It has curiously shaped flowers, as Inset A illustrates, but their yellow and reddish colours stand out well on the bare branches from December to February.

Another interesting feature is that the leaves

produce some marvellous colour in autumn – brilliant yellow or orange and red. The leaves (see Inset B on page 79) resemble those of a hazel, although the two plants are not in the same family. Choose neutral or slightly acid well-drained soil with a little extra peat or leafmould put in before planting.

The most popular is Hamamelis mollis, the Chinese witch hazel. The variety Pallida is strongly scented and has sulphur yellow flowers.

The Japanese witch hazel, Hamamelis japonica, is not so showy and its flowers have less fragrance. However, hybrids between the two species offer some good choices, providing reddish, bronze and orange colour flowers. Jalena, sometimes called Copper Beauty, is the best of the orange colours while Diane is the most red.

Care of Shrubs

The ravages of winter will inevitably play havoc with deciduous shrubs, killing off young shoots and breaking weak ones.

It is shrubs that flower on new growth, not on wood thrown from last year, that need attention in the winter. Buddleia davidii is one example. To keep it in good shape and disease free, cut back the old wood hard.

Cistus, potentilla and hebe will benefit from having damaged shoots cut right out. With Hydrangea paniculata, leave just a few inches of it above the ground.

Hedera and berberis can be lightly thinned to promote growth; fuchsias and Lavatera Rosea should be cut right back.

TUBS FOR SHRUBS ADD DISTINCTION TO THE GARDEN

Small trees, shrubs, and even flowers in tubs add an air of distinction to any type of garden. It is not necessary to be an expert carpenter to make tubs for your garden; we illustrate a simple type, capable of several variations, which anyone can construct. Moreover, our design has graceful lines that won't date quickly.

The tubs may have square tops or may be rounded, as shown in the diagram and explained later. They taper towards the base and are banded with strips of the main timber used. To these strips may be fitted strong metal handles which are both decorative and useful.

The timber must be substantial, of at least 1 inch thickness. Suitable woods are oak, teak or cedar.

Softwoods may be used, but will not stand up to such long hard wear as the hardwoods named.

We show overall dimensions which may easily be altered to suit a special purpose and are assuming that timber 3 inches wide is being used. Each side is exactly the same shape and size. The tops of the strips are easily rounded with a suitable saw (keyhole, fret or bow) and then sand-papered. When fastening the strips to the bands, remember that the bands must 'lap' at the corners, as shown in the drawing, when the sides are assembled. A bracing strip, on which the base is to rest, is attached to the inner surface on each side before assembly, and the base, already drilled with ½ inch drainage holes, is fitted last.

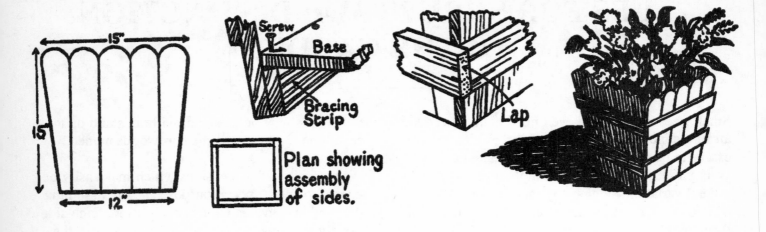

Screw

Base

Bracing Strip

Plan showing assembly of sides.

Lap

The best method of securing the parts is with brass screws, driven from the inside. The snag with driving brass screws is that they snap easily; to avoid this drive an iron screw, of the same length and gauge, into each screw hole before turning the brass screws. Rub all parts smooth before assembly and give the completed tub a rub down after putting the parts together.

The completed tubs may be finished in a variety of ways. If painted, all crevices should be filled with red-lead putty after applying a substantial coat of aluminium priming paint. Follow with at least two undercoats of good quality flat oil-paint, before applying the finishing coat, also oil-paint.

Alternatively, if a decorative wood is used, the tubs may be varnished. Use yacht varnish and give three coats inside and out. The tubs can be finished with wood preservative, but some is not kind to growing plants. Another method of finishing, which will be found best in most cases, is to apply several dressings of boiled linseed oil – this will preserve and beautify. Teak and cedar wood, of course, do not require any preservative finish.

The filling of a tub is quite a simple matter, and provided it is done in accordance with a few common-sense rules, your shrubs should thrive. The drainage holes must first be covered with crocks, which in turn should be over-laid with turf upside-down. The tub is then filled with a mixture of good soil in which there is plenty of leaf-mould or peat and some sand. Do not include manure, as shrub roots should not be allowed to come into contact with it and in a tub there is scarcely room to avoid this. It must also be remembered that some shrubs, particularly the Heathers and Azaleas (now properly Rhododendrons) like peat but hate lime. Your soil mixture must, therefore, be varied to suit the requirements of individual subjects, in accordance with the instructions most growers will supply for plants purchased.

Before planting, examine the roots and cut off cleanly any parts that have been broken in transit. If you cannot plant straight away, stand the shrubs in water until you are ready, as the roots will suffer if left exposed to the air for any length of time.

When we come to the question of what to grow, we are faced with a very wide variety of subjects - much too wide to be dealt with adequately in a short article. Consult a specialist grower, having previously thought about the kinds of shrubs you want. Do you, for example, want evergreens - is the site sunny or shady - do you want fine blooms in spring or summer - or would it be more important to have some blossom in winter?

These and other requirements can all be satisfied by shrubs in tubs, provided you buy the right varieties. That is why the specialist is so important - he will, for example, point out that the Daphne family includes about twenty members that are suitable for tubs, many of which flower in winter. The best-known Daphne, Mezereum, freely produces in February or March, before the leaves appear, reddish-purple, sweetly-scented flowers which are followed in autumn by scarlet berries. There is also a variety, called Alba, which has white flowers and orange berries, while Grandiflora is autumn-flowering. And so on, almost ad infinitum.

By a judicious selection, under expert guidance, tub shrubs can be an almost all-the-year-round attraction.

THE FLOWER GARDEN

Planning the flower garden gives the gardener perhaps his best opportunity of expressing his personality. Small gardens give him a stiff test, however, for what he has to do is to select. The range of choice is enormous, including trees and shrubs, herbaceous perennials, annuals and biennials, bulbs, rock plants, water plants and climbers. These notes are accordingly intended to help the beginner to start off 'on the right foot' and to escape some of the usual mistakes.

First, one or two definitions, omitting those that are obvious.

A perennial is a plant that blooms afresh year after year. A herbaceous perennial is one that dies down to the ground level every winter, remaining alive below ground and sending up new shoots each spring, e.g. delphiniums, lupins, phlox.

An annual grows from seed to full maturity and dies all in one season, e.g. marigold, larkspur, clarkia.

A biennial is sown this year, blooms next year and then dies, e.g. wallflower, sweet william, forget-me-not.

Bulbous plants are forms of perennial that store their energy in fleshy bodies right below ground during their resting periods. In popular parlance, the term includes not only true bulbs, such as daffodils and lilies, but also 'corms', such as gladioli and crocuses, and 'tubers' as in dahlias and potatoes. Irises and some other plants have fleshy stems called 'rhizomes'.

A hardy plant is one that will stand the winter outdoors. Hardy plants are, therefore, the easiest to grow, whether shrubs, herbaceous, annuals, bulbs, etc, but the term does not mean, as so many beginners think, that such plants will stand rough treatment or neglect, or will necessarily succeed in any kind of soil.

It is an old saying that most beginners start their gardening with annuals, progress on to herbaceous plants, and finish up with shrubs or specialist plants. This is not the right policy for the new owner of a garden. Permanencies should have priority.

Having conscientiously prepared the soil, make sure first of your trees and shrubs. They are the most important and permanent features of the garden and take longest to grow. Next should come roses, which surely every gardener will want. Technically, they come in the tree and shrub class, but will give splendid results the very first year.

Then choose your herbaceous perennials, including bulbs; but it is better, as a rule, to leave the spring-flowering bulbs (daffodils, crocuses, muscaris, and snowdrops) until the season after you plant the shrubs and herbaceous things. These bulbs (except tulips) have to be planted earlier in the year than shrubs and herbs (for which planting time is November onwards) and if you plant the bulbs first you disturb them when putting in the shrubs or herbs. Also you may have manured your ground the first year and bulbs hate fresh manure. Don't plant bulbs among your roses, except perhaps very small bulbs; on no account plant tulips among roses.

Annuals are, of course, delightful on their own account, but in small places the best uses for them are as follow-ons for plants that finish early in the year, such as spring bulbs, or as fill-ups between shrubs that are not yet mature, or for the odd corners.

'Bedding' plants are another useful class. 'Summer bedding' refers to plants that are not quite hardy, are raised in a greenhouse and are planted out about the beginning of June. They include such things as petunias, geraniums, antirrhinums, zinnias, begonias, French and African marigolds, etc.

If you have no heated greenhouse, you must buy them from a nursery; a seed-boxful, at the cost of a few pounds, will provide a wonderful display of colour till frost comes.

Spring bedding plants are biennials that include wallflowers, forget-me-nots, sweet williams, Brompton stocks, etc. These you can raise very easily yourself from seed sown in the open in early June, 'pricked off' into a nursery bed and planted out in their final positions in autumn. Bulbs often go in with them.

Choosing perennials for the herbaceous border often gives the beginner a headache, especially when the border is a very narrow one. A first-rate basis for any such border, giving bloom from late May right up to the frosts, is: lupins, delphiniums, phloxes, dahlias, with some low-growing plants in front, of which there are multitudes. Place them in the border more or less according to height, but not too regularly or 'regimented'.

ADAM'S SELECTION OF FLOWERS

ANNUALS

Alyssum	Eschscholtzia	Poppy
Calceolaria	Everlasting Flowers	Redbeckia
Calendula	Godetia	Scabious
Calliopsis	Gypsophila	Statice
Canary Creeper	Hibiscus	Sunflower
Candytuft	Larkspur	Sweet Pea
Chrysanthemum	Love in a Mist	Sweet Sultan
Clarkia	Love Lies Bleeding	Virginia Stock
Convolvulus	Mignonette	Viscaria
Cornflower	Nasturtium	

HALF-HARDY ANNUALS

Ageratum	Marigolds	Phlox
Aster	Mesembryanthemum	Salpiglossis
Begonia	Nemesia	Stock
Cosmos	Nicotiana	Zinnia
Kochia		

Hardy annuals

The approach of March should see warmer weather, and you can start planting some hardy annuals. As garden fillers, or for splashes of massed colour in the garden, it is difficult to beat hardy annuals.

Begin by forking over the beds where seeds are to be sown, raking in a general fertiliser.

Then sow direct into the ground, in drifts or in rows. You can sow the seeds from the packets, or in the easier-to-handle pelleted form, or even in strips (see Inset A). Protect against diseases and pests by mixing the seeds with a combined seed dressing.

A dressing of Growmore at two handfuls to the square yard, and turned into the top inch or so of soil will give the seeds a good start. Then rake over well to provide a fine tilth.

If you wish to achieve the effect of drifts of colour, then mark out the areas for each type of seed you

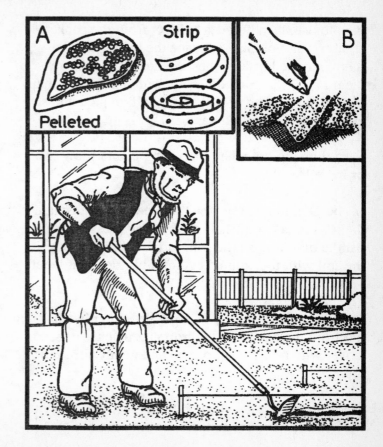

plan to use, then broadcast direct from the packet. If, however, you plan to space the plants and dot them into the borders, then the best way is to sow them in a drill. Draw the drills with a hole (see main picture) to a depth of just about half an inch and sow evenly (see Inset B on page 89).

Start thinning out when the young plants show two or more leaves.

If you plan to nursery-sow the seeds and transplant them later, take out shallow drills by pressing the handle of a rake on the soil, or by cutting through the soil with the pointed end of a plastic plant label – against a cord line, of course.

Sow the seeds as thinly as possible, either by shaking from the packet or by dropping pinches of seed. Cover with a fine layer of soil and gently firm the top.

Since the earlier the sowing, the earlier the display, if conditions are not suitable for planting out, get

things moving by planting under glass.

Among those for early planting outdoors are godetia, calendula, clarkia, cornflower and candytuft (iberis). All of these give a blaze of colour over a long flowering period.

Even in May there is still time to sow hardy and half-hardy annuals outdoors – alyssium, calendula, gaillardia, candytuft and phlox among them – this is the time to get seedlings into their growing positions.

Start by giving the empty beds a good watering. Next, water the young plants which should have been hardened off.

Where seedlings have been grown in boxes, give the box a sharp knock on the ground, and they will be tossed out gently all in one piece.

Otherwise, remove the end of the box and slide the

mat of seedlings out.

The best way to separate the plants is to cut them into strips and then separate them with a sharp knife. Plant without delay and mulch around them as soon as possible.

CHRYSANTHEMUMS

The variety of colour, from the purest white to the deepest bronze and the vast range of size and shape, make chrysanthemums a must in at least one of their forms for most flower beds.

Furthermore, you do not need to be a specialist to grow them.

The spray types are ideal, although Korean varieties and pompoms can look well in the border.

May is the time to purchase your plants. You will need early flowering varieties such as Pennines (in

pale yellow, pink, and salmon), white Adelines or Red Lilian Hoek.

Choose a sunny position sheltered from winds. Fork the plot well and turn in about a handful of chrysanthemum fertiliser to the square yard.

Plant in groups about a foot apart and tie loosely to a stake, as illustrated on page 91.

Pinching out the main stem at 7 or 8 inches high will help to ensure bushy plants which will produce more blooms.

Regular dressings of chrysanthemum fertiliser are recommended during wet weather, through June to the first week in July, when, during dry weather, you should water regularly with a liquid feed.

Leaf miners, capsid bugs and greenfly are the main problems and can be dealt with by an HCH spray applied regularly each week. Once every three weeks, spray with dinocap to control mildew.

There are dangers in leaving chrysanthemums in the ground over winter. One threat is damp and the other is frost, which can kill the root system.

But if drainage is good, leave them in, remove faded flowers and ensure the surrounding area is free from leaves, which attract slugs. Leave top growth to be cut back in spring.

If the plants are to be lifted, cut the stems to within 6 inches of the ground. Cut out any green shoots at the bottom.

Store root systems in boxes of soil or compost. Lift with care, wash them in clean water, label and plant in the box. Then place somewhere light, airy and frost-free.

If you want to propagate chrysanthemums, you should first cut back the plants to ground level in the autumn, to encourage new growth the following year.

To get the best blooms from border types, only the outer new shoots should be used from the divided stools.

Similarly, only the outer new shoots should be used to provide cuttings from those grown under glass. February is a good time to take such cuttings, but certainly by early the following month new growth will allow the taking of cuttings about 2 inches long.

Sever just below a leaf joint, and remove the lower leaves.

Trays or pots, loosely filled with moistened John Innes No 1 will provide a good start. Dip the ends of the cuttings into rooting compound, before planting them, nine or ten to a tray or five or six to a pot.

From the middle of March make regular checks on the root ball, so that once it is well developed the plants can be separated into 3 inch pots, before gradually hardening them off outdoors.

SWEET PEAS

Sweet peas, sporting a myriad of colours, are a superb garden feature. When choosing sweet pea seeds, remember that while recent varieties may provide superb colours, older ones are often best for scent.

February is the time to prepare a site for them. First dig the bed and break up large clods with the blade of the spade.

Tread the area to get a fine tilth and firm the soil to provide conditions for a good root system to develop.

Next, prepare the support system, setting strong posts, each with a 12 inch crossbar at the top, up to 3 feet deep at each end of the proposed row. Attach wires to the crossbar ends.

Put a double row of bamboo canes along the row and tie them in to the top wires.

Short varieties, however, will be comfortably supported by twigs or a coil of netting, whilst miniature types for growing on patios will only need a little raised netting over their containers.

By the end of the month conditions should allow seed planting at the base of stakes where they are to flower.

Sweet peas which have been started in pots will not be planted out until later, but again at the base of stakes.

Sow the seeds in October, in 5 inch pots of compost.

Put a ½ inch mark on a dibber to make holes to that depth, and sow seeds – after treating with a fungicide – ten to a pot. Then water the pots.

If you prefer to sow in boxes, space the seeds 2 inches apart.

The containers should be placed in a cold frame, packing the pots up to their rims with soil or peat. Once the seedlings appear, open up the frame, closing it only when frost is expected.

When planting them, trowel out a hole large enough to take the spread-out roots comfortably.

PERENNIALS

(TREATED AS ANNUALS)

Antirrhinum	Lobelia	Salvia
Carnation	Pansy	Tritonia
Dahlia	Pentstemon	Verbena
Heliotrope	Petunia	Viola

PERENNIALS

Anchusa	Delphinium	Iris
Anemone	Evening Primrose	Lavandula
Aquilegia	Forget-me-not	Lily
Arabis	Foxglove	Lupin
Aubretia	Freesia	Montbretia
Auricula	Gaillardia	Pinks
Campanula	Gentian	Polyanthus
Canna	Geranium	Primrose
Catmint	Geum	Primula
Coreopsis	Gladioli	Pyrethrum
Cyclamen	Gloxinia	Tulip
Daffodil	Hollyhock	Valerian
Daisy	Hyacinth	

Hardy Perennials

Those stock plants of the garden, hardy perennials should be making new growth in late March.

As soon as this starts, clear the areas around them of weeds and loosen the soil close to the plants to allow air and moisture to get down into the roots and mulch by laying compost or peat over the plants (see Inset B).

Though it is best to plant new perennials around September or October, you can add to your stock at almost any time, now that so many species are available, container grown, from garden centres. To get the best effect, group them not in rows but in shaped areas within the border, starting to plant at the centre of the area allotted and working towards the outside (see main illustration).

For the smaller plants a trowel will make a large enough hole in which to plant two or three as a single plant in the groups of, say, six to nine plants.

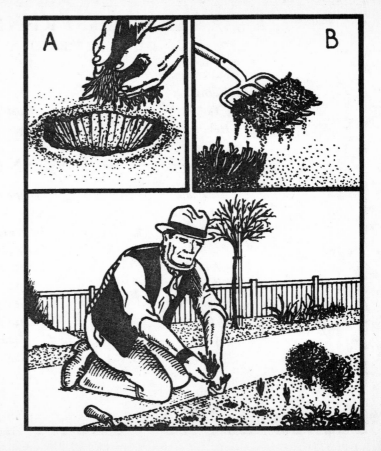

Larger plants such as delphiniums and Russell lupins, require bigger holes to allow for the larger root system (see Inset A on page 96) and also require more space between them.

With the taller growing perennials, set supports as early as possible, either using rings of wire mesh or twine supported by bamboo poles. By setting the support early the leaves grow through them and hide the construction.

DAHLIAS

Dahlias make a super show. In March, to produce the best display, choose a sunny spot, dig it over and dress with bonemeal to boost root growth.

If you are using tubers stored over winter, you can increase your stock by splitting the clumps.

Sever sections, ensuring that each has a bud or shoot already showing growth.

Place the tubers in a box on a layer of potting compost and cover with compost just below the crown.

Water, but do not wet the crowns too much. Then spray every day with tepid water (see Inset A on page 97).

Within a few weeks there will be shoots, 3 to 4 inches long which can be taken as cuttings. Using a razor blade or sharp knife, cut them just above the shooting point, so as not to damage the crown from which further shoots will emerge.

Take off the lower pair of leaves and trim the shoot back cleanly to just below the leaf joint (see Inset B on page 97). Dip the end of each cutting in a hormone rooting powder and place into 3 inch pots filled with John Innes No. 1 potting compost.

Firm in well, tapping the pot on a bench to ensure air is not trapped at the base of the cutting and to ensure that it sits well into the compost – four to a pot.

Cover with glass, or, preferably, place a polythene bag over the pot, supported by twigs or wire, held on by an elastic band.

The cuttings should be well rooted in two to three weeks, when they should be potted up separately to make growth for final planting out in May or June.

For an expansive, but less expensive, display of bedders, it is more practical to raise new plants from seed.

A wide variety, including decoratives and pompoms, can be raised by sowing seed in trays of coconut fibre compost.

Plant out dahlias in June.

Prepare to space them about 18 inches apart. Stake the positions first, then dig holes a little deeper than the root-ball will require, so that you can line the holes with a planting mixture of a bucketful of peat mixed with three or four tablespoons of dried blood

or hoof and horn.

Gently remove the plant from the container so as not to disturb the roots more than necessary, and place in the hole. Then fill around with more planting mixture.

Finally, as in the main illustration, tie in to the stake, and keep tying in as plants grow.

To encourage bushy growth and a longer lasting display of blooms, pinch out the growing tip two or three weeks after planting. Any leaves which are growing near the ground should also be removed. (see Inset B).

Spray fortnightly against greenfly.

TULIPS

Tulips range from pure white through yellows and reds to almost black.

And there is a vast choice from the early Kaufmannians, through April-flowering Early Singles, to the late glory of Parrots.

They will benefit if the ground is first dressed with bonemeal.

Plant in October or November, and arrange the bulb positions on the soil before planting, to ensure the desired effect.

Use a trowel to make a hole about 4 inches deep and leave 6 inches between each bulb.

Set the bulbs firmly on the bottom of the hole and top up to just above the surrounding soil, so that it can be firmed level.

CYCLAMEN

Cyclamen tubers left to dry in the summer will need attention in mid-August.

But first, the production of new plants from seed. Sow separately on a good seed compost in trays. Cover thinly with compost.

Then cover with glass and a sheet of newspaper and stand on moistened gravel. Never let the seeds dry out. Glass and paper should be removed after germination.

When the first two leaves have appeared, prick out and transfer seedlings to trays of John Innes No 1.

As foliage from plants begin to touch, transfer singly to 3 inch and later 5 inch pots of John Innes No. 2.

To re-start a dried tuber, press it gently into the top of a 5 inch pot of John Innes No 2. Water lightly and place in the shade or a cold frame.

Do not allow water to fall on the tuber. When buds appear, feed weekly.

Iris

The iris, or flag, is one of the most colourful and majestic border plants. The flowers are produced on straight stems, surrounded by spear-like leaves, all thrown from rhizomatous rootstock.

Iris are easily propagated by division of the rhizomes in July. But it is also important to divide the rhizomes every three or four years. Left any longer, they will become so crowded that the plants and flowers deteriorate.

Lever the plants gently from the ground with a large fork to lift out a clump without doing too much damage to neighbouring roots.

Leave as much soil clinging to the roots as possible. First, using a sharp knife, take out young, new rhizomes with small leaves.

To increase stock further, sever the best older rhizomes 2 or 3 inches back from new growth.

Prepare the new bed by incorporating leafmould or compost and dress with bonemeal. Level and firm planting area. Before replanting, cut back leaves. Scrape back just enough soil so the rhizomes will be level with the soil. Spread roots, firm them down and take soil back over roots.

Pinks

Modern pinks, such as the popular Doris and border carnations are very rewarding.

Border carnations should be staked and main stems disbudded in June. These have a main bud at the top and side shoots below. Keep the main bud and those at the ends of the side shoots, but rub out any others.

Encourage modern pinks to make side shoots by pinching out main growing points. Increase stocks of pinks by taking cuttings of side shoots with a sharp blade.

Remove the lowest pair of leaves and cut across the stem, just below. Plant the cuttings about seven or eight to a 3 inch pot of sandy soil. Water well and place the pots in an open box in the shade.

Within six weeks they should be ready for potting individually in pots of John Innes No 1.

—— BIENNIALS ——

Canterbury Bells

Cheiranthus

Cineraria

Dianthus

Honesty

Sweet William

Wallflower

Alpines

If you want to replace alpines that are getting old, take root cuttings in February.

Scrape away soil from the plant and cut out some of the roots. To make cuttings from these, the part of the root nearest the plant should be cut straight across and the furthest end cut on a slant .

Root cuttings may be planted in pots or in boxes of sandy compost with the straight-cut tops just above the surface.

Containers should be placed in a cold frame.

When the cuttings develop tuft-like leaves, they can be set out in separate pots.

Among the alpines which can be propagated thus are Crepis, helianthemums, dianthus and some saxifrages.

To grow the high alpine plants it is important to reproduce the root environment that the plants have in their natural surroundings. This should also be done in February.

This involves preparing a special mixture consisting largely of gravel or stone chippings. From this you make a scree (see Inset A on page 103) into which plant roots will penetrate in search of moisture and nutrients.

To make a scree bed choose an open sunny position and excavate the soil to a depth of 2 feet. Fill this with a 6 inch layer of large broken stones at the bottom and the scree mixture on top (see Inset B on page 103), up to the soil surface level. An alternative is to have a raised bed. You can vary the proportions of stone and soil in the mixture if you are growing alpines which are not real scree plants. The usual mixture is about three parts stone to one of soil. The stone may be in the form of chips or, unless lime-hating plants are to be grown, limestone chips.

The soil content should be made up of half and half, peat and loam. Mix together well and then add them to the stone chips to make them a little earthy, but no more. As you fill the hole with the scree mix you might consider dotting a few rocks around in the bed to give it a little extra visual interest.

March is the time to smarten up alpines for Spring.

Start by firming in any plants which have become loose. Where chippings have not been spread around the plants – given that the ground is reasonably dry – gently go between them with an onion hoe.

It is preferable then to hand-drift stone chippings among the plants. These will provide protection, aid drainage and deter slugs.

But if you intend to leave bare earth surroundings, lay slug pellets around the plants.

Where boxes of alpine seeds were placed outdoors to germinate, pay regular attention for signs of life.

Once shoots appear, move the containers into the greenhouse.

May is a fascinating time for those interested in growing alpines.

The ever-popular arabis and alyssum, campanulas, the mossy saxifrages with their high-stemmed flowers and the superb gentian, with trumpet-shaped flowers (see Inset A) in white, yellow and blue can all be started from seed now.

Seeds for most of these are very small, and it is best to sow them in pots (see main picture). To obtain an even better distribution, mix a little fine sand with the seed before sowing. Then cover with just a dusting of seed compost, and finally lay on a sheet of glass, or place them under a cloche or in a frame if you do not have a greenhouse.

Keep a weather eye on established alpines too – water regularly and keep working with the hoe between them. As soon as Alyssum saxatile and

aubretias have finished flowering trim them to keep the shapes neat.

For the latter, a close trim (see Inset B on page 105) will help you to increase your stock again. For it will encourage new shoots which can be used as cuttings in June or July.

Herbaceous Plants

Spring is the time to give special attention to herbaceous plants. Many will be showing new shoots, and may use up the soil if left.

The answer is to lift, divide and retain healthy young shoots and roots. Among herbaceous plants particularly prone to deterioration are Michaelmas daisies. Lift the old plants and separate them. Replant in groups of two or three.

Poppies have thick roots, best divided with a sharp knife. Geum and scabious need to be lifted and

divided every two years, replanted in ground deeply dug and manured. Twigs are adequate for low-growing clumps; taller plants like delphiniums need canes.

Bulbs

Every few years, in May, clumps of bulbs need lifting and splitting up.

Daffodils for instance grow on from year to year, the older bulb producing new ones around it.

Lift the clumps carefully with a fork and split off the smaller bulbs and replant the old and young separately.

The older ones will flower next year, the 'babies' probably needing another year.

Tulips, too, should be allowed to die back naturally, then lift, remove the bulblets and replant the old bulb.

Bulblets need to be planted in a 'nursery' for two or three years to achieve flowering ability.

Tease hyacinths into reproducing. Lift, cut deeply three ways across the bottom of the bulb. When the wounds dry, replant 4 inches deep. Next year they will produce bulblets.

THREE IDEAS FOR MIXED SUMMER BEDS

Plans are shown here of suggestions for three mixed summer flower borders. A combination of herbaceous plants with biennials will enable the beds to make good colour effects throughout early and late summer. When deciding on the placing of such subjects as dahlias, heleniums, etc, consideration must be given to varieties in each case in accordance with their maximum height. Tallest kinds are, of course, planted at the back of the border. Other suggestions for summer beds are two kinds of antirrhinums, tall and intermediate, with an edging of dwarf nasturtiums; cheiranthus, calendula, with white alyssum as an edging; Canterbury bell, mixed colours, with Ageratum, imperial dwarf blue, in the front of the bed.

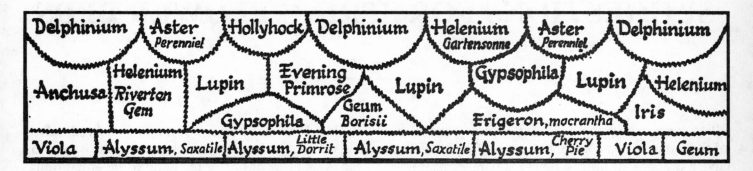

Delphinium	Aster Perenniel	Hollyhock	Delphinium	Helenium Gartensonne	Aster Perenniel	Delphinium
Anchusa	Helenium Riverton Gem	Lupin	Evening Primrose	Lupin	Gypsophila	Helenium
		Gypsophila	Geum Borisii	Erigeron, macrantha	Lupin	Iris
Viola	Alyssum, Saxatile	Alyssum, Little Dorrit	Alyssum, Saxatile	Alyssum, Cherry Pie	Viola	Geum

Phlox	Helenium Chipperfield Orange	Phlox	Chrysanthemum Maximum
Iris, King	Dahlia	Helenium Crimson Beauty	
Calceo-laria	Antirrhinum	Calceolaria	Antirrhinum

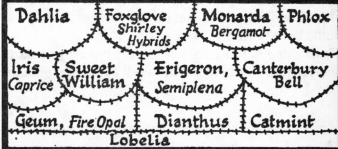

Dahlia	Foxglove Shirley Hybrids	Monarda Bergamot	Phlox
Iris Caprice	Sweet William	Erigeron, Semiplena	Canterbury Bell
Geum, Fire Opal	Dianthus	Catmint	
Lobelia			

SUGGESTIONS FOR SPRING FLOWER BEDS

When preparing spring beds, dig in plenty of material from the compost heap, but use no fresh manure. Give a dressing of lime, 4 oz per square yard. Bulbs should be planted with a groundwork of dwarfer plants, which not only set off the flowers of the bulbs but afford them support.

Think out a definite colour-scheme before you start any planting. Get the groundwork and edging plants in first. Wall-flowers, forget-me-nots, aubretia, double white Arabis all make settings to May-flowering tulips. A mass of one of the giant trumpet daffodils in the centre of a bed, as shown here, is very effective. In a bed of hyacinths surrounded by a border a central group of scarlet or orange tulips is charming. Many beautiful schemes are possible on similar lines.

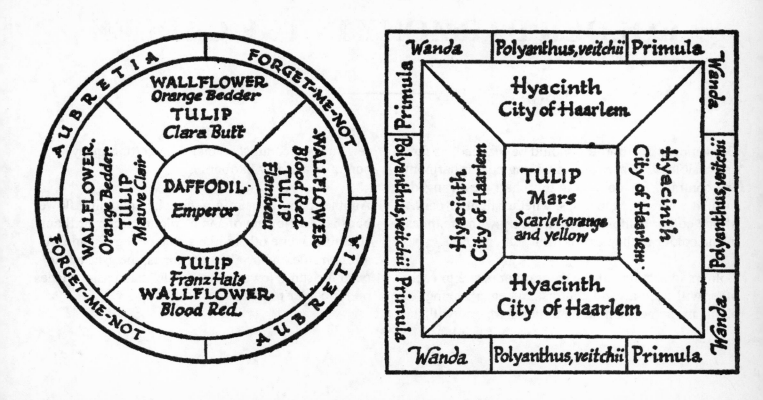

Left diagram (circular bed):

AUBRETIA

FORGET-ME-NOT

WALLFLOWER
Orange Bedder
TULIP
Clara Butt

WALLFLOWER
Blood Red
TULIP
Flambeau

WALLFLOWER.
Orange Bedder:
TULIP
Mauve Clair

DAFFODIL
Emperor

TULIP
Franz Hals
WALLFLOWER.
Blood Red.

FORGET-ME-NOT

AUBRETIA

Right diagram (square bed):

Wanda

Polyanthus, veitchii

Primula

Primula

Wanda

Hyacinth
City of Haarlem

Polyanthus, veitchii

Hyacinth
City of Haarlem

Hyacinth
City of Haarlem.

Polyanthus, veitchii

TULIP
Mars
Scarlet-orange
and yellow

Primula

Hyacinth
City of Haarlem

Wanda

Wanda

Polyanthus, veitchii

Primula

111

COLOUR HARMONY IN THE GARDEN

Garden beds and borders should be planned, as far as possible, with a view to attaining colour harmony and contrast. The colours in this chart are arranged in such a way that the tones, whether light or dark, of one colour combine harmoniously with the tones of the colour in the next or near section.

Colours in sections of the diagram opposite to each other will form a vivid contrast. When arranging plants in the bed, aim at obtaining harmony with a few striking contrasts rather than getting many contrasts and few harmonies.

Another point to bear in mind when planning flower beds is that flowers of some colours prefer brilliant sunshine, while others like shade or semi-shade. As a rough rule, the brighter the tones, the greater the need for sun. Flowers of more delicate pastel shades prefer cooler positions.

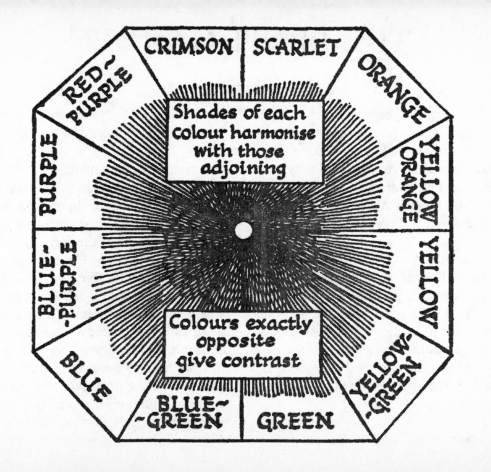

CRIMSON   SCARLET

RED~PURPLE

ORANGE

PURPLE

YELLOW-ORANGE

BLUE~-PURPLE

YELLOW

BLUE

YELLOW-GREEN

BLUE~-GREEN   GREEN

Shades of each
Colour harmonise
with those
adjoining

Colours exactly
opposite
give contrast

THE FRUIT GARDEN

Fruit trees and bushes are best kept apart from vegetables. This makes for easier management and is for the good of both. Strawberries are an exception. On the other hand, there is no reason at all why some fruits, such as apples, pears and standard redcurrants, should not be grown among flowers, where they have a happy, 'cottagey' effect.

Most fruits should be allocated to a sunny area, but gooseberries, blackberries, raspberries and especially redcurrants and 'sour' cherries, will also do well in partial shade. The redcurrant and Morello cherry will thrive in the full shade on the north wall of a house and are thus both decorative and economical of space. Blackberries and loganberries are admirable for training on a fence and thus also fulfil a dual purpose.

The strawberry is best treated as part of the vegetable garden 'rotations', moving on from plot to plot each year as the runners develop.

For ease of management, except for those growing on walls, arrange your fruits in orderly rows, running north and south if possible. If you are starting a new garden, you are strongly advised to grow your apples and pears in the form of cordons, not as standard trees or bushes. Cordons are far easier for pruning, spraying, thinning, etc. They cancel out the need for expensive ladders and powerful sprays which the amateur cannot afford and without which the fruit on large trees gets neglected. You can plant cordon apples and pears as close as 18 inches apart in straight lines bent over (gradually) to an angle of 45° on a strong post-and-wire framework. Choose varieties suitable for the cordon form (not all are) on what are called 'dwarfing stocks'. A good fruit nursery will advise you, but some of the best dessert apples are Cox's Orange Pippin, Orleans Reinette, Laxton's Fortune, Ribston Pippin, James Grieve and Ellison's Orange. Most pears are readily adaptable and the best for beginners is Conference.

Gooseberries and redcurrants (the latter especially) are also admirable in the (upright) cordon form. They produce an abundance of exhibition fruit. You can plant them a foot apart, or less.

All cordon fruits depend for success on the system of summer pruning. Stop the laterals when they have grown about five leaves, and in winter prune hard back to one or two buds. Don't summer prune the 'leading' shoot, but cut it back half-way in winter.

Where space compels limitations, omit cherries first. They grow very big and the birds get most of the fruit.

Also, with eating cherries, you must have at least two trees, as they are self-sterile. Plums also take up a lot of room, but if you have any, choose Victoria – the best all-rounder and self-fertile.

In the choice of all apples, pears, plums and cherries, bear in mind that you must nearly always have two different varieties, as very few are self-fertile.

FRUIT TREES, BUSHES AND PLANTS

Apple	Damson	Plum
Blackberry	Gooseberry	Raspberry
Blackcurrant	Loganberry	Redcurrant
Cherry	Pear	Strawberry

Fruit Trees

November is a good time to plant new fruit trees. When digging the hole, keep top and subsoil separate and, to avoid harming the roots, drive in a stake to support the tree before planting.

Spread the roots across the hole, fill over them with the finer topsoil, and then finish off with the subsoil.

After planting, young apples and pears should be cut back by about two-thirds. Cut just above a bud which you would like to provide a new shoot.

Until the trees are about five years old, cut back leaders and, where further growth is desired, reduce laterals to about four buds. To increase next year's fruit production, thin out fruit spurs.

May is the time to care for apples and pears. This will repay you with healthy crops.

To guard against scab on either, use a benomyl spray, such as Benlate, every ten to fourteen days. Use a portable container with a lance spray for best coverage, particularly under leaves.

When the apple petals fall, watch out for sawfly (use an HCH spray) and red spider mites (a malathion spray). The latter will also combat greenfly attacking pears.

A major disappointment is shortage of fruit buds.

Solve this by bark ringing at blossom time, which diverts the food supply to the branches. Take out a quarter-inch wide strip around half the trunk or side branches, and another, 2 or 3 inches either above or below. Cover the wounds with adhesive tape immediately.

As apples ripen in July, remember that heavy crops may break branches. And since the wealth of this year's fruit crop should be obvious by now, time will need to be taken to ensure its security.

First bear in mind the need to tend the trees themselves.

Probably the easiest way to provide support for heavily-laden branches is to use props. They should have deep forks padded with foam material to cradle the branches.

The quality and size of the fruit can be improved by thinning. Some fruit will fall naturally – this is the so-called 'June drop', though it usually happens in early July.

After this has taken place, you can further improve the size of fruit by removing some of the remaining apples by hand.

The aim is to reduce the number of fruit to one per cluster and then allow about 4 inches between each dessert apple. Cooking and other large apples will need more space.

Carefully pinch off the unwanted fruit with finger and thumb. Attacks by codling moth caterpillars may now be apparent. Damaged fruit should be removed and destroyed.

Having dealt with thinning crops of apples and pears, we should now turn to summer pruning around mid-July.

This is particularly important where trees are being trained, or grown in a restricted form.

The first aim of summer pruning is to contain the tree's size, without fostering new growth.

Secondly, one aims to open up the centre of the tree to make way for light and air – helping to produce healthy fruit. This also allows space for thorough spraying and easier picking.

Using sharp secateurs, cut back new laterals to leave shoots with just four or five leaves on each. Laterals are shoots from the main branch or leader.

Such laterals as may be needed to extend the branch framework of the tree can, of course, be left.

The leaders should not be pruned.

Fruit Bushes

To get the best results in the fruit garden you should feed the bushes, canes and trees every February.

As a general principle use 2–3 oz per square yard and apply this evenly over the area covered by the branches of the bush or tree.

If you suspect that certain fruits are suffering from deficiencies to which they are known to be susceptible (such as gooseberries and red and white currants having insufficient potash) you might choose to use a fertiliser to suit. For potash you could use a rose or tomato fertiliser, for instance, or you could apply sulphate of potash around the bushes at ¾ oz per square yard.

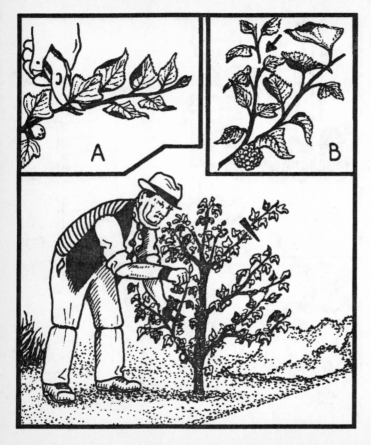

A

B

Remember that watering and preventing moisture loss by mulching (see Inset on page 119) during the summer months is as important as fertiliser applications. And if you use rotted manure or compost, the mulch will increase soil fertility as well.

After the June harvest of the fruits of gooseberries and red and white currants, it is time to start preparing for next season.

Main pruning is, of course, left until autumn or winter, when, in the case of gooseberries, the bush is opened up and good shoots cut back up to three-quarters.

In the autumn too, you will need to tend the currants, cutting out older wood at ground level and removing any overhanging shoots.

Summer pruning is a fairly light operation.

In the case of gooseberries, take out the few branches that cut across the centre of the bush (see main illustration on page 120). Then cut back sideshoots to five leaves from the base, cutting cleanly with secateurs at a leaf joint (as in Inset A and indicated in main illustration on page 120). The leaders, however, are not touched until the autumn when they should be cut back to about half.

Red and white currants – either bushes or those grown as cordons – which are two or more years old should receive similar summer pruning. As new growth starts to take on a brownish hue, cut back again to four or five leaves, but just above a leaf joint as shown in Inset B on page 120.

In nature one method of propagation occurs when long branches lying on the ground, such as those of strawberry plants, strike roots.

A man-made variation is tip-layering, by which blackberries and loganberries are propagated. This should be done in early August.

Choose canes that have grown since this spring.

Bend the tips and bury them.

If the soil is too heavy, add compost or leaf mould.

Now make a vertical cut with a spade and another at 45°.

The shoot is then fed down the slope of the hole and soil put on top.

Roots form at the tip and a new shoot grows up the vertical side.

It's exciting when you can grow fruit or vegetables earlier or later than your neighbours. One late producer is the autumn-fruiting raspberry and late January is the time to plant or prune.

The raspberry called September fruits from August to October. You need to dig the ground deeply, working in compost or well-rotted manure.

Plant new canes 18 inches apart in a trench deep

enough for a good 3 inches of soil over the spread-out roots. Firm in well as the trench is filled. Cut the canes back to about a foot and tie to a cord attached to stakes at the trench ends.

In March apply Growmore to encourage growth.

Autumn raspberries, unlike summer ones, produce fruit on new canes, so pruning is simple. In mid-February, just before growth begins, cut the canes back hard, to ground level.

THE VEGETABLE OR KITCHEN GARDEN

A few simple rules of planning and management are most necessary for the success of the kitchen garden, especially where space is limited.

The first need, whatever the size of the garden, is to carry out some simple system of 'rotation of crops'. To grow the same crop year after year in the same plot of ground (except onions) invites very bad diseases and pests, and impoverishes the soil. Big growers adopt elaborate systems of rotation, but the amateur can content himself with some quite simple change-over system. Be especially careful in the case of the group of crops knows as 'brassicas' (cabbages, Brussels sprouts, cauliflowers, broccoli, kale and turnips – not lettuces).

Next, as far as the space allows, plan for a succession of vegetables all the year round. Avoid having a glut of one sort of vegetable one month and nothing at all next month. Of the non-keeping vegetables, adopt a system of 'successional sowing' according to your space. Sow only a small pinch of lettuce seed at a time, but repeat every two or three weeks from March to September. This also applies to summer spinach. Sow only one or two rows of peas at a time, and follow with others of later varieties. There are cabbage varieties for all seasons of the year.

Where space is very limited you have got to be ruthlessly selective, cutting out for preference those vegetables that are least economical to grow oneself. The first to omit (on these grounds) is potatoes, which take up a lot of room and are reasonably cheap in the shops. Other examples are beetroot and cucumbers, of which one wants, as a rule, only one or two at a time. Another tip in limited places is to concentrate first on the vegetables of winter, when they are at their most expensive in the shops. This means chiefly the brassicas (including winter turnips), leeks, parsnips, winter spinach, celery, together with the 'keeper' vegetables – mainly onions, carrots and potatoes (if grown).

All these suggestions are based purely on economic grounds, but it is equally important that you should enjoy your garden by growing the things that you most like.

Other dodges for making full use of ground are inter-cropping and catch-cropping. Inter-cropping means sowing a quick-maturing vegetable (spinach, radishes, lettuces) between rows of slow-growing ones (celery, leeks, winter cabbage, etc.) before they have approached maturity. Catch-cropping means sowing a quick crop in a plot of ground from which one main crop has been harvested and before another main crop is sown.

ADAM'S SELECTION OF VEGETABLES

Artichokes	*Endive*	*Pea*
Beans	*Garlic*	*Potato*
Beet	*Horseradish*	*Radish*
Broccoli	*Kale (Borecole)*	*Salsify*
Brussels sprouts	*Kohlrabi*	*Seakale*
Cabbage	*Leek*	*Shallot*
Carrot	*Lettuce*	*Spinach*
Cauliflower	*Marrow*	*Spinach Beet*
Celery	*Mushroom*	*Swede*
Chicory	*Onion*	*Tomato*
Corn (sweet)	*Parsley*	*Turnip*
Cucumber	*Parsnip*	*Watercress*

LETTUCE

August or September is the time to ensure an early salad crop for next year. You do not need a large space or cover to grow lettuce, provided you choose a hardy variety.

Hardy varieties which will stand the winter well without protection include Arctic King and Valdor. Before sowing, work the ground to a fine tilth and rake in bone-meal at 4 oz to the square metre. Draw drills just about ½ inch deep and 12 inches apart. Sow the seeds at 9 inch intervals. Those in the north can set out spring cabbages. Choose a plot that was manured for its previous crop. Lift the soil in ridges 8–10 inches high and dust with bone-meal.

Put the plants in so the lower leaves are just above soil level. Leave 6 inches between each plant, in rows 18 inches apart. March thinnings can be used as spring greens.

To grow under cloches, choose a forcing variety such as May King or Novita. These should be sown thinly in drills ½ inch deep and 4 inches apart, in October.

They will be ready to transplant, again under glass, in December.

BEETROOT

Beetroot, that popular addition to salads, is an easy grower which can fill in between other crops.

Not all are red and round. Burpees Golden, whose leaves can also be cooked and eaten, has a golden hue, while Cylindra is long and oval.

Moneta appeals to the new gardener; it produces only one seedling per cluster so needs no thinning out!

Forono, however, has cylindrical roots which cut to give uniform slices.

Beetroots need to be grown in soil which has been
deeply dug. Do not manure it, but dress with
Growmore. Sow the seeds in April when the ground
is warm, 2 inches apart in drills an inch deep and
rows a foot apart. Thin out to 6 inches.

POTATOES

You should be preparing for the earliest sowing of
seeds in February.

As soon as it is dry enough, lightly fork over the
ground to something just under 4 inches to allow the
top soil to dry out.

When the soil has dried out, gentle treading will
break down most larger lumps. Then rake to a fine
tilth.

Make sure, too, that the soil gathers as much
warmth as possible. Polythene sheetings held up
with stakes can help over larger areas, but generally,

cloches are ideal.

However, for an early crop, make sure you close the ends. A square of glass placed (as shown in the main illustration on page 127) will help to retain the captured heat.

Prepare for early potatoes. Seed potatoes should be set up in trays to sprout with the 'eye' or 'rose' end uppermost (see Inset on page 127).

Dry newspaper between the rows will help to keep them in position while stored in a light, airy, frost-free place.

In about four weeks they should have sturdy shoots up to about ½ inch long and will be just right for planting.

Tubers for main crop potatoes should be showing sprouts in mid-April, ready for planting before the end of the month.

A reasonable crop will require an area not used for potatoes last year, well manured during the autumn. And it will benefit from general fertiliser, raked in now at about 4 oz to the square yard.

Using a hoe, draw out drills about 4 inches deep and just over 2 feet apart. Large tubers may be cut in half, ensuring that each half has two or three sprouts, and that the cuts are allowed to heal before being put in the drills. When you place them, do it firmly, allowing 15 inches between each.

When the row is complete, draw the soil over the tubers with a rake, so that the light does not turn them green, leaving a ridge over the drills. Begin drawing soil up around the plants when they are about 9 inches high.

Rain in late July can pose problems for potato and tomato plants.

Potato blight is the culprit. The plants will have brown blotches on the leaves, with a white coating underneath. If left, rot will set in. Using a lance spray, treat potatoes, before their tops meet, with Bordeaux mixture at 10–14 day intervals.

Earthing up will ensure that blight spores do not get washed from the leaves down to the tubers which, as a result, may have sunken parts and finish up with brown rot inside.

Wet weather may make wireworms more active – making a maze of holes in the tubers.

Prevent this in future by growing first earlies, which are not usually affected by them.

Slugs do more unsightly damage. So lift the tubers in August, before conditions become too damp.

CABBAGE

Regular production of cabbages is the result of seasonal sowing and, therefore, careful planning. There are many varieties to choose from among the four main groups of summer, autumn, winter and spring cabbages.

If you want fresh cabbage in the winter, start sowing and planting at the beginning of May.

Christmas Drumhead Early, the F1 Celtic and the F1 Winterton (very like January King, which is usually listed under savoys) are well tried and popular.

The most successful way of growing any of the brassica family is to sow the seeds in a seed bed.

When they are about 4 inches high they will need to be transplanted to their final quarters, but before planting out, dress the area with fertiliser at 3 oz to the square yard.

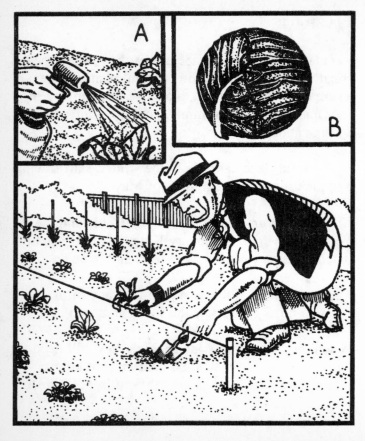

Using a hoe, draw out a drill about 4 inches deep and make holes in the drill into which the seedlings are planted.

The seedlings need watering well and firming in, too. Allow about 2 feet between plants. For earlier cutting you can now sow the F1 Hispi, or Pixie.

June is the time to set out later winter varieties such as Winter White, which stores well in airy and cool conditions (see Inset B), January King and Christmas Drumhead. Winter White will be ready for harvesting in mid winter, whilst January King will go on through to early spring.

Before planting, rake in a general fertiliser together with Bromophose (to deal with cabbage root fly) and calomel dust (to control club root).

When the soil is moist, set out the plants leaving about 20 inches between them (see main illustration).

Watch out for caterpillars, white fly and the flea beetle and at first sign spray regularly with malathion (see Inset A on page 130), and dust with derris until coarser leaves form.

As the plants grow, remove leaves which show decay or yellowing.

MARROWS

Marrows and their relative, courgettes, are among the most succulent vegetables.

Bush marrows include Long Green Bush, which has a dark green and cream striped skin.

Zucchini is a heavy cropper and there are trailing varieties, including Long Green and Long Green striped.

Sow in early June, planting three seeds 1 inch deep at each station. Stations should be about 3 feet apart. Only the strongest of developing plants will be left.

Healthy spare seedlings can be grown on and, like bought-in plants, be set out under a cloche if necessary, to harden them off.

An easy way to grow small varieties of courgettes is to train them up a tepee, with canes put in at each station.

ONIONS

February is the right month for planting several members of the onion family, providing the soil is not too wet and sticky.

Shallots (see Inset A) definitely require February planting. Set the bulbs 6 inches apart in rows 9 inches apart, pushing them into the soil so that most of the bulb is buried.

Garlic is gown in a similar way. A bulb of garlic (see Inset B) is composed of a number of individual sections called cloves, which should be planted individually at 4–6 inch intervals along an inch deep drill. Leave the plants to grow until the foliage dies down and the bulbs ripen in summer.

Onions are grown either from seeds or sets. Plant sets now or in March, like shallots, 4–5 inches apart in rows 1 foot apart. Gardeners who grow for showing usually sow their onion seeds under glass in December or January, but February sowing under cloches or March sowing in the open ground will give satisfactory results.

Onions demand plenty of water. They also need help in the ripening process starting in August.

Nature will give the first hint that ripening has begun. As foliage starts to turn yellow, the tops should be bent over.

After two weeks partially lift the bulbs with a fork. Gently prise them to break the roots and lift them a little higher above the soil level.
After another fortnight, the onions can be lifted and spread out to dry.

Lay them on a net stretched between four posts, so that air can circulate freely around them.
After a few days of drying out, the tops can be cut off and any loose skin removed.

They will then be ready for storing in nets or on wooden slats, so that they have good air circulation.

CARROTS

Carrots, sown in April, should be lifted in September. Make sure that the fork does not damage the crop.

Set aside any that are damaged for eating immediately. To store, cut off the leaves near the growth point, clean off any soil and place, alternately tip and crown, in deep boxes on ½ inch of slightly damp sand. Cover with another ½ inch of sand, then put in another layer of carrots. Continue until the box is full. Place in a cool, well-ventilated shed.

Store beetroot (see page 126) in the same way, but do not cut the leaves as this will cause them to bleed. Just twist them off.

BROAD BEANS AND PEAS

Sow broad beans and peas in November for an early crop next year. Given well-drained soil, they are hardy enough to withstand the rigours of winter, particularly when given some protection.
Fork ground previously composted and dress with sulphate of potash at ½ oz per square metre.

Choose Aquadulce and Sutton beans. Dust with a captan dressing and sow Sutton in single rows at 6 inch intervals. Use cloches and close the ends. Aquadulce are best in double drills 9 inch apart; 2 feet between each pair.

For peas, take out two or three drills just over 1 inch deep and 3–4 inches apart. Sow the peas at 2 inch intervals.

Choose Meteor or Feltham First, both first-rate under cloches.

CUCUMBERS

April is the time to start sowing ridge cucumbers. For this early sowing, it is perhaps best to set the seeds in 3 inch pots of John Innes seed compost covered with glass. Plant about ½ inch deep. In May you can harden off for planting in June.
The bed for growing on should be well prepared, for all cucumbers like rich soil conditions. So dig the ground thoroughly and work in plenty of well rotted manure and garden compost.

When planting out, space about 2½ feet apart and scatter slug pellets about.

When the plants have made five or six leaves, start training by pinching out the growing tip (see inset A on page 135) to allow them to throw side-shoots which can be tied into a trellis (as in the main illustration on page 135). The new shoots should again be pinched out when they have shown seven or eight leaves (see Inset B on page 135).

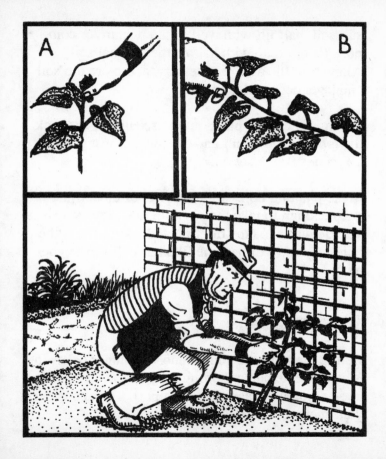

You will need to pollinate by picking off the male flowers and introducing the pollen to the female flowers by dusting the male flower on to the female. You can tell which is which because the female flower petals have the semblance of a baby cucumber behind them.

LEEKS

Early to mid-April is the best time to start some leeks, either from seed or from plants available at local nurseries and garden centres.

Whether you are using your own seedlings or bought plants, prepare the bed for planting out in June or July, early enough for it to settle. Where only a comparatively small number of leeks are required dig the bed to allow for, say two rows 15 inches apart and with about 8 inches between each plant in the rows.

Dig a trench to about a spade's depth, loosen the

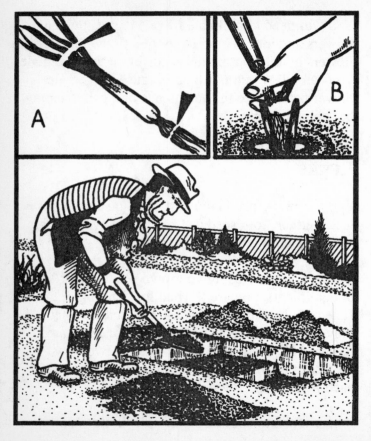

sub-soil, half fill with well rotted manure or compost, then top up with half of the original soil. Allow to settle and, if necessary, add more top soil and level before planting.

When it is time to plant out the seedlings, cut back the tops by about half and the roots to just about 1½ inches (see Inset A).

Make planting holes with a trowel or dibber just deep enough to take the plant up to its lowest leaves. Trickle water in (see Inset B) and do not fill in the holes as they will become filled as cultivation goes on.

RUNNER BEANS

Before planting out your French or runner beans in May, give the bed a thorough digging and turn in a good amount of manure or compost. Then consider your method of support.

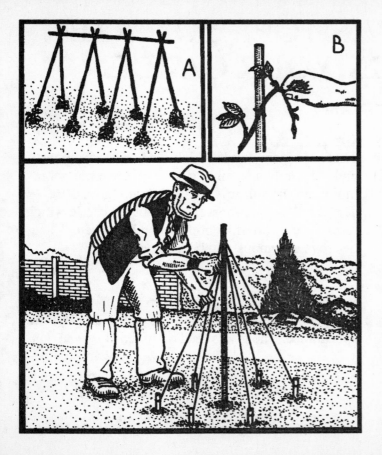

You can use a traditional arrangement of poles (see Inset A), or there is the maypole type, where a 4 foot central pole acts as top tether for up to 10 strings (not plastic-covered material) attached to pegs (see main picture).

If you are only at the sowing stage, plant two beans per pole, later discarding the weaker at the base of each string.

However, if you are planting out beans raised under glass, put in only one.

Ensure there is a good supply of slug pellets around each plant. Water often.

When the plants reach the top of the supports pinch out the growing tips (see Inset B). Regular spraying of the flowers with either a syringe or the hose set on fine spray, should guarantee a good crop.

137

HERE ARE SOME VISITORS YOU ARE LIKELY TO FIND IN YOUR GARDEN

These are always welcome:

Centipede
Yellowish-orange in colour, moves rapidly, and has one pair of spiny legs on each segment all along the body. Feeds on soil pests.

Earthworm
Drains and aerates the soil, particularly in flower beds and vegetable plots, but on lawns the worm casts are unsightly and, if too numerous, the worms must be destroyed.

Ground Beetle
There are many kinds which feed on harmful pests, and, generally speaking, if an insect can run about rapidly in the soil it is a friend, hunting its prey. The Devil's-coach-horse, a long black beetle which turns up the end of its body when disturbed, destroys enormous numbers of pests.

Hover-fly
Has yellow bands on its body, giving it a wasp-like appearance. The grubs feed on green-fly.

Ichneumon-fly

Lays its eggs inside caterpillars. The grubs, which are legalises, eat their way out and spin yellow cocoons around their dead victims.

Lacewing-fly

Has two pairs of net-veined wings. The grubs prey on aphids.

Ladybirds

Some have black spots, others yellow or red. The grubs have dark, elongated bodies, often marked with spots. Both beetles and grubs feed on green-fly (aphids), scale insects and other pests.

Spiders, Frogs, Toads and Lizards

These are friends of the gardener, for they are all insect eaters.

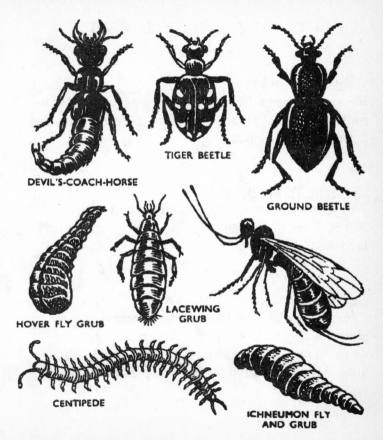

DEVIL'S-COACH-HORSE

TIGER BEETLE

GROUND BEETLE

HOVER FLY GRUB

LACEWING GRUB

CENTIPEDE

ICHNEUMON FLY AND GRUB

Be sure to destroy these:

Cabbage Root Fly
Resembles a small house-fly; the maggots tunnel roots and stems. Treat with calomel, dust weekly for three weeks after planting.

Cabbage White Butterfly
The yellowish-green caterpillars eat and destroy leaves. Control by hand picking; spray with liquid Derris.

Carrot-fly
Ravages of these small dark-green insects cause plants to flag. Grubs are found on roots. Sow whizzed naphthalene (1 oz per square yard) when thinning, and twice more at 14-day intervals.

Chafer Beetle (May Bug)
Grub is dull white; beetle is brown. Attacks roots and leaves. Dig in 1 oz naphthalene per square yard in early spring.

Eelworm
A microscopic pest; affected plants become stunted and should be burned. Sterilise soil.

Leather-jacket
The grub of Daddy-long-legs; feeds on roots. Control by mixing ¼ oz crushed Metaldehyde with ¾ lb bran. Lay in tiny covered heaps near plants. Slugs can be treated similarly.

Onion-fly
The white maggots destroy bulbs. Treat by dusting naphthalene along rows at 10-day intervals.

Pea, Bean and Turnip Weevils

Resembling beetles in appearance, weevils eat leaf edges. Dust with Derris or DDT.

Wireworm

Recognised by its yellowish colour; attacks roots. Insert small pieces of Paradichlorbenzene in 6 inch deep holes, 2 feet apart, and cover.

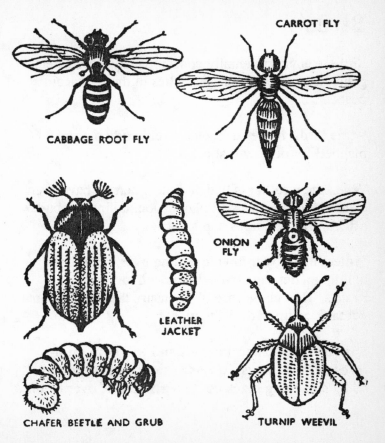

CABBAGE ROOT FLY

CARROT FLY

LEATHER JACKET

ONION FLY

CHAFER BEETLE AND GRUB

TURNIP WEEVIL

141

Birds

In these environmentally conscious days, gardeners generally welcome birds as allies in the war against pests.

Some birds, however, seek a livelihood on crops planned for our own tables.

When the weather is bad and most berries have been cleared, bullfinches will play havoc, taking the buds off fruit bushes, trees and shrubs.

Protect these by throwing netting over them, or by building a net cage over shrubs and low fruit bushes. Though be careful to ensure the birds do not get tangled up with the netting.

Sparrows also take fruit buds and will strip prim-roses or Polyanthus flowers. These are best protect-ed by stretching black cotton, criss-cross, over them.

Action also needs to be taken to keep wood pigeons away from gardens and vegetable plots.

Their fare is varied, including wild seeds and berries. Once these have been cleared, however, they will turn to crops such as spring cabbage seedlings.

This time netting can be stretched over the rows, supported at the ends of stakes covered with upturned plastic lemonade bottles.

Woolly-leaved alpines should be covered in damp weather with a sheet of glass raised on stakes.

WEED KILLERS AND ARTIFICIAL FERTILISERS

Good gardening must always depend upon providing the soil with a certain amount of organic matter. This means animal and vegetable matter of some sort – dung, peat, old turf, leafmould, hops, seaweed, or the compost that you make in your own garden from accumulations of waste vegetable or animal matter. These organic substances impart valuable physical properties to the soil, giving it bulk, moisture-holding qualities, aeration, etc. They also, after decaying, provide food for the plants. Organics have drawbacks, however. Nowadays they are expensive and often hard to obtain, and they are very seldom perfectly balanced in all the chemical qualities that a plant requires. Therefore, those fertilisers that we call artificial, or chemical or inorganic, are invaluable, either as a supplement to the organic foods, or as a substitute for them for short periods.

The chemicals needed in a plant's earth-food are numerous, but the most important ones are: NITROGEN, which stimulates foliage, PHOSPHATES, which build up root systems and ripen seed, and POTASH, which gives balance and stability to the whole structure of the plant, and is valuable for fruit. The other chemical elements needed by the plant – iron, boron, manganese, etc. – are called 'trace elements', as they are required in small quantities only.

The first and basic lesson to be taken to heart by beginners in these matters is to be very wary of making their own fertiliser mixtures until they are more advanced. It is necessary for a plant's food to be properly balanced. A deficiency of potash and an excess of nitrogen, for example, may have disastrous effects on the plant's constitution. It is, therefore, sound and sensible practice to buy your fertilisers ready blended from a manufacturer of good repute.

Since the needs of all plants, however, are not identical, there are special fertilisers for special crops, such as tomatoes, chrysanthemums or roses. And there are fertilisers devised for the peculiar needs of lawns.

There are some very important laws to obey in the use of artificials:

1. They must not touch the foliage of a plant, with the exception of grass fertilisers and the granulated types.

2. They must be applied a little at a time, never exceeding 'what it says on the packet'.

3. Never use them at the same time as lime – not until at least fourteen days after the lime. Remember that, as compared with organics, artificials are powerfully concentrated, quick in action, but quickly spent. So 'little and often' is the rule, hoeing or raking the material into the top inch of soil while the plants are actually growing or very shortly before they are put out.

Weed Killers

Modern weed killers fall into two main groups –
selective and non-selective. Selective weed killers,
also called 'hormone' weed killers, are used chiefly
on lawns. For this purpose the substance used is
known as '2,4-D', and there are several good
proprietary makes. 'MCPA' is much the same sort of
thing. They have the odd faculty of not affecting
grasses, but causing distorted growth and slow death
to broader-leaved plants and sometimes to fine-
leaved weeds as well. This type of weed killer is
usually (and best) applied to the lawn in liquid form.
Do not use a fine spray. Use an ordinary watering-
can, but take care not to use it for any other purpose
until after copious purgings. Apply when there is no
wind, for the drift of any particle of the liquid onto a
plant in a nearby bed is liable to be fatal. Apply
while the weeds are in active growth – say, from late
April until August. If the weed growth is bad,
dressings may be given at about six-week intervals –
not more often. Apply when the soil is moist and
rain not imminent.

Don't use a 2,4-D dressing in the preparation of a
new lawn, or for at least a year afterwards.

2,4-D may also be used to kill some of the more
odious weeds of the flower border – thistles,
dandelions, docks, etc. It works extremely well on
bindweed (or bellbind), which need no longer be
considered a menace. On ground elder it is effective
only after two or more dressings. The method for all
these is to paint the foliage with the solution at the
stated strength (not concentrated), taking GREAT
CARE not to let drips fall on a cultivated plant.
There are also 'pre-emergence' concoctions to kill
young weeds in vegetable seed drills.

Non-selective weed killers may be used only on
paths or on patches of ground that are quite free of
any cultivated crops. The most powerful of these
(and indeed of all weed killers) is SODIUM
CHLORATE, which is deadly to all vegetation.
Follow the directions on the tin carefully,
remembering also that it is volatile. If used in liquid
form, which is the best, take care not to wet your

145

clothes with it. Sodium chlorate penetrates deeply and is effective for six months or so.

Several other weed killers under proprietary names are available for use on paths and waste ground, some of them with a sodium chlorate base, and some for use in dry powder form. All you have to do is to obey the instructions on the tin.

Soil Pest Destruction

Great advances have been made in recent times in dealing with soil pests. The two most important are BHC (Benzenehexachloride) and Aldrin.

BHC, available under many proprietary names, deals with a wide variety of soil pests. In its cruder forms, however, it imparts a taint to many vegetables, and if needed on or near them it should be used in the special form known as 'gamma' BHC, though more expensive. 'Lindane' is the American name for the same thing. Gamma BHC is particularly valuable for onion-fly, carrot-fly, cabbage-fly, flea beetle and wireworm and is a sure protection. For these uses gamma BHC has replaced the older remedies.

Aldrin covers many of the same uses as BHC, but is specially valuable for cutworms, chafer grubs and leather-jackets, which have defied the efforts of the gardener for so long. Get a good proprietary brand and follow instructions.

Artificial Fertilisers

Artificial fertilisers are most useful when natural manures are not available, and as a supplement to vegetable refuse. The six main kinds are numbered here. Nitrogenous manures, 1 and 2, stimulate foliage and roots. Phosphatic manures, 3, 5, and 6, have the opposite effect, checking rampant growth, but promoting fruit and flower growth. Potassic manures, 4, including wood-ash, benefit plants in all stages of growth. Artificials are in concentrated form; only small dressings, such as 1–2 oz per square yard must be applied, and then hoed in. Don't allow them to come into contact with leaves, or they may scorch the plants. Use No. 1 around growing plants only; it dissolves quickly. Nos. 2 and 3 should be used only in ground containing lime; No. 6 is best for soil deficient in lime. When making up artificial fertilisers, remember that, although most chemicals can be mixed safely, others should be used at once when mixed, while some should not be mixed at all. Fertile soil with a good supply of humus will produce good crops on artificials alone for some years, but natural manure is necessary after a period.

1. Sodium Nitrate (Nitrate of Soda)

2. Ammonium Sulphate (Sulphate of Ammonia)

3. Superphosphate

4. Potassium Sulphate (Sulphate of Potash)

5. Bonemeal

6. Basic Slag

GARDEN GADGETS

A Garden Line

Cut a pair of pointed stakes. On the top of each fit a large cotton or thread reel. One of these is made fast for winding; the other left loose for winding the line, which should be of strong twine.

A Planting Dibber

A dibber for planting bulbs, potatoes, etc., can be made from an old spade-handle. By boring holes at measured points and inserting a wooden pin, as shown, the depth of the hole can be regulated accurately.

An Earwig Trap

Fold small pieces of corrugated cardboard. Insert them into match-box covers. Tie them to the stakes supporting chrysanthemums, dahlias, etc. Earwigs will shelter in the traps and can be shaken out and killed.

A Seedling Bed-Marker

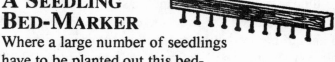

Where a large number of seedlings have to be planted out this bed-marker will save time. Strong wire nails are driven at equal distances into a long strip of wood. With this a number of spaces can be marked out at the same time.

An Adjustable Tool Handle

An easily adjustable handle which will fit any tools with a tapered socket can be made by shaping the end of a broom-handle to a long tapering point. Drive a nail into the tip. Twist a length of wire tightly round in a spiral, securing the end. Twist the handle into the tool socket to secure it. To release the handle when needed for another tool, twist it in the opposite direction.

An Adjustable Drill-maker

A home-made drill-maker will save time and work on your plot. A board is needed in which holes are made at various distances apart. The adjustable wooden "teeth" are fastened to the board by wing-nuts, enabling them to be moved to other holes. The broom-handle fits into a hole in the centre of a block fixed to the board.

Wing nut→

A Seed Protector

Two boards with supporting pegs are each studded on three sides with nails. The boards are set at the ends of the row. Black thread is stretched from end to end of the row, twisting it around the nails. This forms a protecting cover to the seed-bed from birds.

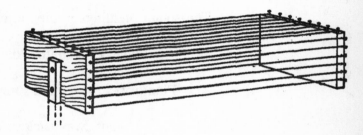

149

A DOUBLE PAGE OF 'DOs'

Burn all dead and diseased wood after pruning.

Transplant seedlings in the morning or evening, and not at midday.

Stake plants before the wind blows them down.

Plant roses firmly and spread their roots when doing so.

Cut away suckers directly they appear.

Pick off dead flowers; your border will have colour much longer.

Keep your eyes open for pests at all times, and deal with them accordingly.

Water cacti and greenhouse plants round the side of the pots, and not over them.

Remove weeds from the lawn directly they are seen.

Thin seedlings to the right distance apart, or your crops will suffer.

Keep the soil well hoed round onions, parsnips and carrots in the summer.

Pinch out side shoots of tomatoes immediately.

Keep greenhouse glass clean in winter.

Provide good stakes for fruit trees.

Wash all flower-pots before and after use.

Keep all tools clean and in good condition.

A DOUBLE PAGE OF 'DON'Ts'

DON'T sow thickly or too deeply. The smaller the seed, the shallower the sowing.

DON'T work on soil when it is very wet.

DON'T forget the undersides of leaves when spraying.

DON'T neglect to thin out seedlings.

DON'T neglect drainage, or the soil will remain cold owing to constant evaporation.

DON'T dig at an oblique angle. Drive your spade down vertically.

DON'T omit liming. It helps organic decay and neutralises acidity.

DON'T bury fertilisers too deeply or they will soon be wasted.

DON'T omit to soak ground before applying liquid fertilisers.

DON'T sprinkle water in dry weather. If you use water then give a soaking.

DON'T remove soil from roots of plants when transplanting.

DON'T use lime and farm manure at the same time.

DON'T use fresh soot; it should be weathered first.

DON'T use a dibber when planting bulbs; a trowel is better.

DON'T prune roses with frost about.

DON'T leave water lying on floor or staging in the greenhouse during the winter. Mop it up.

A GLOSSARY OF GARDENING TERMS

Annuals: Plants which bloom, produce seed and die during the same season.

Hardy Annuals: Plants which pass through all stages of growth in open ground, needing no protection. Sown March or April for July and August blooms, or in August for June flowering.

Half-hardy Annuals: Plants which, in their early stages of growth, need artificial heat; later they are planted out in the open for flowering and seed ripening. Sown in greenhouse or frame in January, February or March. Seedlings planted out of doors in May for summer blooming.

Biennials: Plants which need two seasons to arrive at full maturity. Sown in the open on reverse border in May or June; plants are set out in flowering quarters in autumn.

Perennials or Herbaceous Plants: Plants which continue to live and increase in the open for several years. Stems die down each season and grow up again from the roots each spring. Sow in greenhouse in March or in the open in April, May or June.

Spit: The length of a spade blade as a measure of depth in digging.

Rod: 30¼ square yards.

Suckers: Useless shoots from the stock on which a tree is budded. On rose, plum and lilac, suckers form freely. Sever them at their source. Rose suckers are thorny, usually have seven leaflets of pale colour. A true rose leaf has five leaflets.

Subsoil: The soil lying below that which is cultivated.

Taking the Bud: The removing of superfluous flower-buds on chrysanthemums which form below the first, so that this chief bud may develop.

Tilth: Soil broken down finely to make it suitable for sowing or planting.

Tap-root: Main root of a tree or plant.

Humus: Decayed vegetable matter.

Blind: A plant or shoot which fails to produce flowers or leaves.

Crown: The bud-like centre of strawberry plant or the top of root-stock of hardy herbaceous plants.

Lateral: A secondary shoot which develops on a main branch.

Loam: The top spit of turf decayed, after a year's stacking, into mellow soil.

Mulch: A layer of manure, lawn cuttings or other material laid around trees and plants to keep the soil moist.

Offset: Small bulbs attached to parent bulbs or small rooted pieces of hardy plants. In each case they are detached for propagation.

INDEX